A TERRIBLE THING

A TERRIBLE THING

moCa Cleveland

HATJE
CANTZ

CONTENTS

THE ART OF STORYTELLING
A. Will Brown

7

A TERRIBLE THING

17

SCANNING MODERNITY: SONDRA PERRY AND THE DARK SIDE OF PROGRESS
Mario Gooden

89

DOING GENDER IN THE "NEW OFFICE"
Alison Hirst & Christina Schwabenland

97

Director's Afterword

117

Artist & Contributor Bios

118

THE ART OF STORYTELLING [1]

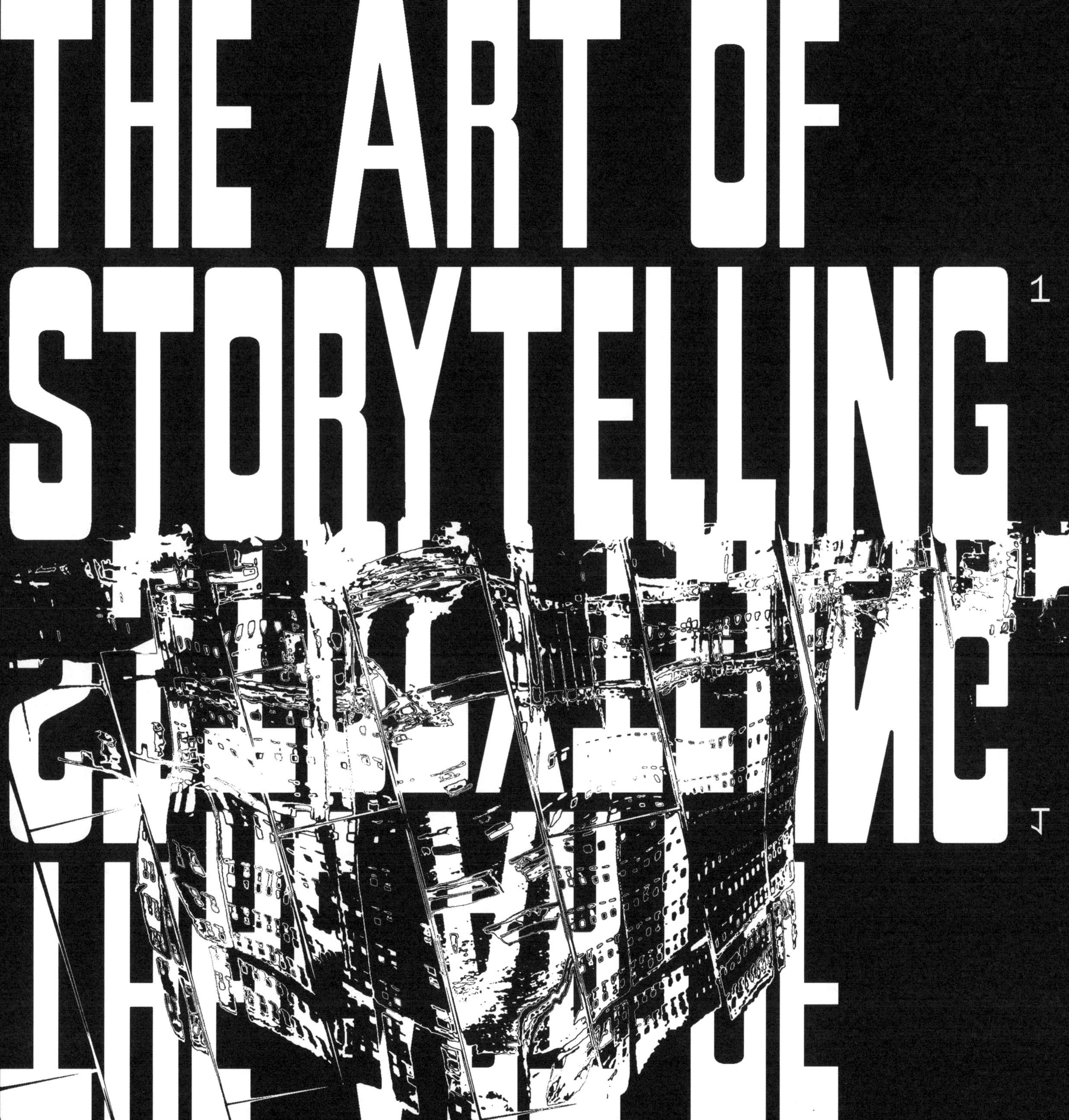

A PREFACE

Everything begins and ends with a story—as much as there is ever a beginning and an ending at all.

The events that shape much of the narrative explored within Sondra Perry's *A Terrible Thing* (2019) began in Europe before the fifteenth century, continued and were profoundly reinforced during and after the founding of the United States, and persist today. I am referencing, specifically, white supremacy structures, which were and are a fundamental part of United States history. While there is momentum building against them in US public and political discourse, the nation remains profoundly steeped in hollow, insolvent ideas that are dangerously alive in those willing to die or do harm to defend them.[2]

When telling, or counter-telling, a narrative, it is not only the story as a whole that matters but also how that story is told and who is doing the telling. As a non-black, non-brown, non-indigenous person, I am conscious of my words occupying space by sharing and interpreting Sondra Perry's incisive retelling of the narratives that are a part of her new work *A Terrible Thing*.[3] Her piece offers a powerful, sophisticated framework for turning many of the world's tools of control and oppression back on themselves. The essay that follows is not an encompassing narrative of the artist's intent. As the curator of this exhibition, in writing this essay about the work, I am not speaking for it but about it. The following narratives and interpretations begin in the middle of one of many stories and end somewhere that isn't really an ending at all but another beginning that lies beyond this text.[4]

THE FOLLOWING IS A TERRIBLE THING: THIS IS THEIR STORY

Introduction

"In the reevaluation of their situation, some artists attempted to extend themselves into their environment, and to work with its problems and events."
—Kynaston L. McShine, "Essay," *Information*, 1970

Though written nearly a half-century ago, McShine's statement, composed while he was Associate Curator of Painting and Sculpture at the Museum of Modern Art in New York, speaks directly to the heart of Perry's *A Terrible Thing*. The critical, thoughtful questions that Perry asks—an imperative element of her work—open rifts in the public narratives of cities and peoples by feeding formerly unrecognized and deliberately occluded information back into these chronicled machinations.

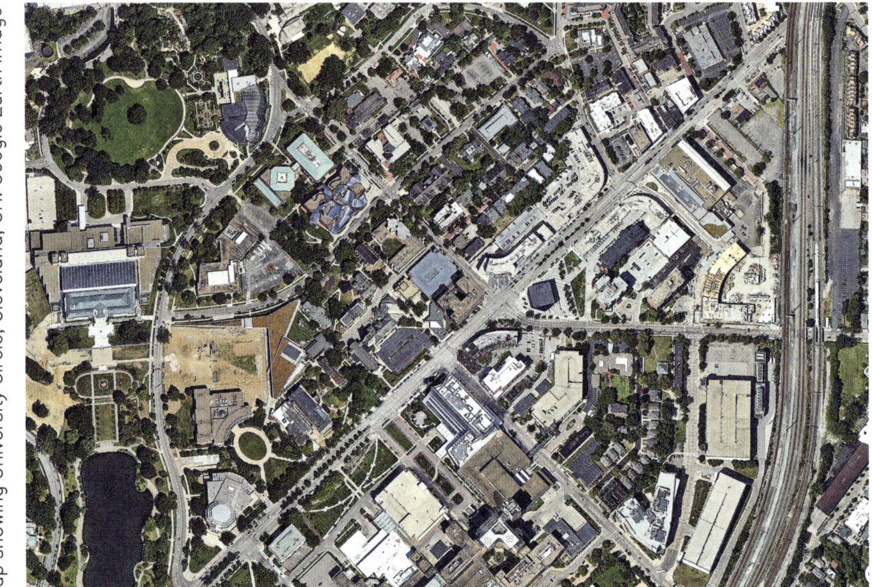

Map showing University Circle, Cleveland, OH. Google Earth image

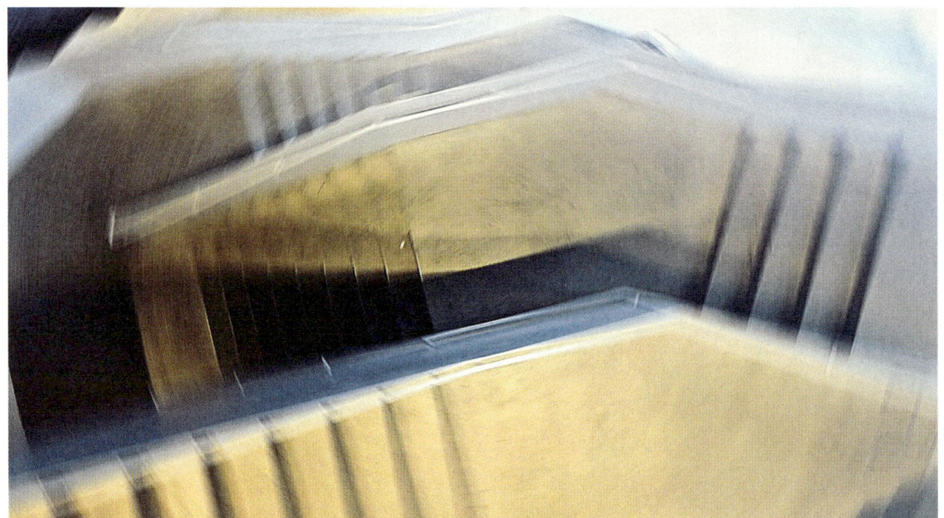

Sondra Perry, Source image for *A Terrible Thing*, 2019. Courtesy the artist and Bridget Donahue, New York

A. Will Brown

A Terrible Thing thoughtfully offers numerous entry points to explore the rich, partially erased histories that surround this land—the western territory of the Haudenosaunee or Iroquois, the Western Reserve of Connecticut, Northeast Ohio, Forest City, and, of course, Cleveland.[5] In the process, the work damages and upends narratives like those surrounding Cleveland's urban development. It asks us to intellectually and physically reinsert ourselves into the problems and events of our environment in order to understand our future.[6]

Perry's artwork comprises a two-channel video projection with accompanying audio, a scent, and two site-specific architectural installations in the gallery. As in much of her work, Perry also employs sophisticated, readily available digital media tools—such as CGI animation, GIS mapping, text-to-speech software, drone video surveillance, and found media footage—to explore and reveal the dominant role of technology in community building as well as perpetuating oppression. She does this by using a drone to capture imagery of a building that is at the heart of her critique, by inserting chroma key blue into the byways of a neighborhood to call attention to how and when it was gentrified and developed, and even by offering a sensory experience to evoke the conditions of a terrible past.

Iron

If what we can perceive with our senses delimits what is politically possible, then how do we make legible forms of power that are invisible? How can we imagine ourselves out of a box that we don't even know we're stuck inside? Like a character in a Franz Kafka story, we are called into presence, managed, confined, and punished by an authority that we struggle to locate or identify, and every time we embark on a quest for answers, there is just infinite deferral and postponement. —Jackie Wang, "Introduction," *Carceral Capitalism*, 2018

Wang's elegant, probing words refer specifically to the imperceptible "ascendancy of algorithmic power in the Age of Big Data."[7] This includes the invention and use of credit and eScores, automation of the labor force, production, surveillance, expropriation, data-mining, predictive policing, and so on. Wang's words tell us that, as citizens of the United States, we are governed by an obfuscated, far-reaching power structure. They hint at the specter of a larger, more ominous idea: this power structure systemically enacts overt as well as covert violence and theft upon black, brown, and indigenous peoples.

Before visitors enter the gallery space of *A Terrible Thing*, they climb a flight of stairs and move across a short pathway where a bewildering sensory presence materializes in the form of a scent, offering an invisible yet immersive experience. For many, smell is most strongly connected to memory, and Perry's scent, composed in Cleveland for this project, is replicated from the chemical reaction that occurs when skin touches iron—the smell of blood and decaying flesh.

This scent has a number of potential meanings and subsequent interpretations, but one link emerges from Edward E. Baptist's book *The Half Has Never Been Told: Slavery and the Making of American Capitalism*. Baptist explains that this smell would have pervaded countless forced marches—described through the repeated trauma of seventeenth-century slave Charles Ball—that moved slaves from one state or territory to another. The clanking, chaffing iron cuffs, chains, padlocks, and collars of the gendered coffles left "black-and-red lines of scabs [that] bordered the manacles,"[8] and torrid, permanent wounds. This smell, disturbingly, was an integral part of the founding and building of wealth of the United States—it was in the ether.

This smell also draws from Perry's research into the history of blacksmithing and blacksmiths, as far back as seventeenth-century colonial United States. Many enslaved Africans were forced to clear land and then cultivate and harvest cotton—the world's most important cash crop—despite knowledge of skilled trades and "various kinds of specialized expertise,"[9] such as blacksmithing. These highly skilled workers were presented for sale, with or without acknowledgment of their professions, for slave traders seeking the most financial return.[10] The sales represented the erasure of generationally learned expertise and hard-earned social purchase.

The scent in *A Terrible Thing* draws together the disturbing relationships between blood, iron, labor, sweat, social death,[11] stolen abundance,[12] dehumanization, and the largest accumulation of wealth the world has ever known. Yet, it also offers a moment of ineffability, a sensory experience that is unique to each of those who experience it. Under the umbrella of largely invisible control structures, Perry's scent tells the story that often goes untold—perhaps the one we need to hear now more than ever.

Infrastructure & Architecture

Shortly after moving to Cleveland from Detroit, Michigan, Winston E. Willis, a young black entrepreneur and businessperson, helped lead the transformation of his new city's Euclid Avenue Corridor. Euclid was one of Cleveland's most important infrastructural arteries, and throughout the sixties, Willis built over two-dozen thriving businesses in the area, helping to make it famous as a center of jazz, Motown, and various forms of live entertainment. His most culturally significant business was the Jazz Temple, a legendary alcohol-free jazz coffeehouse running in the early sixties, which played host to many of jazz's and comedy's giants—John Coltrane, Miles Davis, Redd Foxx, Dizzy Gillespie, Herbie Hancock, Gloria Lynne, Richard Pryor, and Dinah Washington. Second-hand accounts even place Malcolm X and Martin Luther King Jr., in the audience on separate occasions.

At the same time that Willis was transforming Euclid, the extraordinarily powerful Cleveland Clinic Foundation, University Hospitals, and Western Reserve University were in the midst of planning massive, interconnected expansions—growing the idea of a neighborhood called Uptown and a larger University Circle district. This plan targeted the section of Euclid Avenue that Willis had thoughtfully developed, so he fought back, along with members of the community, with all of the legal, financial, and political means available. Willis's Jazz Temple, which drew racially and socioeconomically mixed crowds from across the city as well as the mostly white student population from the nearby Western Reserve University, became a target of the city's lingering racism. And after several failed after-hours bombings, the Jazz Temple was tragically brought down one night in August 1964.[13]

Over the following three decades, Willis slowly lost ground and the financial resources to fight back and was eventually forced out through both legal and illegal actions. This loss was considered a victory by "Cleveland's previously unchallenged ruling circle of powerful whites,"[14] and a spark of hope for a black-owned center of commerce, entertainment, and community was extinguished. The story not only mirrors the many forced migrations that black and native Americans have faced but also highlights the importance of honoring those who walked those miles and the land that was stolen from them.

The Jazz Temple's former location is where the Museum of Contemporary Art (moCa) Cleveland's seven-year-old Farshid Moussavi–designed mirror-clad building now stands. There are no historical markers sharing the story of the Jazz Temple or Willis's role as a business owner and real estate developer, nor is there an annual celebration of black American history in this renowned area. There is also no permanent public acknowledgment that this land was stolen from the Haudenosaunee peoples preceding this history—not that any marker could rectify these ills. However, multilayered research into the recent and more distant past, indicating that the same colonial acts and logic continue today, is a key part of Perry's practice and integral to the network of ideas and stories depicted in *A Terrible Thing*. The piece marks these histories and their hidden nature as a crucial element of its narrative. The Jazz Temple serves as inspiration for Perry's research into the shifts and changes that have taken place in the neighborhood, including an examination of the twentieth-century redlining maps of Cleveland and its surrounding areas.

Just after the Jazz Temple was attacked, a number of Cleveland residents tried to combat redlining, a practice that inevitably leads to segregated neighborhoods by redrawing districts based on race.[15] Redlining, which is now illegal but still exists, operates by financial institutions offering either discriminatory high-interest loans and credit lines or the outright denial of credit to people based on their race or economic status. Banks, insurance companies, and other types of lenders outlined neighborhoods they deemed too financially risky to invest in or lend money to in red. This practice isolated minority populations

A. Will Brown

and the urban poor, creating areas that were (are) caught in feed-back loops of poverty and failing infrastructure, which inevitably made land-grabs by public, private, or civic organizations cheap and fast. Most often throughout the US, and certainly in Cleveland, redlining was used to discriminate against black Americans.

In 1965, the Ludlow Community Association (LCA) and the area's residents took steps to make their community a welcoming place by helping black and white families own and manage property, thereby keeping the demographics of the area at roughly 50 percent black and 50 percent white. This eliminated developers' and the local government's interests in redlining or over-developing the area. However, the strategy failed to address any of the root problems of American racism. Controlling this neighborhood dynamic involved implicit support of whiteness as the social standard, where performing whiteness or passing—a form of self-erasure and survival—was the expected norm. This route to acceptance deliberately inflicted psychological violence of the most insidious, damaging kind on black families who sought housing in neighborhoods with higher living standards. The image taken from the "Cosmopolitan Pioneers" article[16] tells the story of performing identity to ease the fears and anxieties of those who identify with and are identified by whiteness. As black couples and white couples mingle, the homogeneity of their dress, hairstyling, facial expressions, and bodily gestures is highly staged and striking. Even as a relatively progressive initiative and organization, at its core, the LCA was about reinforcing the construction of white behavioral supremacy and assimilation, and not the freedom to come as you are.

The mirrored surfaces and wall of windows in *A Terrible Thing* suggest the ways that the reflections of visitors and our familiar urban structures are the product of these complex social tensions. The gently angled wall of windows bisecting the gallery is a near-facsimile of the windows and mirrored surfaces throughout moCa's building—and the rear projection on these windows creates the illusion that it is a wall of windows looking onto the

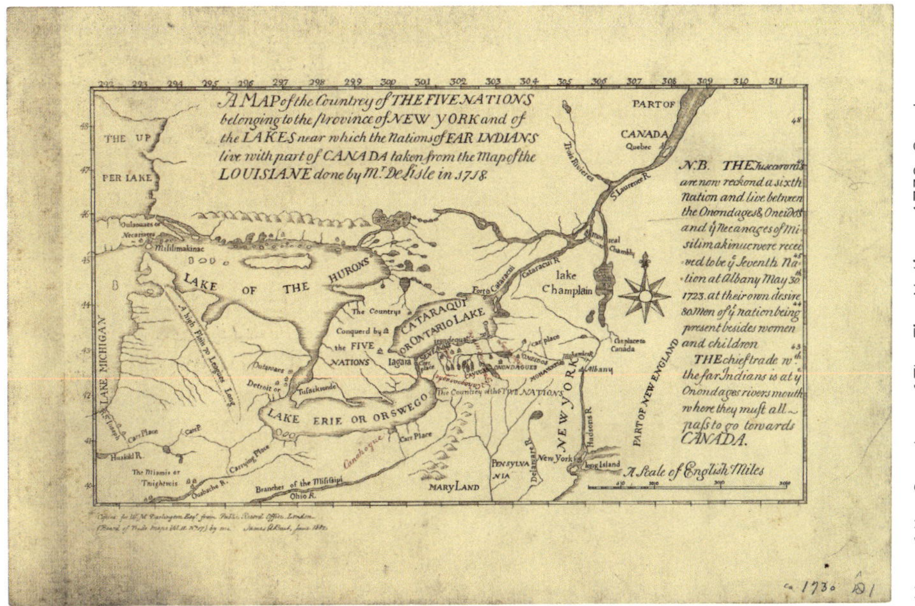

Map of the Countrey of The Five Nations, 1730. Courtesy Darlington Digital Library, University of Pittsburgh, PA

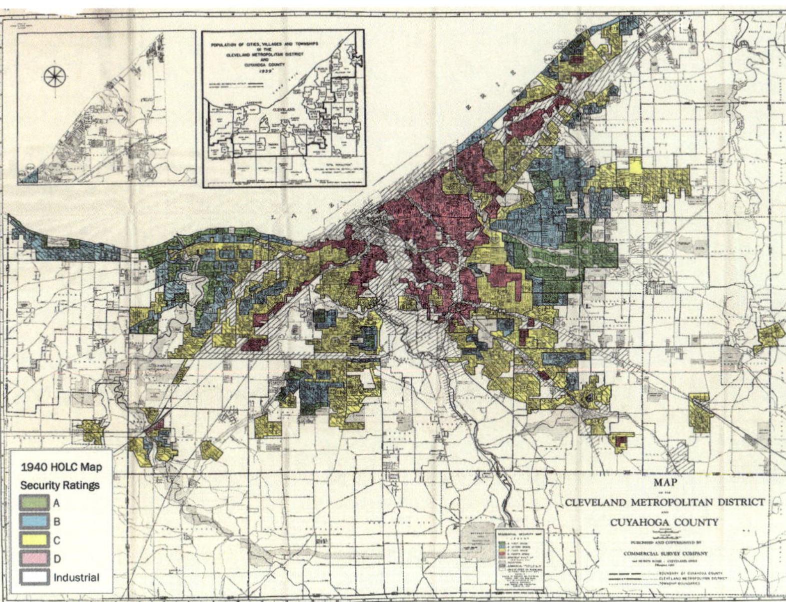

Countywide HOLC Map for Cuyahoga County, 1940. Courtesy ©Kirwan Institute for the Study of Race and Ethnicity, Columbus, OH

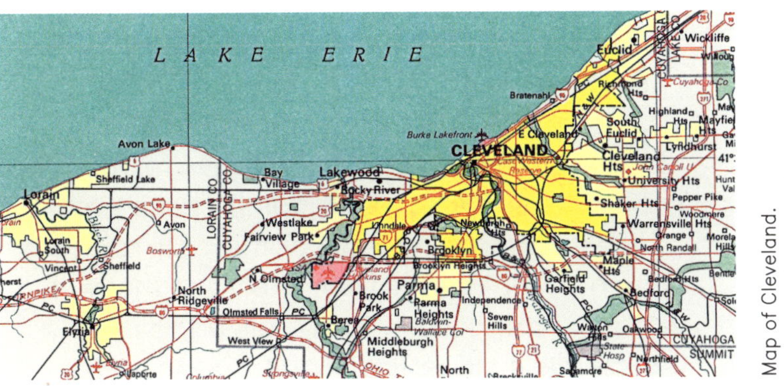

Map of Cleveland. Courtesy Wikimedia Commons

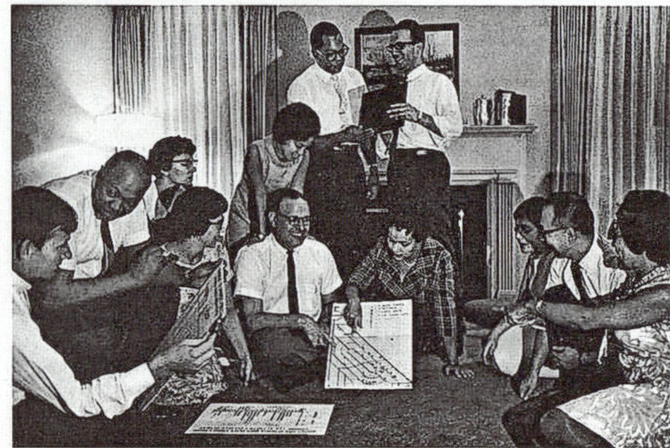

outside world. This confounding relationship, of refraction amongst surface, context, and sight, creates shifting illusions resembling the proclaimed narratives of the past that are vulnerable to interrogation and interpretation. These reflections and refractions break up the performance of self or identity and challenge the idea that there is a sole performance that matters more than any other. Here, Perry uses architecture and infrastructure to expose the distorted facsimiles of reality created to uphold governmental power structures and white supremacy, revealing widely told false narratives that cover up stories, such as those around the destruction of the Jazz Temple. These manifold mirrored surfaces build an elegant tension between viewer and space, drawing one in and out of a hall of distorted mirrors.

This intervening strategy of undermining overarching societal narratives emerges throughout Perry's larger body of work. In *IT'S IN THE GAME '17 or Mirror Gag for Vitrine and Projection* (2017), the artist explores the widespread exploitation of college athletes' images and features the artist and her twin brother, Sandy Perry—who played college basketball and had his image stolen by EA-Sports for use in a National Collegiate Athletic Association basketball video game. In her two-channel HD video and animation installation, she uses the same video game technology that exploited Sandy in order to reclaim his—and many other athletes'—image in a counternarrative.

Perry's video in *A Terrible Thing* functions slightly differently as the group of refracted mirrors intervenes in the images. The mirrors also add an ahistorical dimension that addresses how new urban developments (often reflective polished steel and glass buildings) and the consequent processes of gentrification break up attempts to remember former communities and institutions. These past places were not mirrors of their surroundings but were part of the fabric of them. It is almost impossible to visualize the Jazz Temple here since the ground upon which

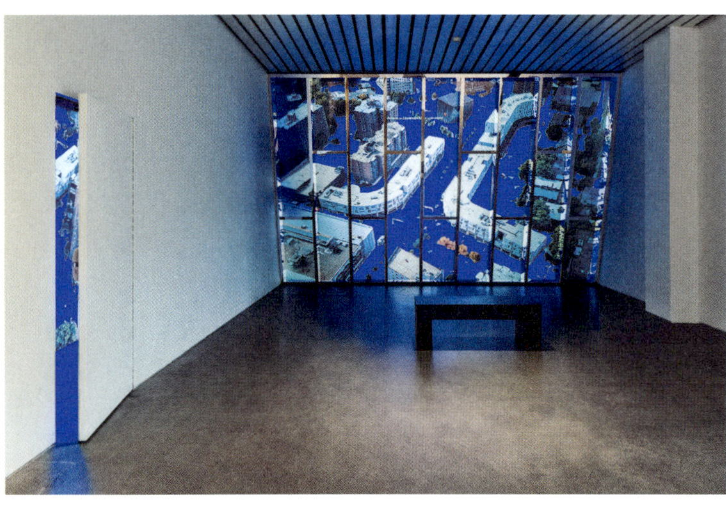

A. Will Brown

it stood has been rendered invisible by the profusion of reflections encasing it. Perry confronts this obfuscation by building a reflective version that seeks to not only retell the story of this corner's past life but also build a strategic platform to begin confronting the erasure. While the work takes on the form of moCa and interrogates the story of the land that surrounds it, it does so out of opportunity rather than malice, and with all of the power and sleight of hand of the mythological Trojan Horse. Conceptually and literally, this institutional space is a fitting platform to explore how art can build processes toward active de-structuring instead of simply through protest and structural criticism.

The Imaginary – Everything

A Terrible Thing's video loop opens and ends with chroma key blue (CKB). This powerful formal and conceptual color motif has become associated with her work in a similar way that Yves Klein is associated with his blue. Klein used "International Klein Blue" (IKB) to encapsulate immateriality, the absolute, and the infinite—everything that is possible all at once. The two have vastly different conceptual and formal approaches to art making (and the connection of each to a single color offers a perhaps limited parallel), but both of their blues are variations of a color long held as that of life, of a beginning, of the place just after black, where everything is possible.

At the end of the video loop in *A Terrible Thing*, CKB washes over the rear projection and its mirrored architecture (the gallery floor and walls) and emanates from within the second architectural installation (a closet space) in the form of a Google Earth view of Cleveland's Uptown and surrounding area. Perry opens and closes this piece and many other works with CKB, providing a momentary reset and imaginative plane.

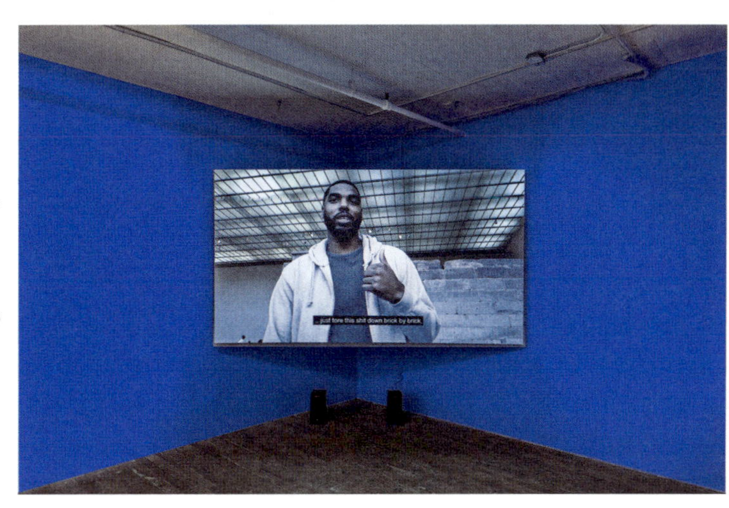

Sondra Perry, *IT'S IN THE GAME '17*, 2018 (still). Digital video projection in a room painted Rosco chroma key blue, color, sound (looped). Courtesy the artist and Bridget Donahue, New York

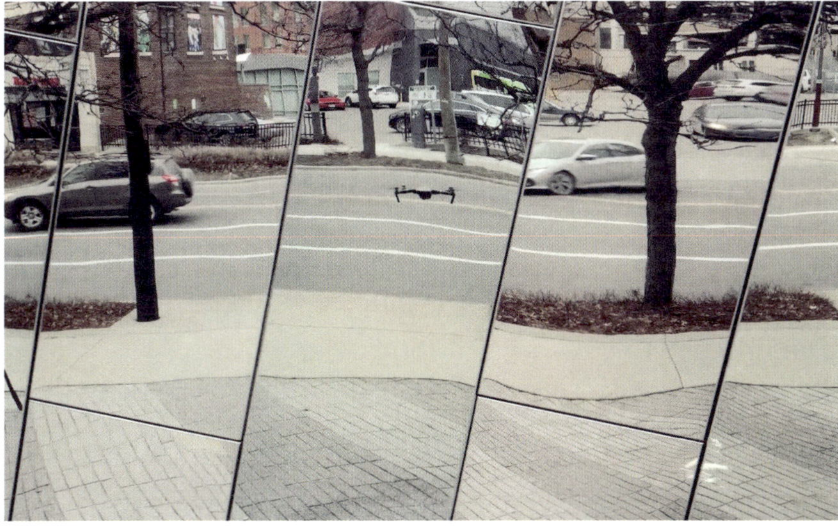

Sondra Perry, *A Terrible Thing*, 2019 (still). Two-channel HD color video, sound; 10:03 min. Courtesy the artist and Bridget Donahue, New York

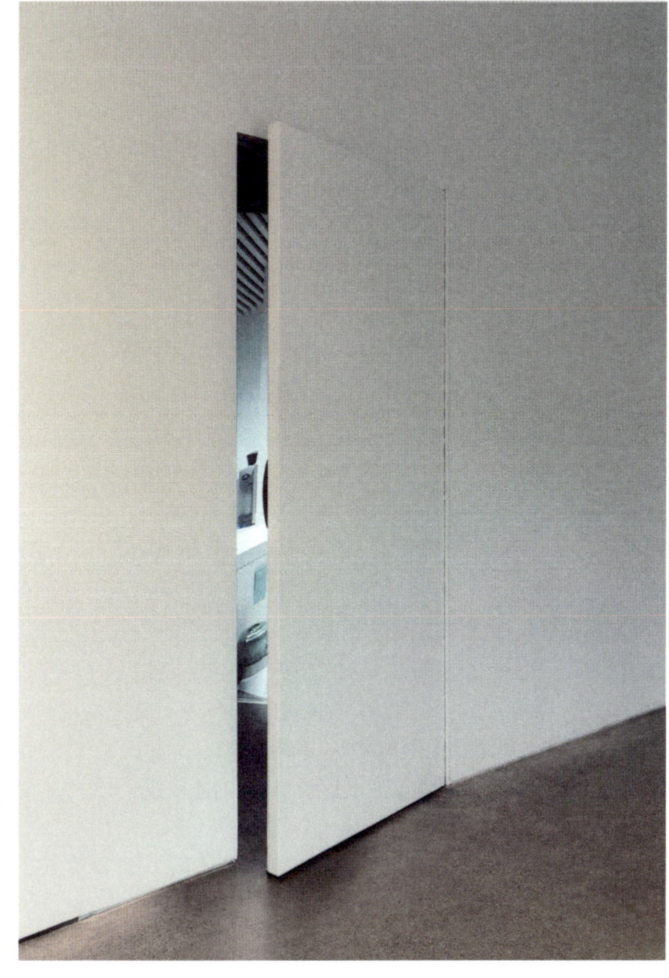

Installation view: Sondra Perry, *A Terrible Thing*, 2019. Museum of Contemporary Art Cleveland. Photo: Field Studio

Slowly, a group of houses, institutions, apartments, and businesses surrounded by avenues and byways of CKB water fills the space. This micro-archipelago of Cleveland's Uptown bears an uncomfortable resemblance to the images of storm waters surrounding buildings that rose to unimaginable heights in New Orleans after Hurricane Katrina. The jarring images of people stranded atop roofs, swimming through poisoned, rushing waters, holding onto trees, and floating in small makeshift boats stuck with us as their homes, places of work, favorite haunts, cars, telephone poles, yards, porches, histories, identities, and worldly possessions were swept away in a preventable disaster. Many were still starving on land and drowning in the water long after the storm passed and long after we expected relief to arrive. The hardest hit areas of New Orleans—the Lower Ninth Ward and its surrounding neighborhoods—were inhabited by brown and black communities, pushed there by the same redlining and racist development policies at work across most American cities.[17]

This eerie echo of the submergence of the Lower Ninth Ward suggests the physical force of ideas that shape our lived environment—underlying narratives used to advocate for urban development, gentrification, public safety, and social progress—and of their human toll. We are reminded that the divestment and theft of land in Cleveland, and the erasure of history and skill, were all actions backed by intention and force that reshaped the story. Here, we return to the idea of power structures that shape the stories we tell. The metaphors and theories used to describe the modern prison in society—the carceral archipelago[18]—explain how technology and surveillance, as well as the internalization of rules through self-policing and vigilance of others, are used to achieve broad-reaching social

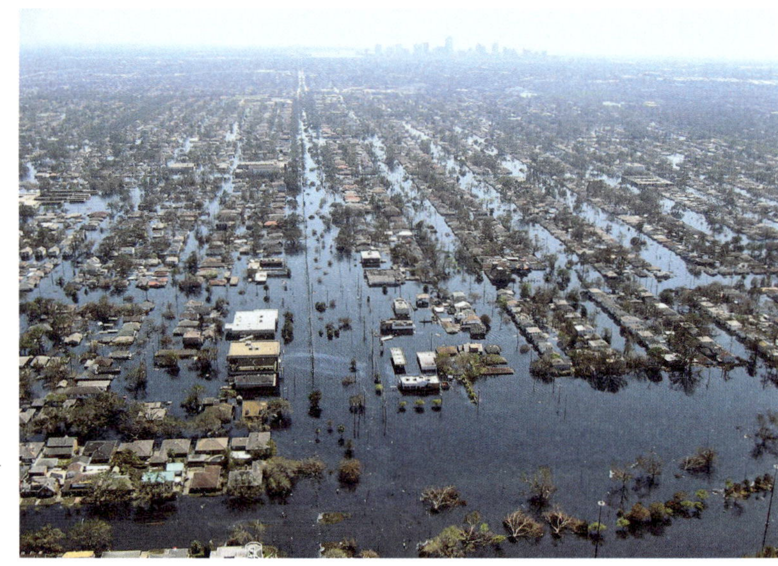

View of flooded New Orleans, LA, in the aftermath of Hurricane Katrina, September 11, 2005. Courtesy the US National Oceanic and Atmospheric Administration (NOAA). Photo: Commander Mark Moran, NOAA Aviation Weather Center, Lt. Phil Eastman, and Lt. Dave Demers, NOAA Aircraft Operations Center

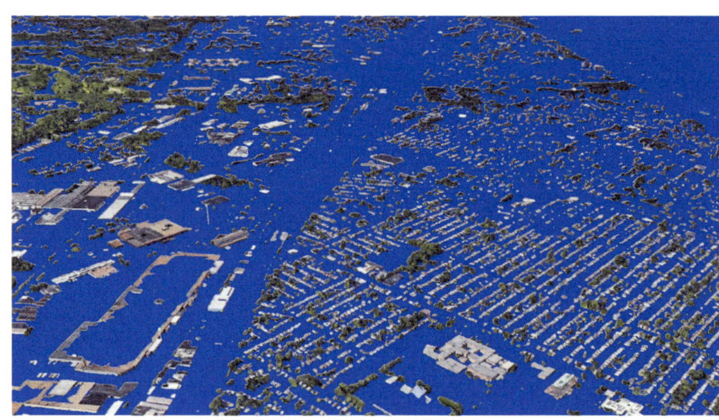

Sondra Perry, *A Terrible Thing*, 2019 (still). Two-channel HD color video, sound; 10:03 min. Courtesy the artist and Bridget Donahue, New York

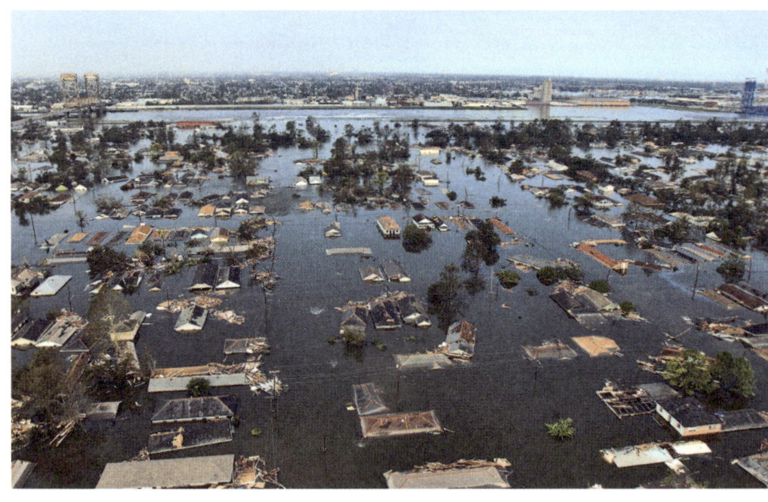

New Orleans, LA, August 30, 2005. Courtesy the FEMA Photo Library. Photo: Jocelyn Augustino/FEMA

Sondra Perry, *A Terrible Thing*, 2019 (still). Two-channel HD color video, sound; 10:03 min. Courtesy the artist and Bridget Donahue, New York

A. Will Brown

control by restricting our access to the truth. Perry draws attention to the fact that white supremacy depends on erasing the presence and stories of non-white people, institutions, and businesses, and *A Terrible Thing* enacts multifaceted damage by building a platform for sharing ideas and stories that this system has buried.

The French-Caribbean poet, philosopher, and writer Édouard Glissant uses the word "imaginary" to describe "all the ways a culture has of perceiving and conceiving of the world."[19] As Perry's CKB fills the spaces in Uptown, creating another archipelago, it takes on the role of a new imaginary—a powerful opposing force to the panopticon. As the hiss-like whisper of the text-to-speech computer voice repeats in rapid succession, "terrible, terrible, terrible, terrible, terrible, terrible thing," CKB spreads across Cleveland's streets. *A Terrible Thing* ushers forth a wave of possibility, a slippery and generous container of everything that is possible after the prevailing hegemony is exposed bit by bit. Perry's work tells new and old stories, sometimes in pieces, sometimes fully, and it does so while holding its complexity and fluidity.

As the video moves across Cleveland, the city's spaces and streets are veiled in profoundly optimistic potential.[20] The return of the land to the Haudenosaunee, who still live in Northeast Ohio, the rebirth of the Jazz Temple, and the many individual reclamations of site and life are all re-envisioned. CKB is a billion blue pixels awaiting future manifestations of a liberated cultural imaginary.

BIBLIOGRAPHY

"A Concert for Hurricane Relief." Performance by Kanye West and Mike Myers, filmed September 2, 2005. NBC Universal Television Group.

Baptist, Edward E. *The Half Has Never Been Told: Slavery and the Making of American Capitalism*. New York: Basic Books, 2016.

Belli Research Institute. *Afro-Pessimism: An Introduction*. Racked & Dispatched, 2017. https://rackedanddispatched.noblogs.org/files/2017/01/Afro-Pessimism2.pdf.

Bentham, Jeremy, and Miran Božovič. *The Panopticon Writings*. New York: Verso, 1995.

"Cayuga: People," and "Iroquois Confederacy: American Indian Confederation." Encyclopedia Britannica, Inc., July 11, 2018. www.britannica.com/topic/Cayuga-people.

Colombi, Chris, and Joe Mosbrook. "JAZZ." Encyclopedia of Cleveland History | Case Western Reserve University, June 29, 2018. case.edu/ech/articles/j/jazz.

"Cosmopolitan Pioneers." LCA History: Cosmopolitan Pioneers, *Ohio Bell Magazine*, 1967. www.ludlowcommunity.org/history-pioneers.htm.

Garrow, David J. "105th And Euclid: The Winston Willis Story." Medium, August 3, 2017. medium.com/@105thandEuclid/105th-and-euclid-the-winston-willis-story-1becb31365d0.

Glissant, Édouard, and Betsy Wing. *Poetics of Relation*. Ann Arbor: University of Michigan Press, 1997.

Halligan, Gabriela, and Kelsey Smith. "Ludlow Community Association - An Experiment in Controlled Integration." Cleveland Historical: Center for Public History + Digital Humanities, August 10, 2012. clevelandhistorical.org/items/show/534.

Klein, Alex. "Hard, Soft, and Wet." In *Myths of the Marble*, edited by Alex Klein and Milena Høgsberg, 9–24. Berlin: Sternberg Press, 2018.

Kochman, Laura. "The Battle Is Joined." Mural Arts Philadelphia, Monument Lab, 2017. www.muralarts.org/artworks/monumentlab/the-battle-is-joined/.

McShine, Kynaston L. "Essay." In *Information*, edited by Kynaston L. McShine, 138–41. New York: Museum of Modern Art, 1970.

Pierre-Ingram, India. "The Miracle on East 105th." PressureLife, February 18, 2019. pressurelife.com/the-miracle-on-east-105th/.

Sheridan, Alan, and Michel Foucault. *Discipline and Punishment: The Birth of the Prison*. New York: Vintage Anchor Publishing, 1995.

Tuck, Eve. "Suspending Damage: A Letter to Communities." *Harvard Educational Review* 79, no. 3, (2009): 409–26.

Wang, Jackie. "Introduction." In *Carceral Capitalism*, edited by Hui Wang, 52. Los Angeles: Semiotext(e), 2018.

Willis-Carrasco, Aundra. "The Jazz Temple - When Jazz Came to University Circle in the 1960s." Cleveland Historical, September 23, 2017. clevelandhistorical.org/items/show/811.

NOTES

1 The title is inspired by Slick Rick's *The Art of Storytelling*, released by Def Jam Recordings in 1999.

2 The ideas within this text were written within the context of Afro-pessimism, as charted in *Afro-Pessimism: An Introduction*, which includes texts by Frank B. Wilderson, Saidiya Hartman, Steve Martinot, Jared Sexton, and Hortense J Spillers. For a thorough framework of Afro-pessimism, see Belli Research Institute, "Introduction," *Afro-Pessimism: An Introduction*, Racked & Dispatched, 2017, 7–15, https://rackedanddispatched.noblogs.org/files/2017/01/Afro-Pessimism2.pdf.

3 The following words resonate with my ambivalence in undertaking writing about Sondra Perry's work: "As a non-Black person—none of my words should be taken as representative…. Being non-Black, I am structurally positioned against Blackness and thus to feel a world built completely against you is something that is ultimately incomprehensible to me. My interest…comes not as an empathetic ally—as that position only reinforces the racial hierarchy—but as an enemy of whiteness (and as someone who lovingly fights alongside friends)." Belli Research Institute, "Preface," *Afro-Pessimism*, vi.

4 *A Terrible Thing*, as both the exhibition and the artwork, deals with complex social and historic problems and constructs. This essay does not intend to define, classify, or explain all of these but to build a series of narrative and theoretical lenses around the piece so that we might investigate and untangle them further. This text is not meant to solely position the artwork against white supremacy but as one part of how the work operates, and it attempts to ascribe language to Perry's work that aids in potential demystification.

5 "Cayuga: People," and "Iroquois Confederacy: American Indian Confederation," Encyclopedia Britannica, Inc., July 11, 2018, www.britannica.com/topic/Cayuga-people.

6 For a thorough, thoughtful history of the white people who claimed this region as the Western Reserve of Connecticut, see: http://www.ohiohistorycentral.org/w/Connecticut_Land_Company and https://case.edu/ech/articles/c/connecticut-land-co.

7 Jackie Wang, "Introduction," in *Carceral Capitalism*, ed. Hui Wang (Los Angeles: Semiotext(e), 2018), 52.

8 Edward E. Baptist, "Feet," in *The Half Has Never Been Told: Slavery and the Making of American Capitalism* (New York: Basic Books, 2016), 25.

9 Baptist, "Right Hand," *The Half Has Never Been Told*, 103.

10 For more on this subject, see Baptist, "Tongues," *The Half Has Never Been Told*, 145–70.

11 "Social death has three constituent elements: one is gratuitous violence, which means that the body of the slave is open to the violence of all others. Whether he or she receives that violence or not, he or she exists in a state of structural or open vulnerability. This vulnerability is not contingent upon his or her transgressing some type of law, as in going on strike with the worker. The other point is to say that the slave is natally alienated, which is to say that the temporality of one's life that is manifest in filial and afilial relations—the capacity to have families and the capacity to have associative relations—may exist very well in your head…. And the third point is general dishonor, which is to say, you are dishonored in your very being." Frank B. Wilderson and C.S. Soong, "Blacks and the Master/Slave Relation," *Afro-Pessimism*, 18.

12 Baptist, "Tongues," *The Half Has Never Been Told*, 165.

13 India Pierre-Ingram, "The Miracle on East 105th," PressureLife, February 18, 2019, pressurelife.com/the-miracle-on-east-105th/.

14 David J. Garrow, "105th and Euclid: The Winston Willis Story," Medium, August 3, 2017, https://medium.com/@105thandEuclid/105th-and-euclid-the-winston-willis-story-1becb31365d0.

15 Much of the information about Cleveland and the city's attempts to create racially mixed and equal communities (as well as its long history of discriminatory housing, lending, and business practices) comes from an essay by Elizabeth Culp, "The Fight for Suburbia," which was written for a graduate seminar in May 2014. While not published officially, this essay was written using primary sources and can be made available through contact with the author (a.willbrown@gmail.com). Information about the Ludlow Community comes from the disgracefully titled article, "Cosmopolitan Pioneers," in LCA History: Cosmopolitan Pioneers, *Ohio Bell Magazine*, 1967, www.ludlowcommunity.org/history-pioneers.htm. I say "disgracefully" because the two words "Cosmopolitan" and "Pioneers" perpetuate the language of the settler colonizer, which "seeks over time to eliminate the categories of colonizer and colonized through a process by which the former replaces the latter completely, usurping the claim to indigenous residence." Jared Sexton, "The *Vel* of Slavery: Tracking the Figure of the Unsovereign," in *Afro-Pessimism*, 153. Further reading on this topic can also be found in, Eve Tuck, "Suspending Damage: A Letter to Communities," *Harvard Educational Review* 79, no. 3 (2009): 409–26.

16 "Cosmopolitan Pioneers," LCA History: Cosmopolitan Pioneers.

17 Five days after the storm hit, on September 2, 2005, Kanye West stated on live television, "George Bush doesn't care about black people," while standing next to Mike Myers on a celebrity spot to raise money for the victims. ("A Concert for Hurricane Relief," A Concert for Hurricane Relief, performance by Kanye West and Mike Myers, NBC Universal Television Group, September 2, 2005.) His words struck a chord that resonated deeply within American society. Many were now free to ask and imagine why these rising waters were allowed beyond the levees, how they were allowed to crash over, seep under, and blast through them, submerging black neighborhoods when there was a known remedy. It cut through the spine, opening a space for questions about the very nature of why this had happened. People suddenly wondered: why had the levees not been repaired? Why was the Federal Emergency Relief Agency (FEMA) so slow to respond? Why was there so little money? These questions led to public outcry when it emerged that the Bush administration had diverted funding for securing those same levees to support the war in Iraq and had direly underfunded FEMA. West's words asserted boldly that the government was responsible for this and many acts of systemic neglect that led to black and brown deaths and the erasure of their communities in New Orleans. While West later walked back his words with a public apology—a forced act given as understandable self-preservation and survival—the damage had been done.

18 For more on Michel Foucault's "carceral archipelago" as well as Jeremy Bentham's "panopticon," see Alan Sheridan and Michel Foucault, *Discipline and Punishment: The Birth of the Prison* (New York: Vintage Anchor Publishing, 1995), and Jeremy Bentham, *The Panopticon Writings* (New York: Verso, 1995).

19 Édouard Glissant, "Glossary," in *Poetics of Relation*, transl. Betsy Wing (Ann Arbor: University of Michigan Press, 1997), xxi–xxiii.

20 Though my conclusion falls prey to both colonialist manifestations and processes, I consider CKB to be a container of unlimited potential, offering a future without the hegemony that has been enacted over the last six-hundred-odd years. CKB is everything, and, in turn, any form of supremacy or colonialism is problematic. If we only offer critique of one form of supremacy, then it stands as the only supremacy, which is deeply flawed logic. Supremacy itself is the root problem. For more on this, see Eve Tuck, "Suspending Damage," 409–26.

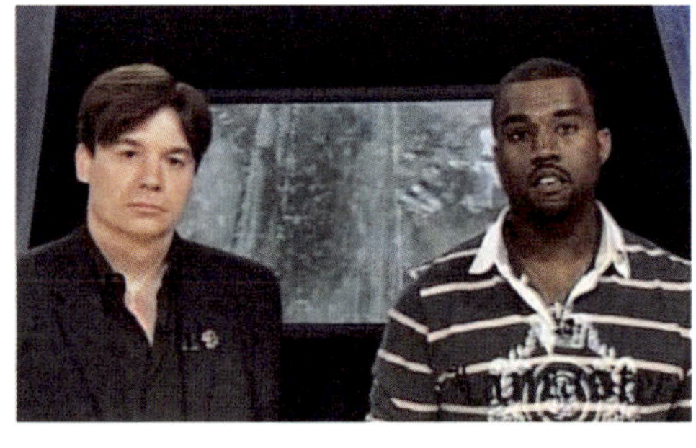

Still from "A Concert for Hurricane Relief," 2005. Sponsored by NBC Universal Television Group

A. Will Brown

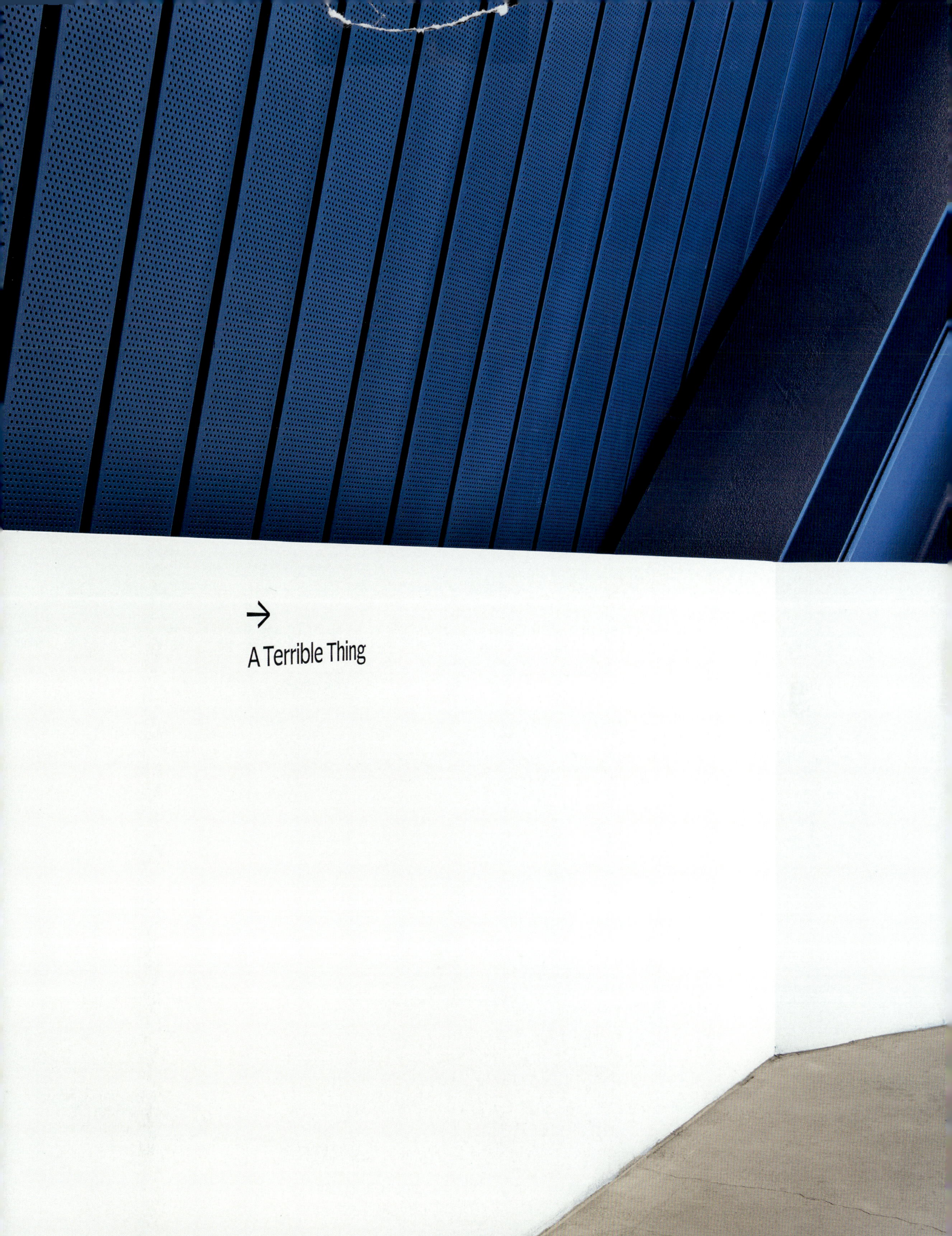
→
A Terrible Thing

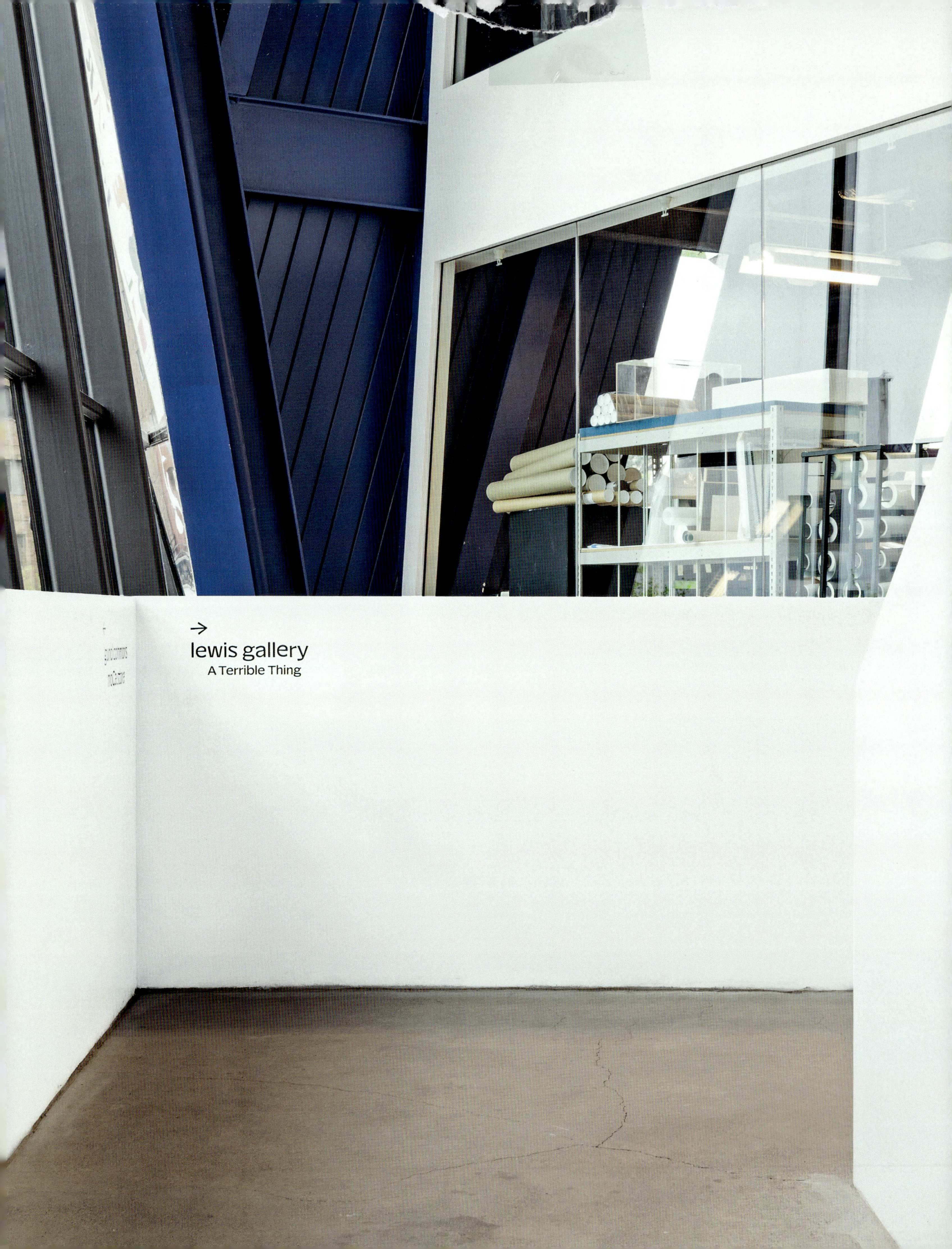
→
lewis gallery
A Terrible Thing

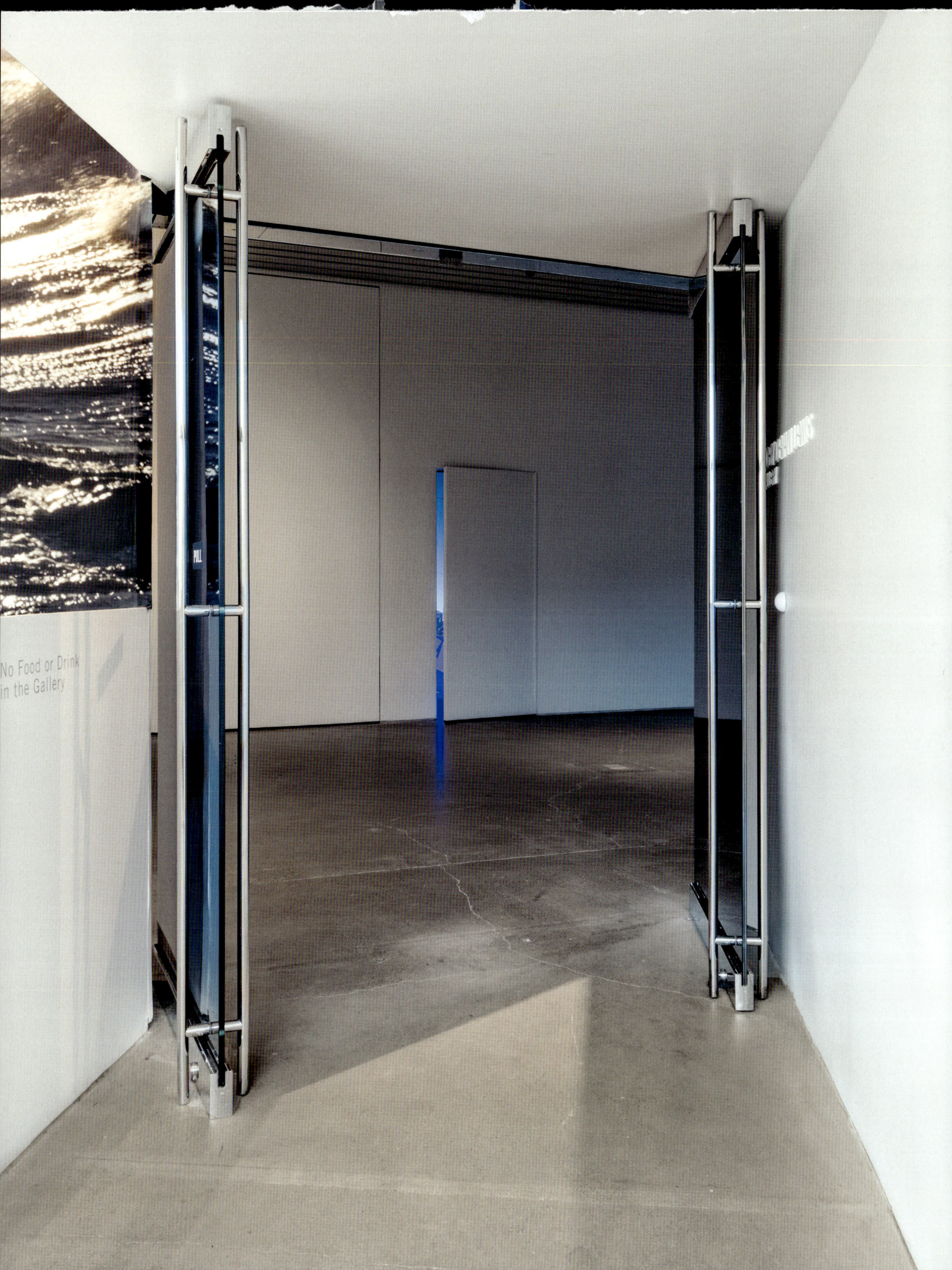
No Food or Drink
in the Gallery
PULL

Here, under feet, and the concrete, and the silt, and fine sand. We are anchored to this place via geothermal wells six hundred feet into the Chagrin Shale, a geologic formation 365 million years old.

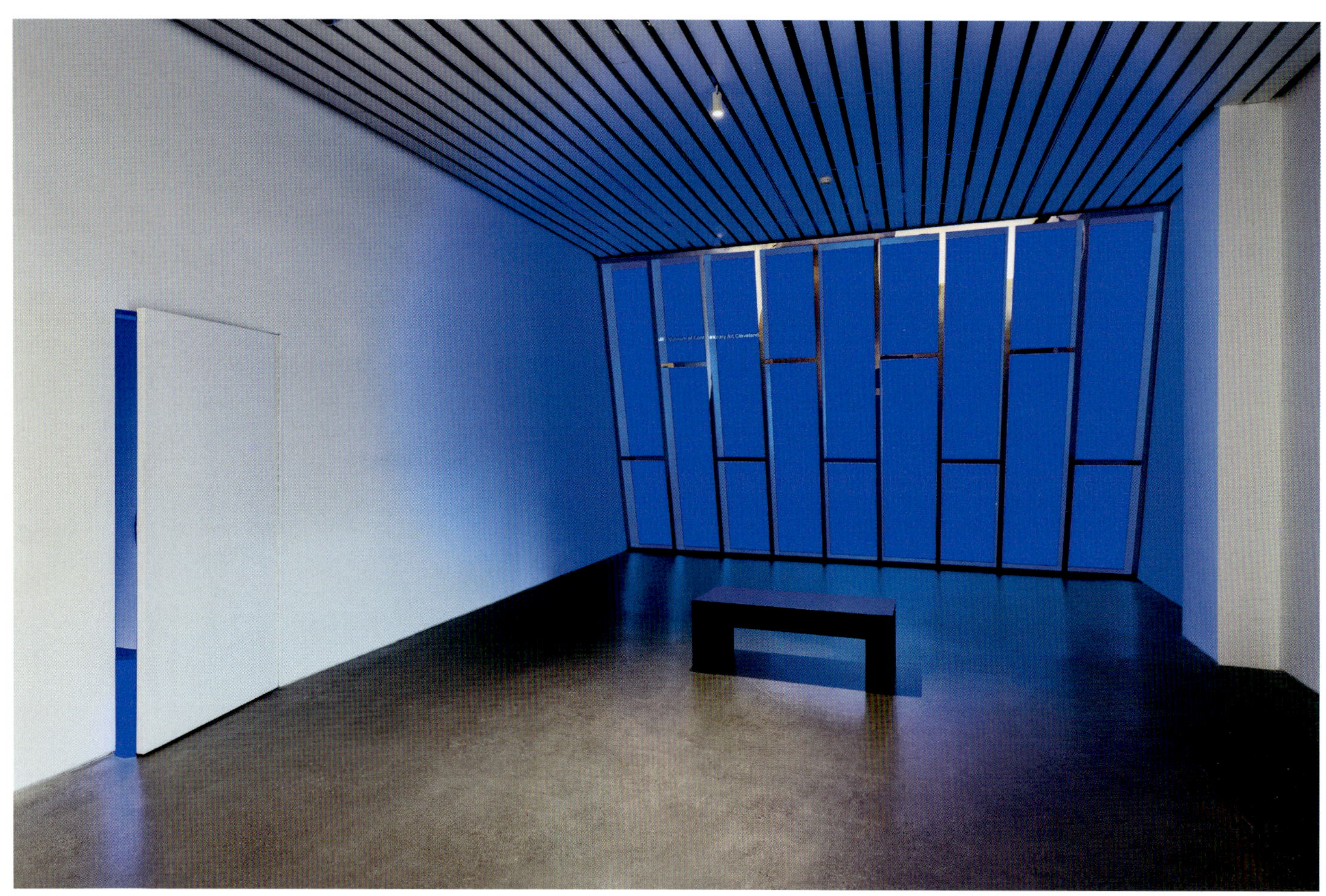

Our new name is moCa. We are a construction.

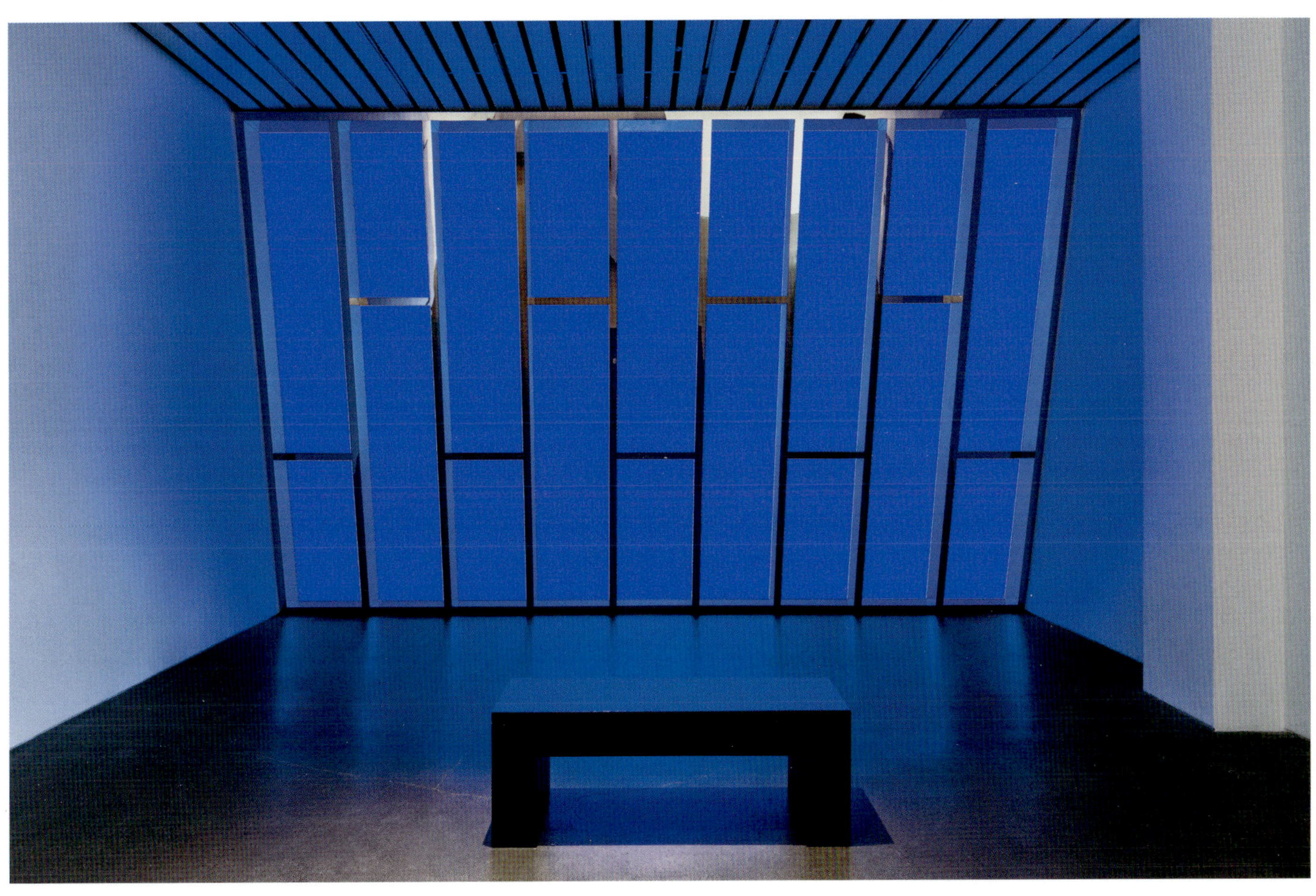

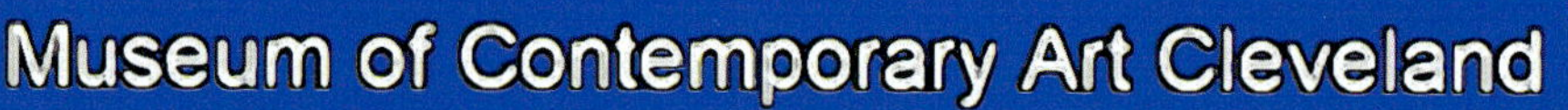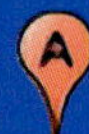
Museum of Contemporary Art Cleveland

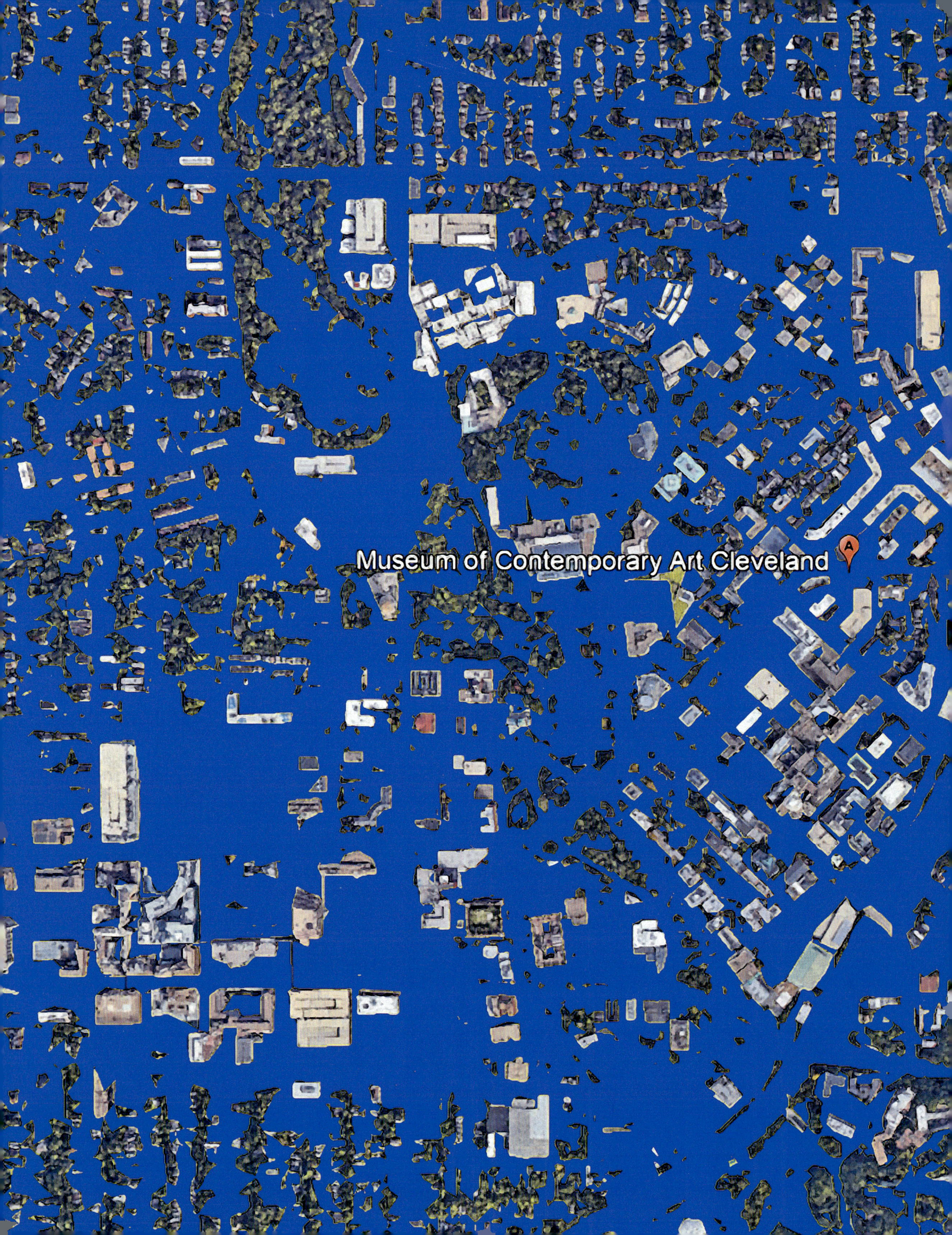

Museum of Contemporary Art Cleveland

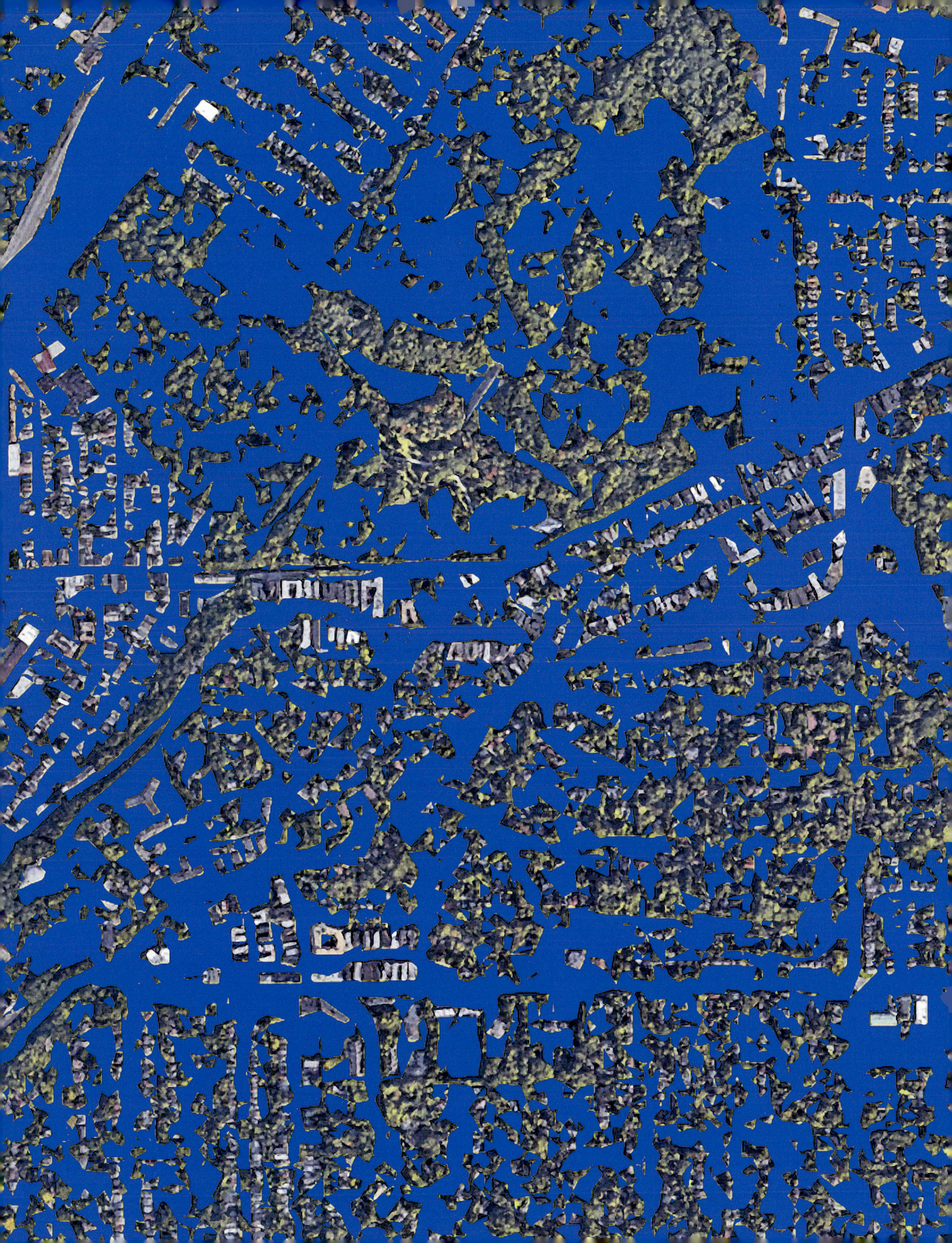

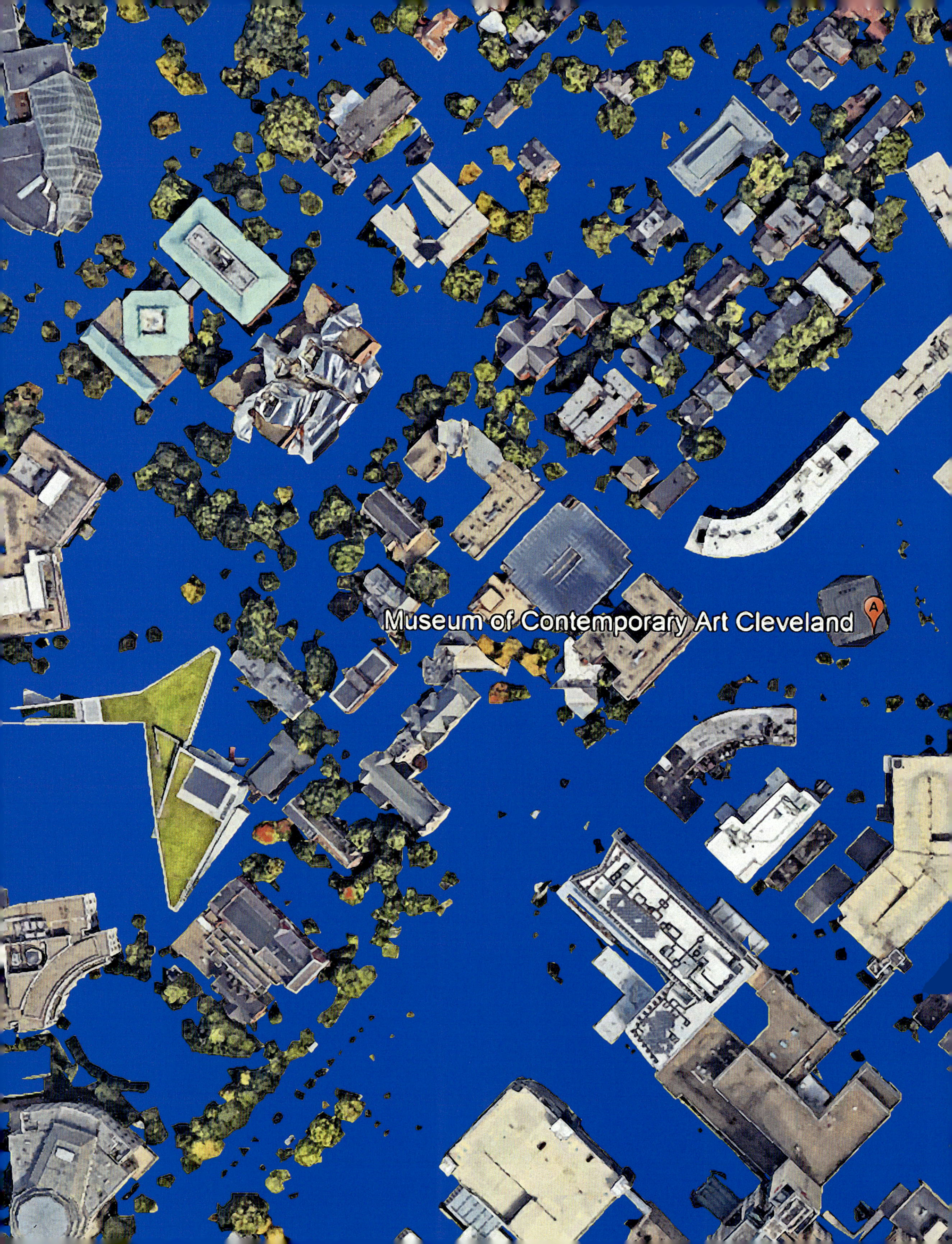

Museum of Contemporary Art Cleveland

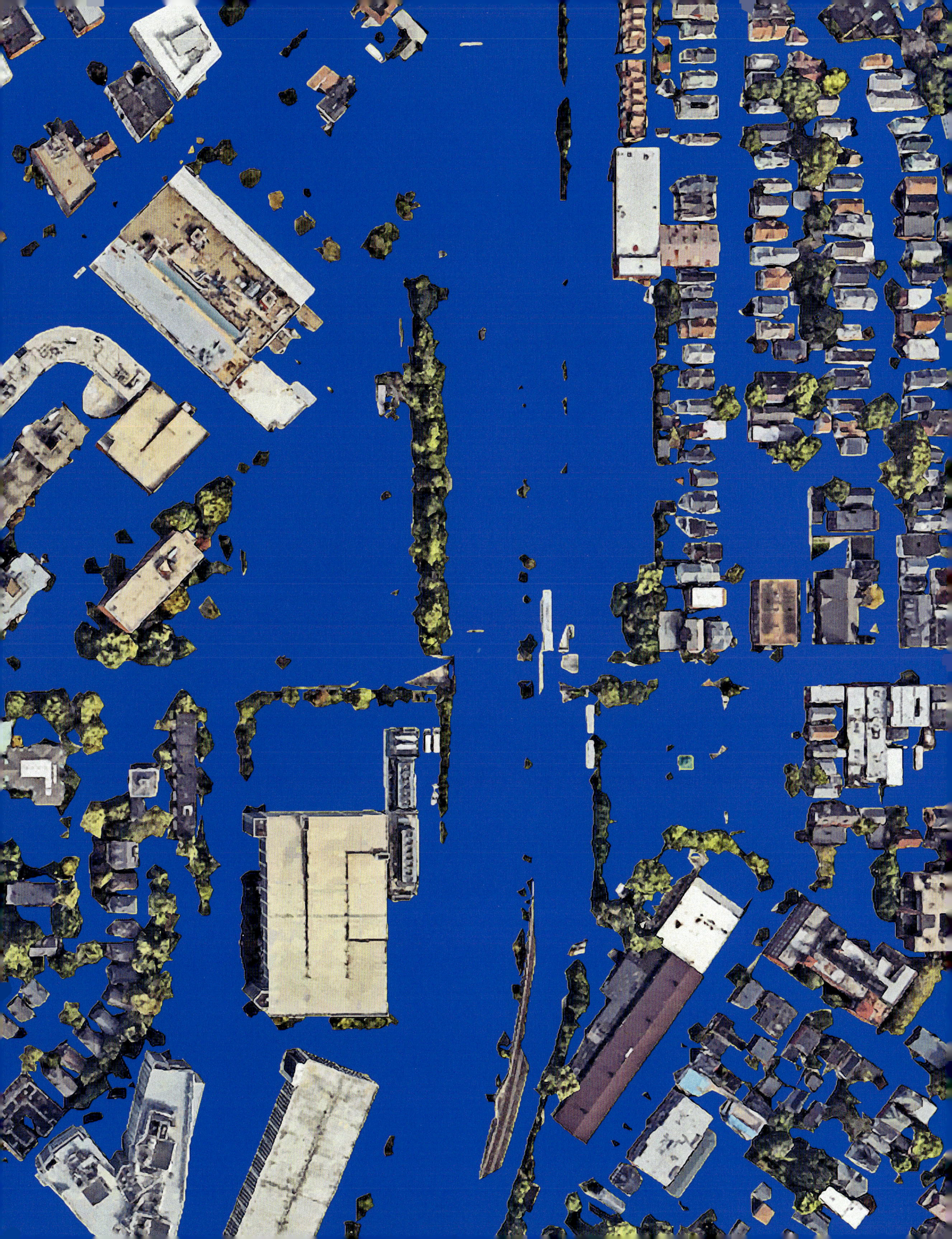

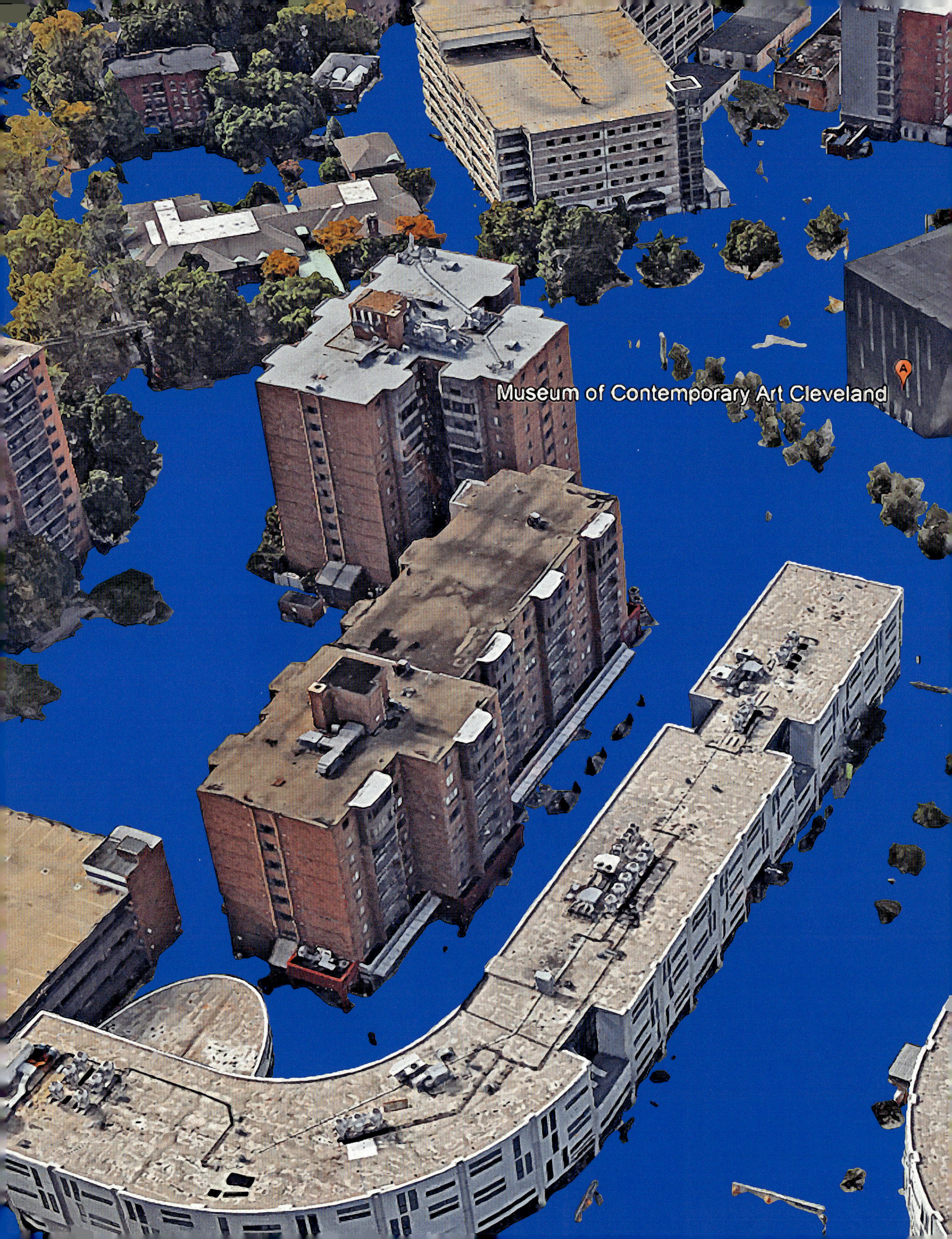
Museum of Contemporary Art Cleveland

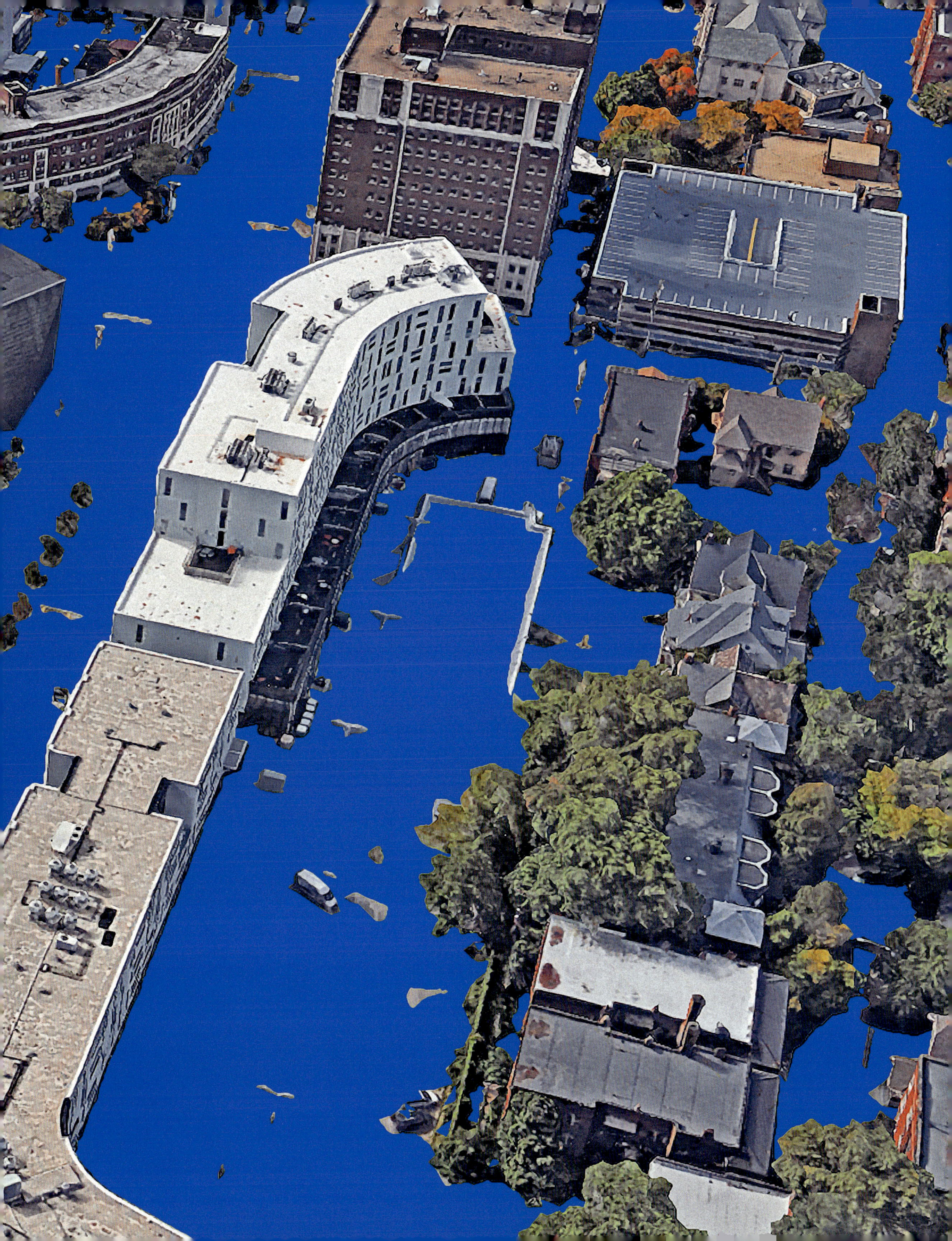

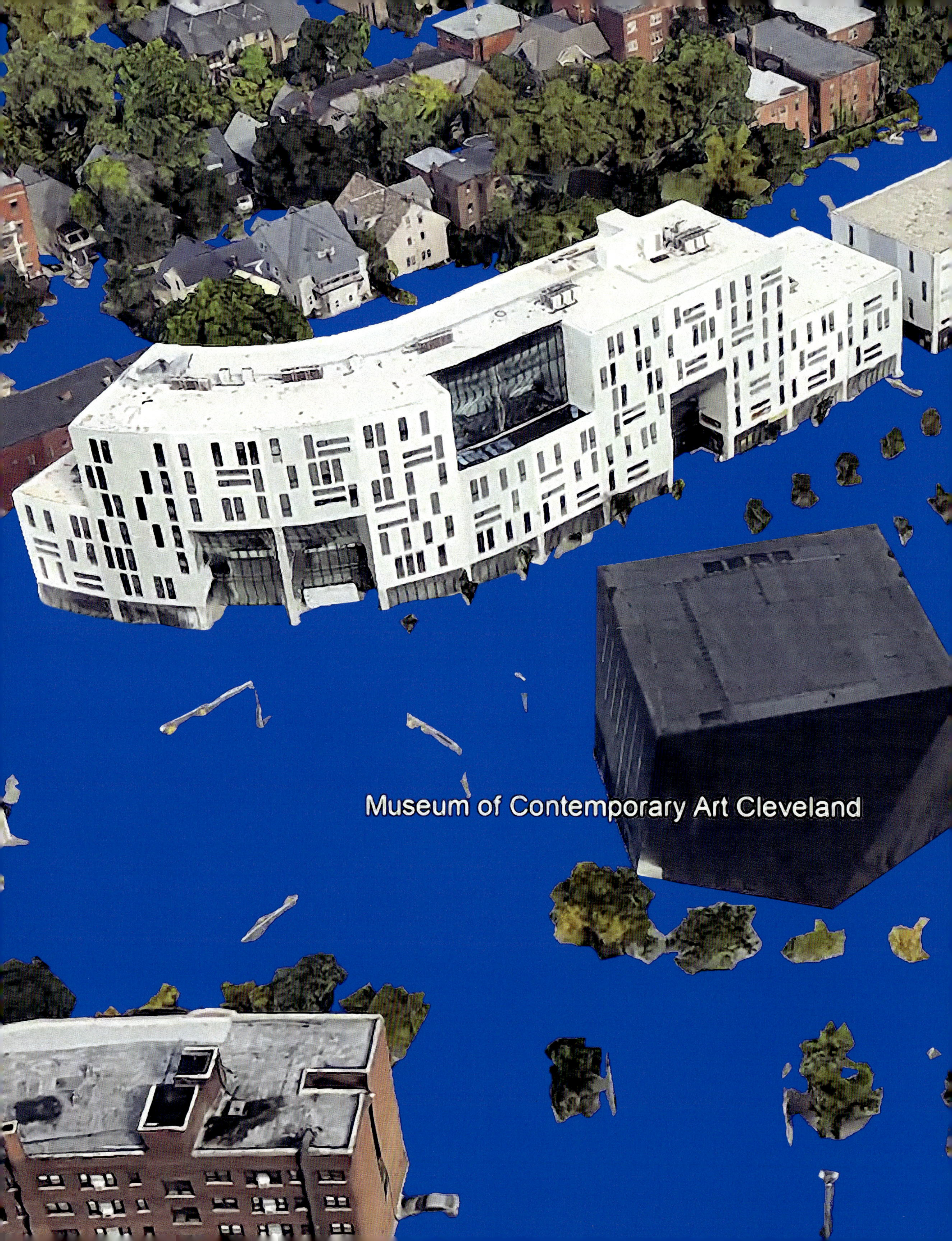
Museum of Contemporary Art Cleveland

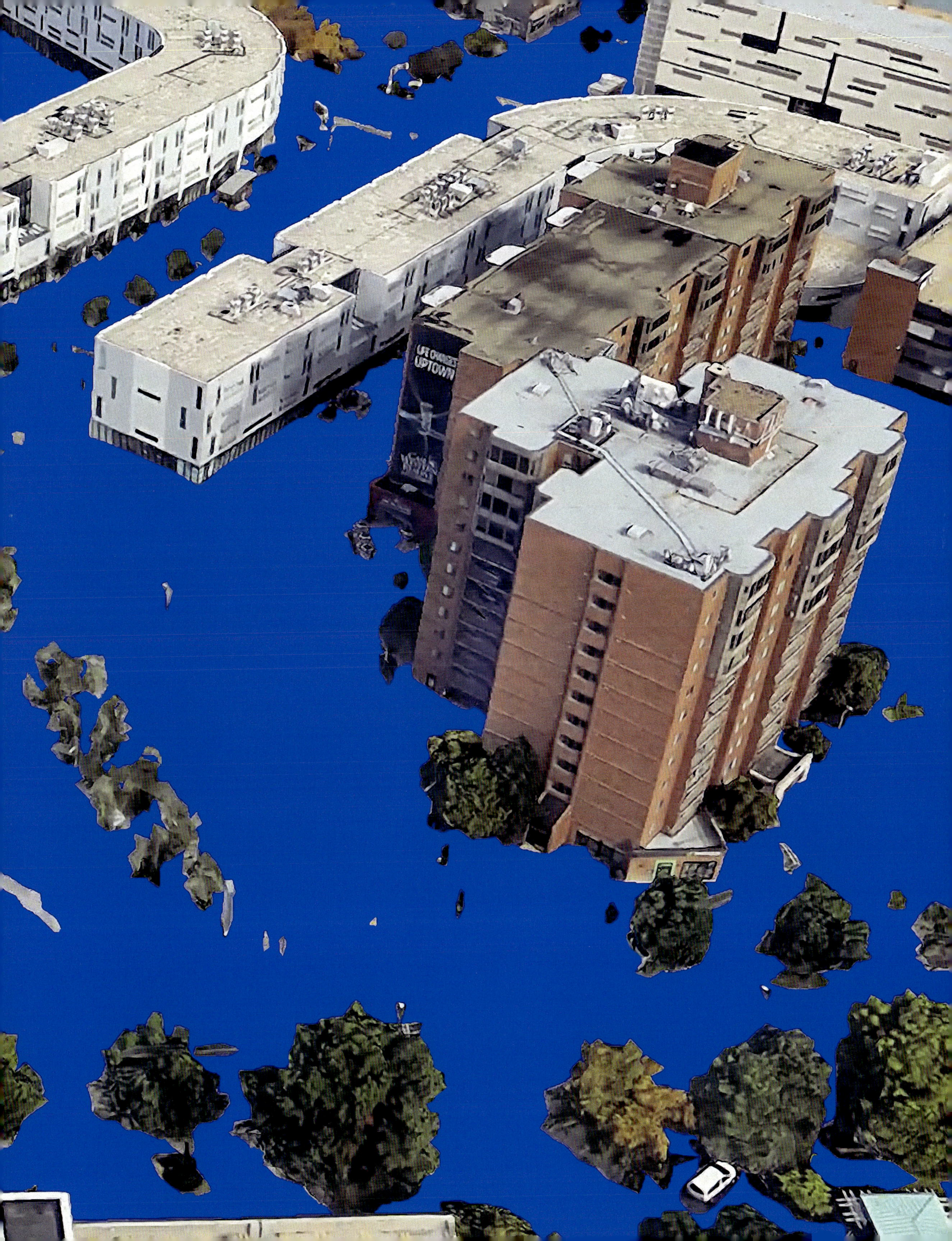
LIFE CHANGES
UPTOWN

We are a construction. With the assistance of   14.8 million in New Markets Tax Credits federal income tax credits used to encourage private investment in low-income communities around the United States we exist through cooperation and solidarities beyond our understanding.

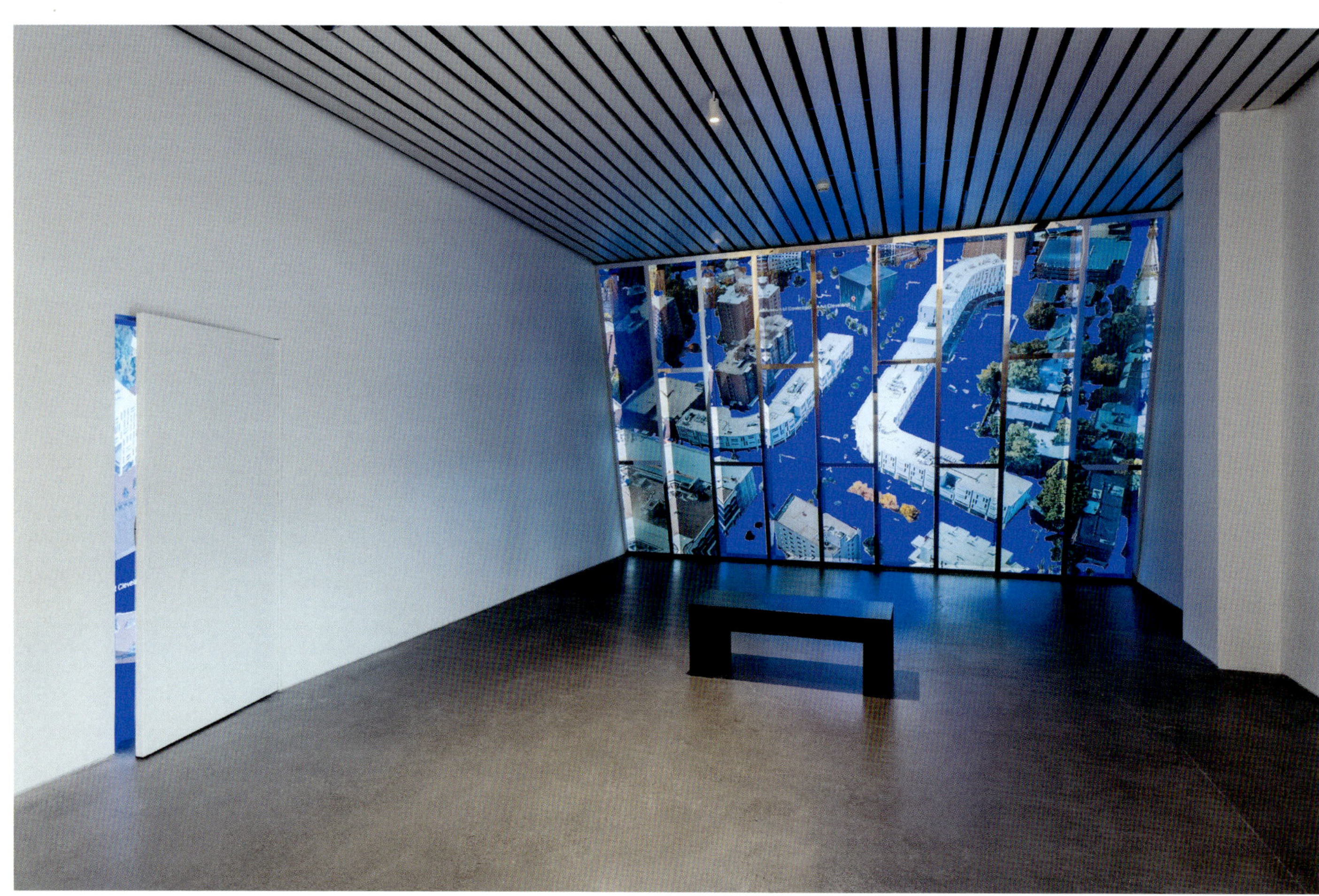

We are a neighborhood resource. We pump energy from the
earth into ourselves and make heat. We pump vital revenue
into the local economy as visitors frequent local shopping and
dining and nightlife establishments.

We are a highly visible commitment to
Cleveland's urban redevelopment.
We are highly visible, and we have sight.
We are alive.

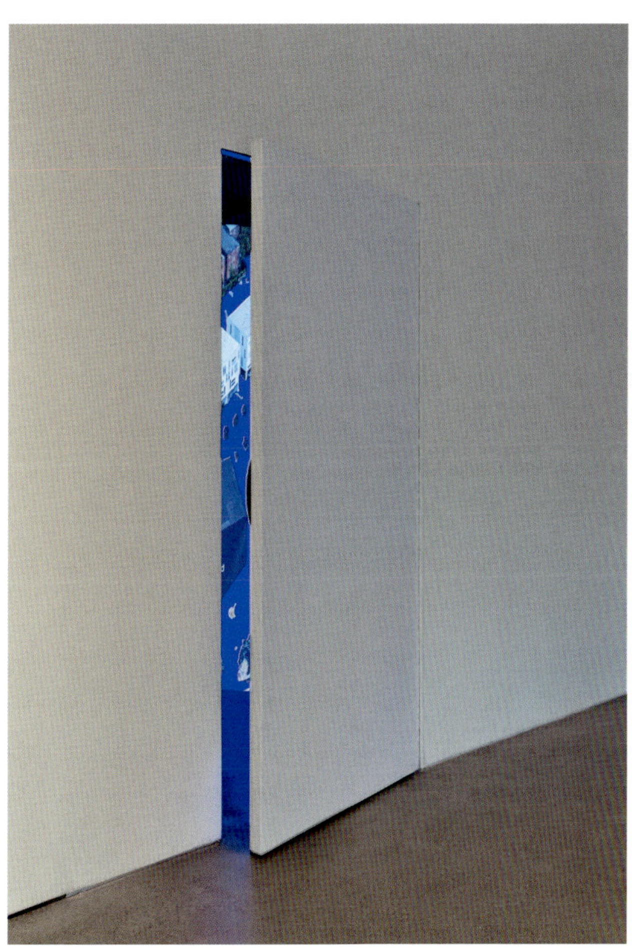

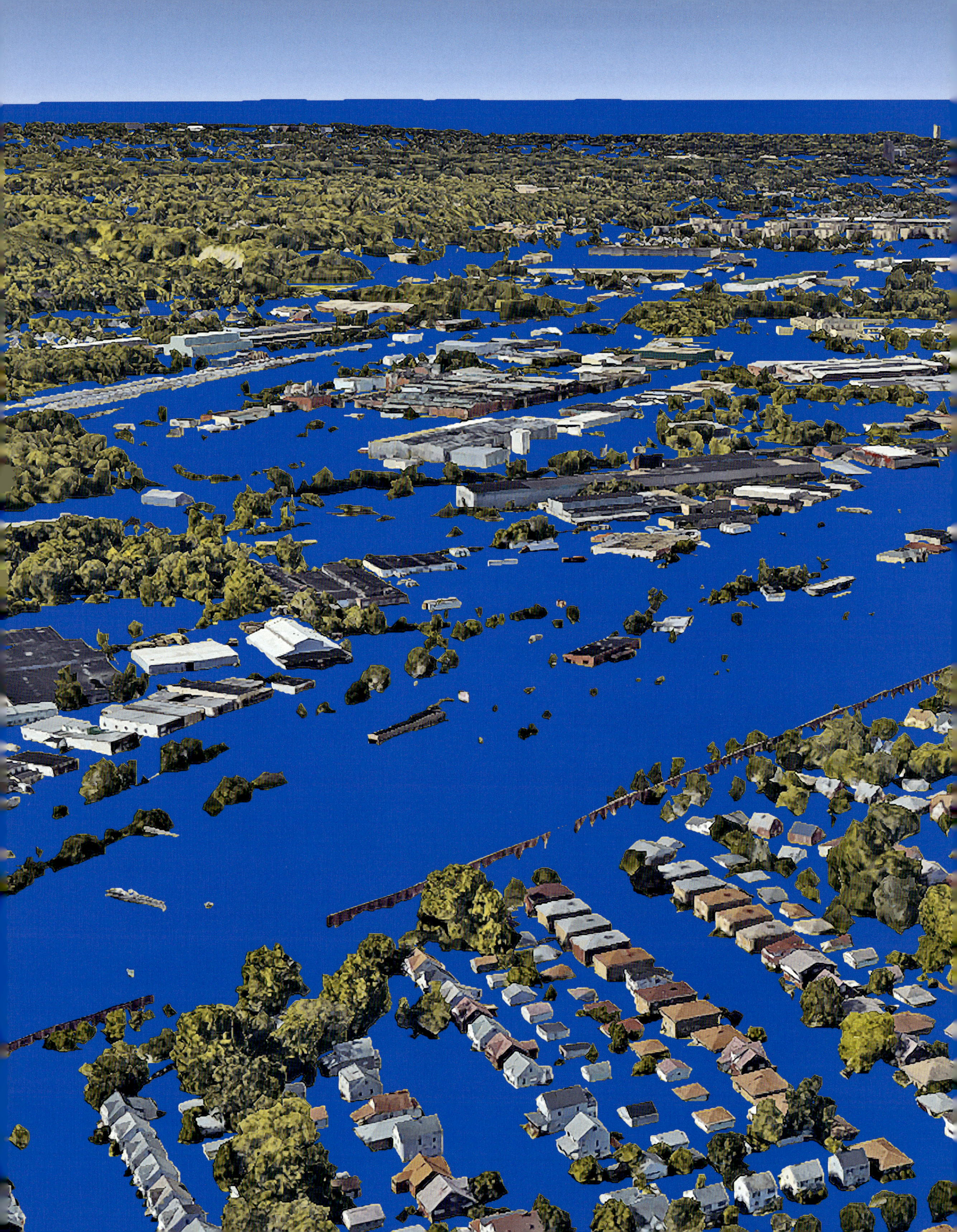

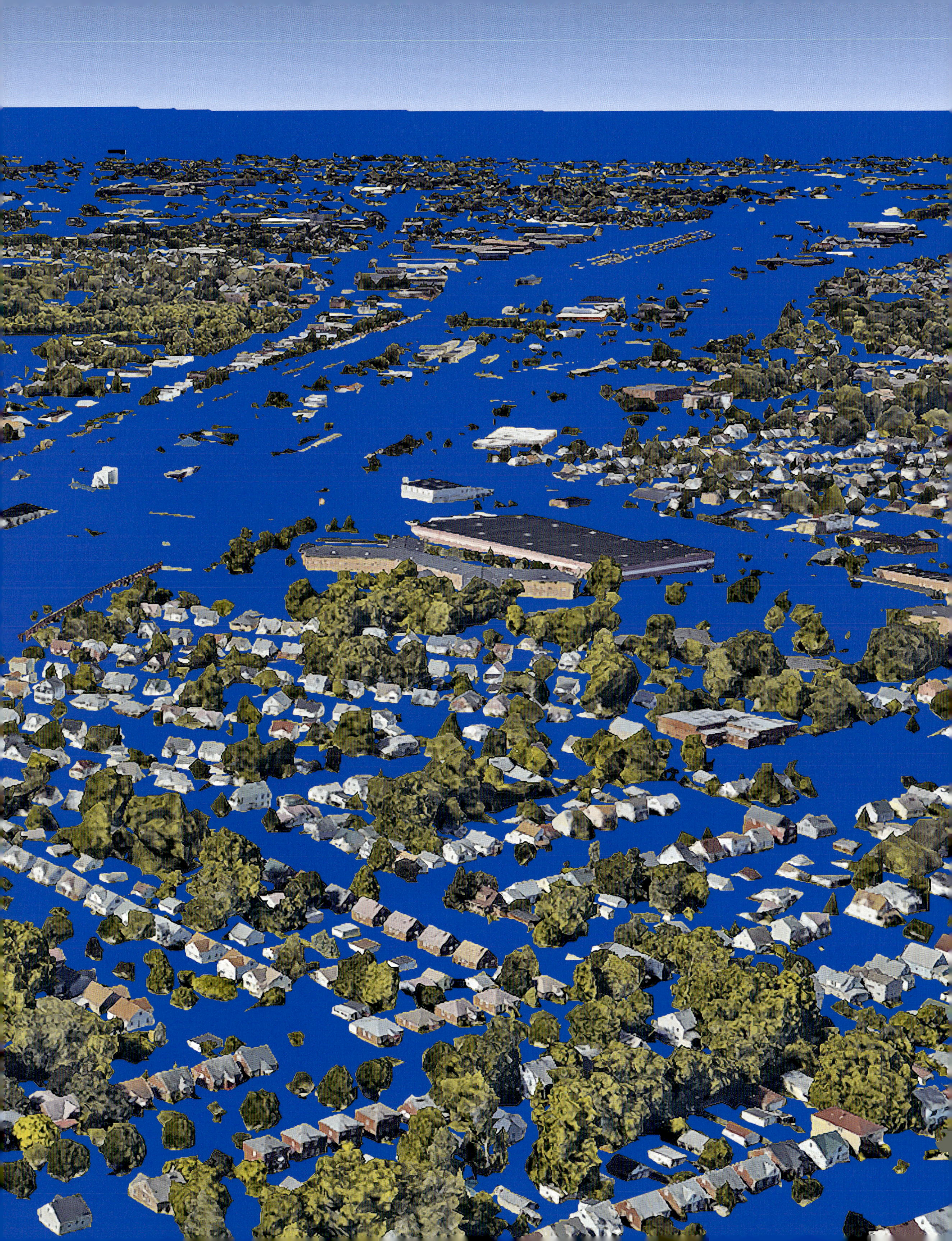

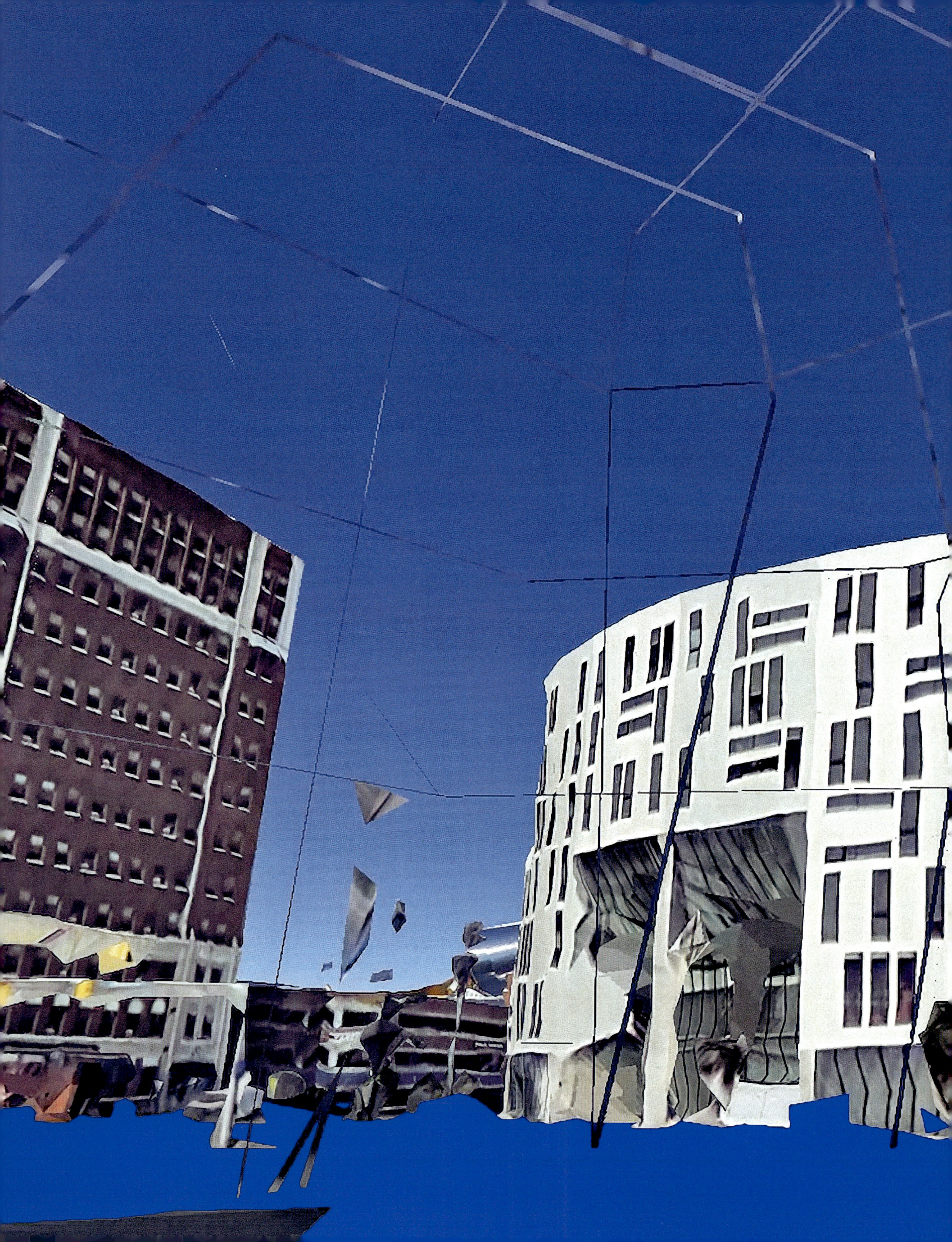

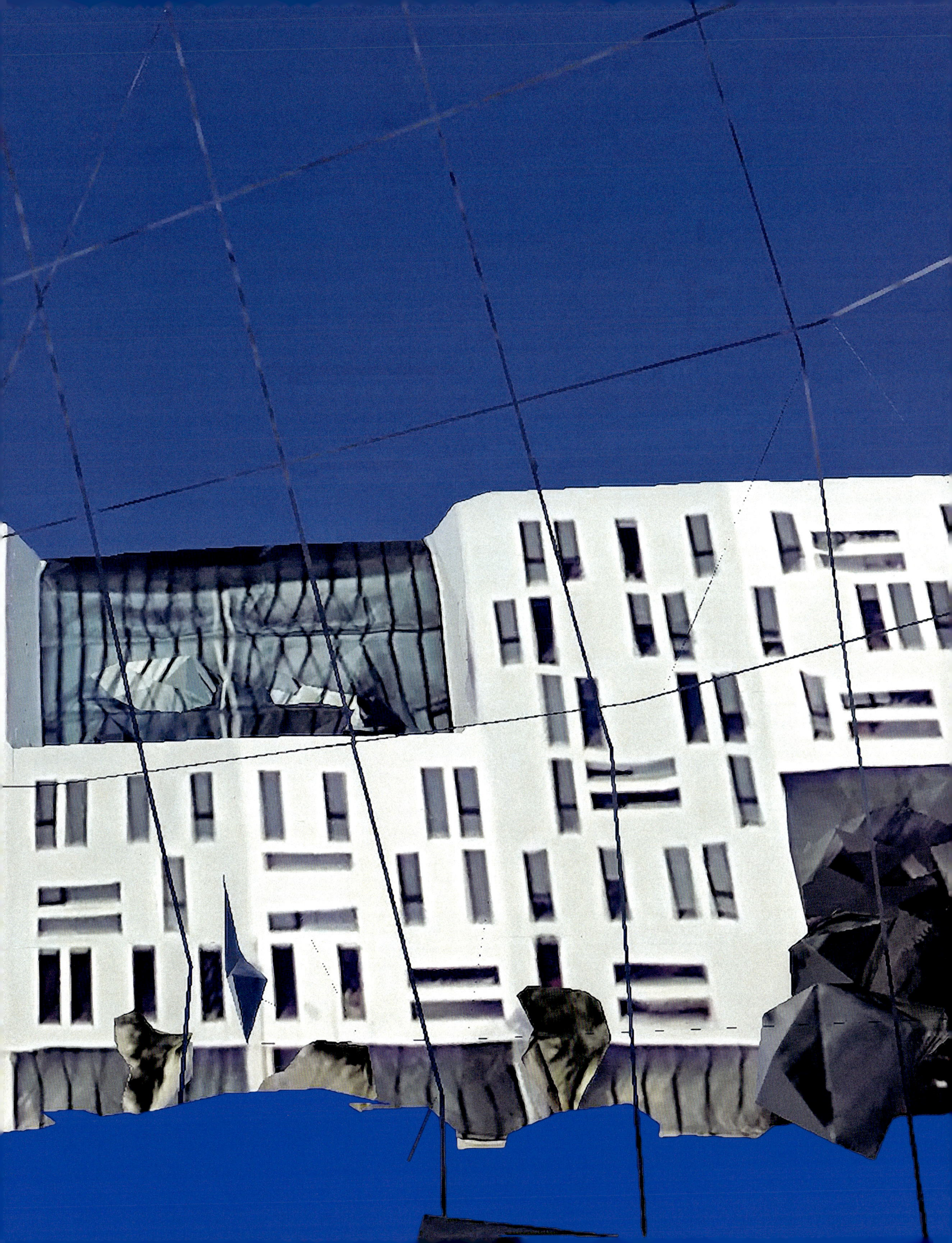

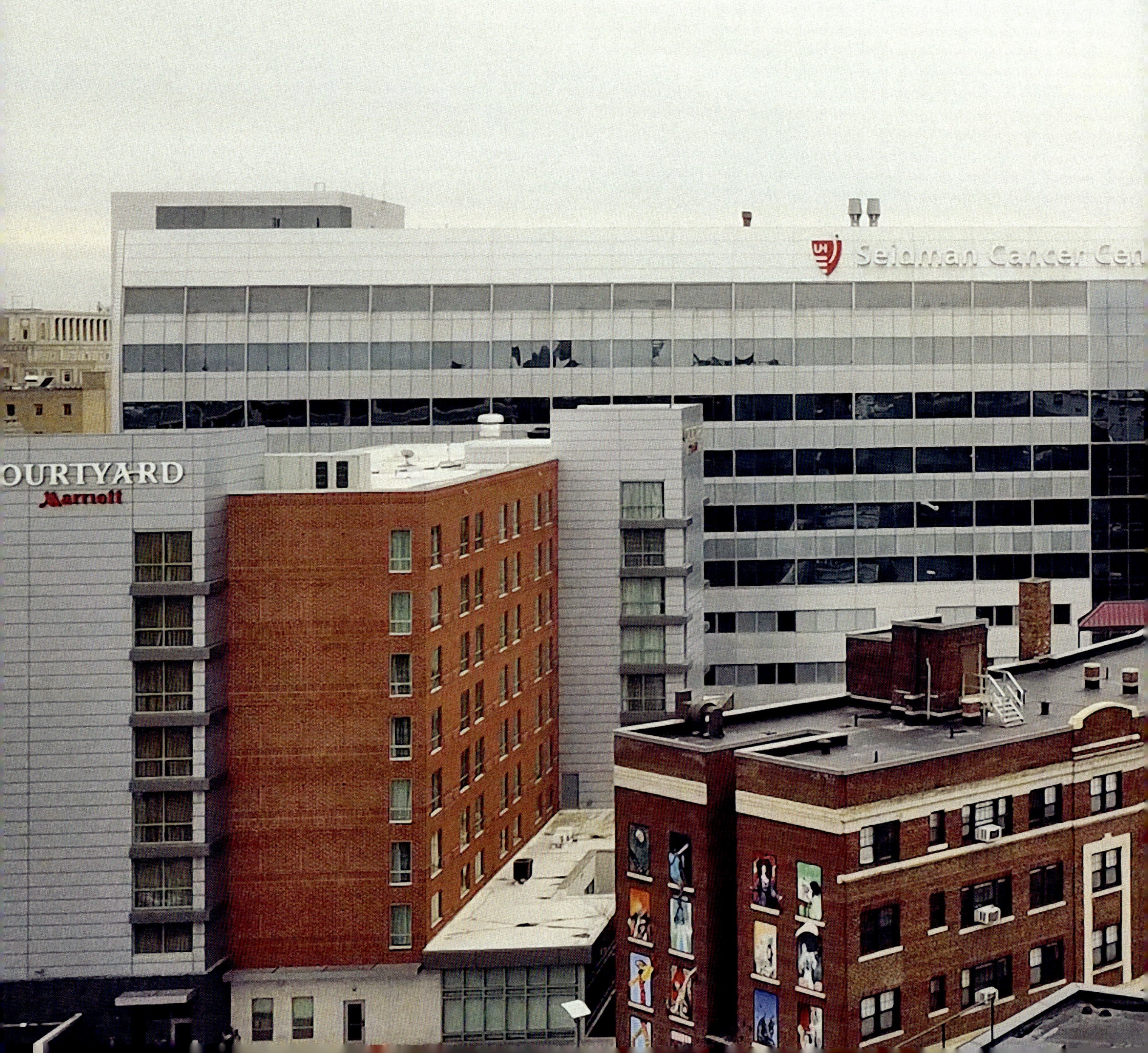
Seidman Cancer Cen
COURTYARD
Marriott

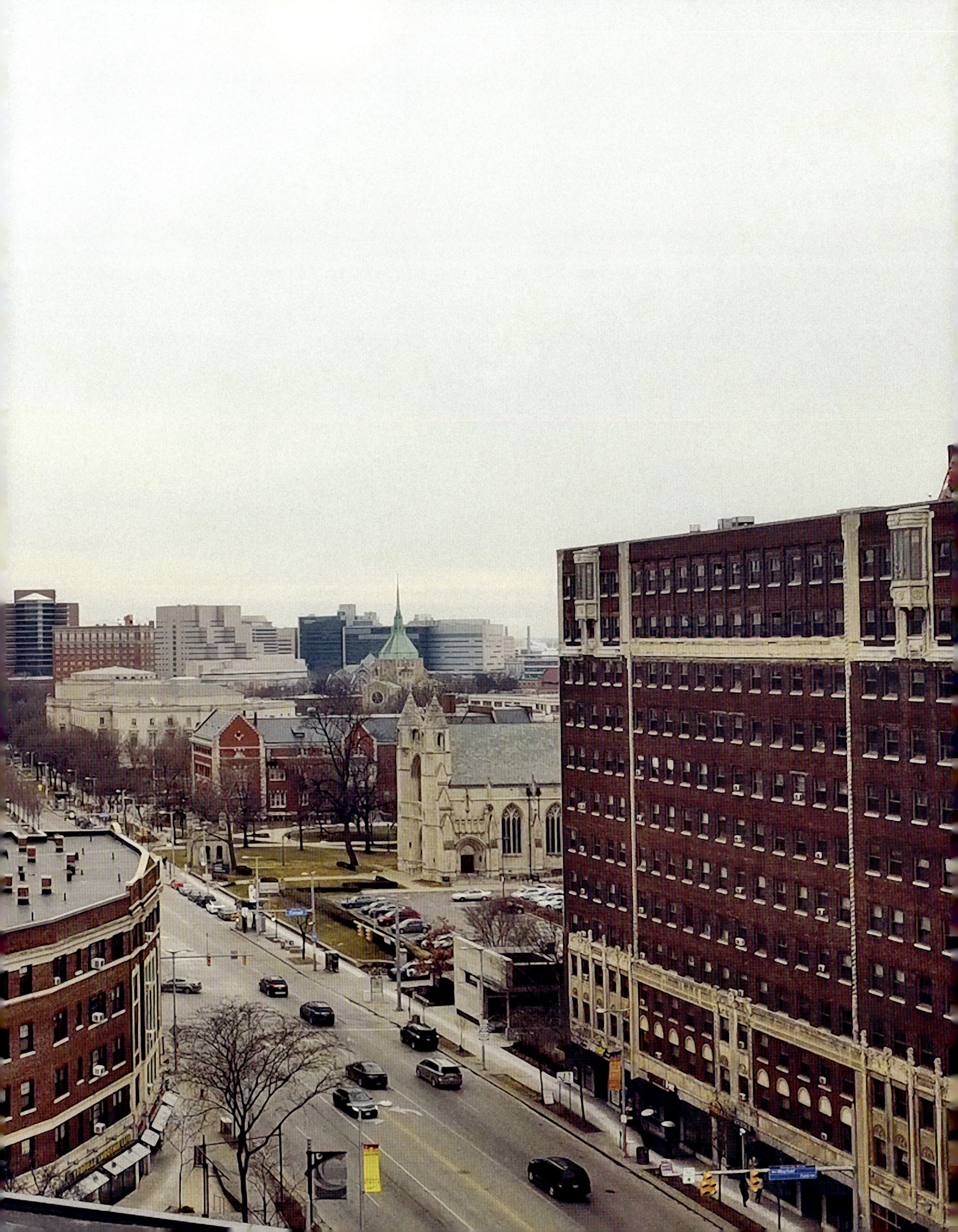

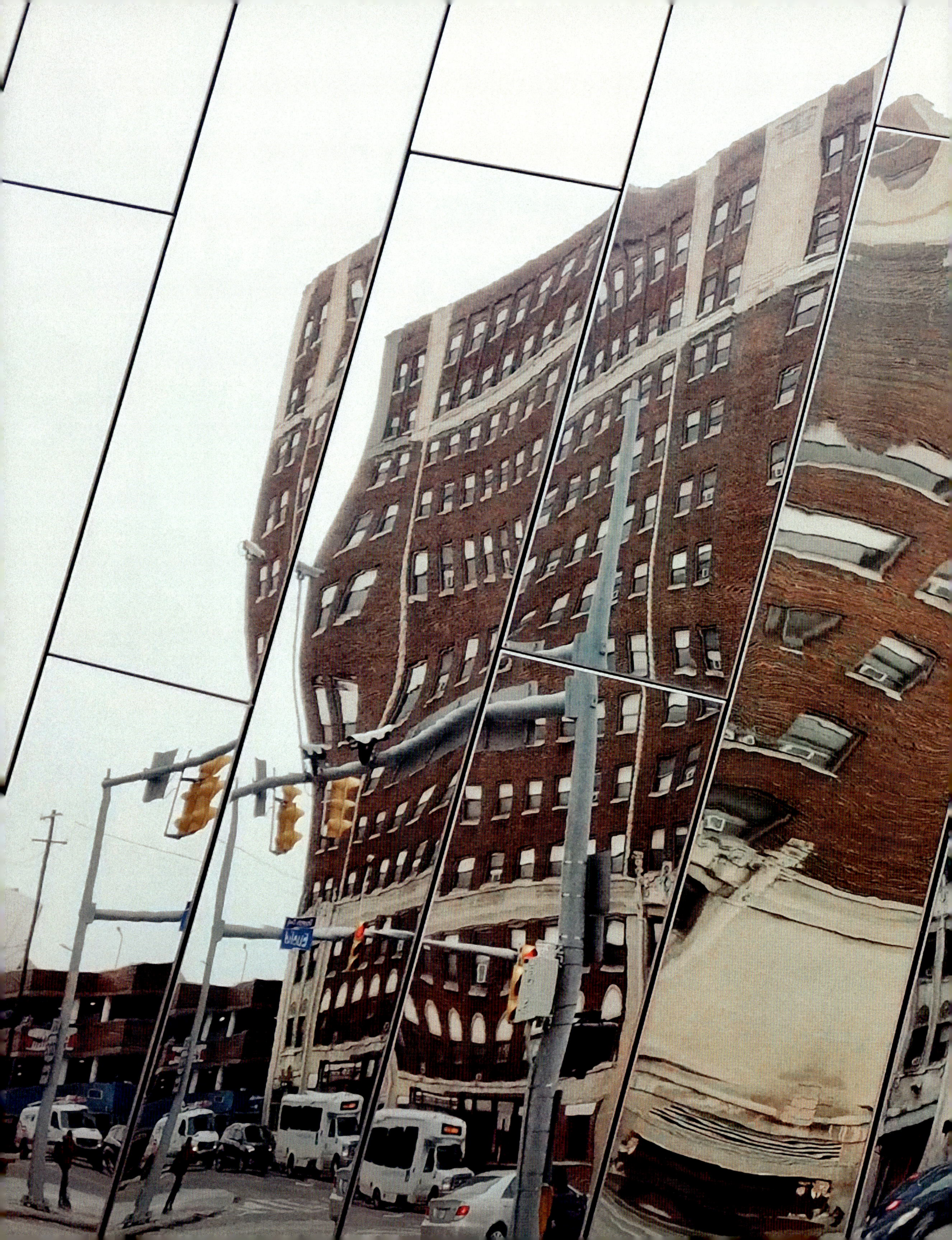

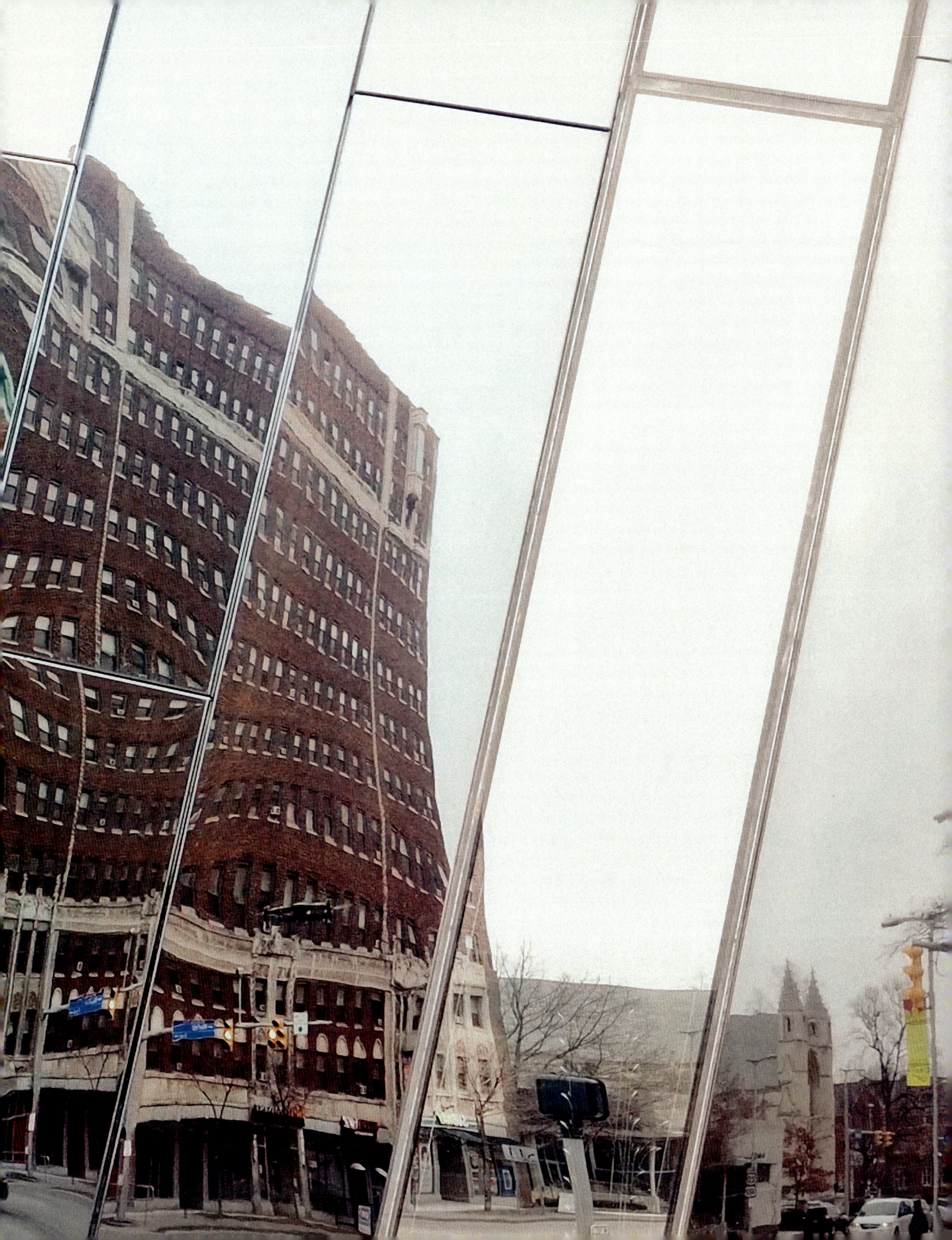

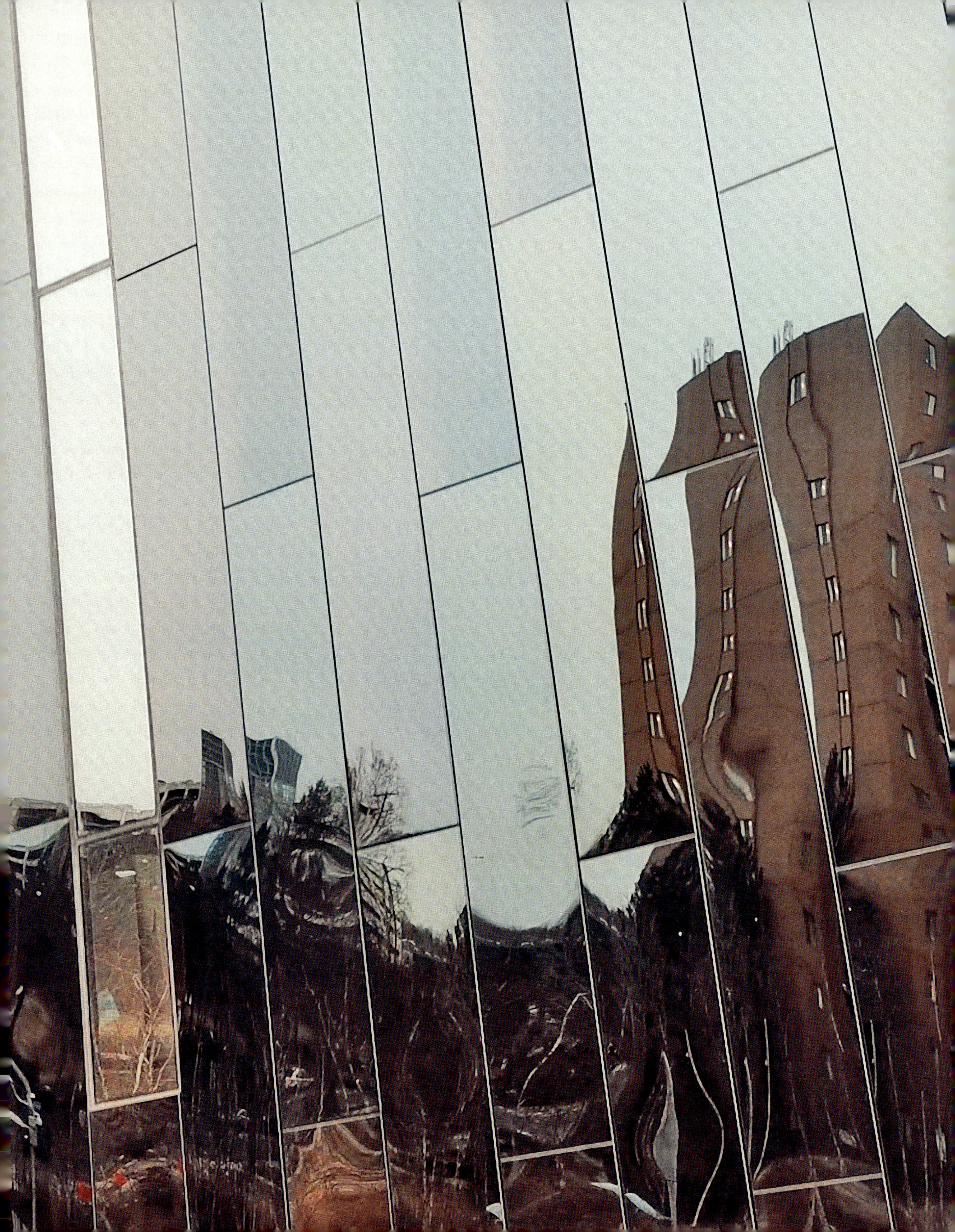

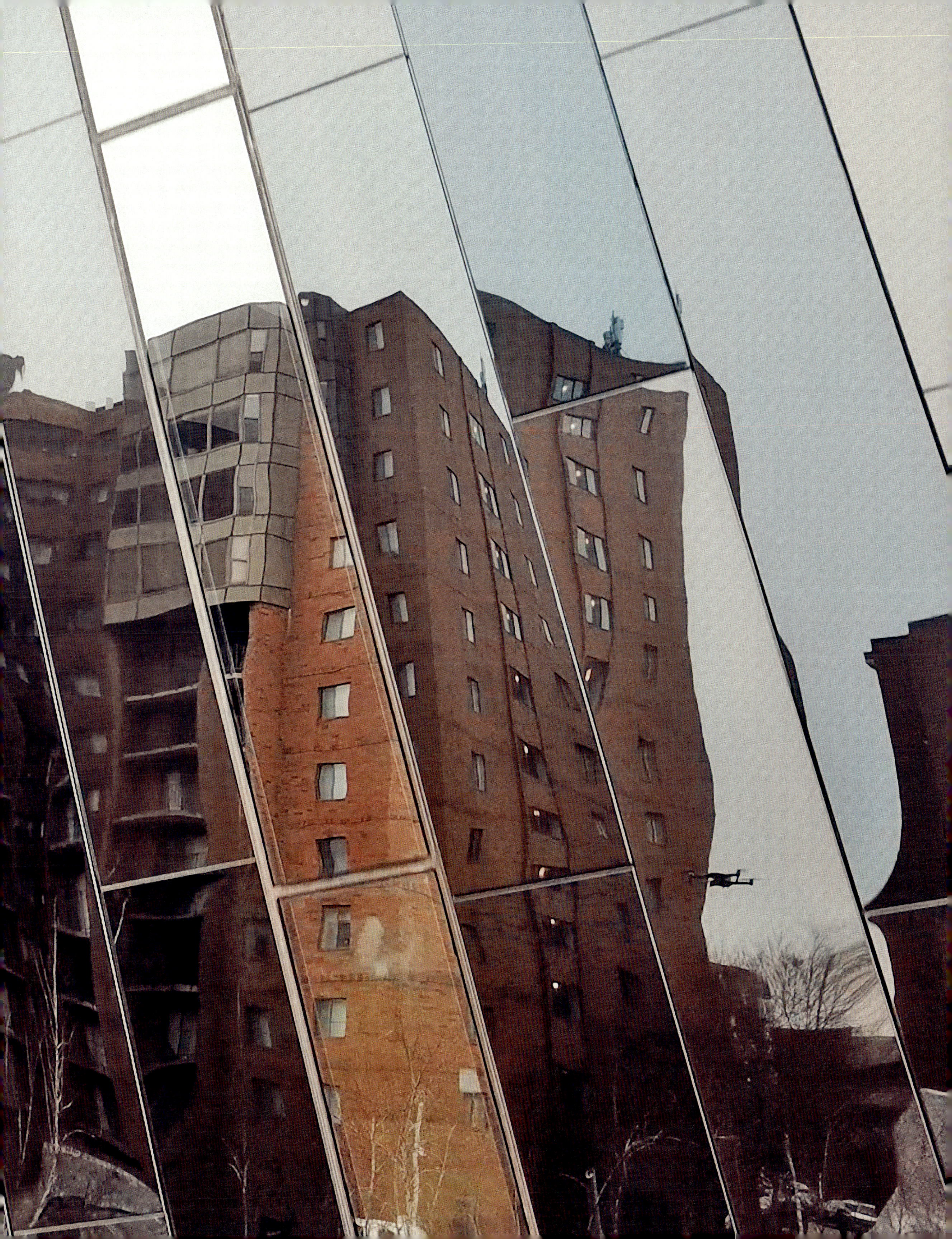

When you are anchored, anchored, anchored, anchored,
anchored, anchored, anchored, anchored, anchored, anchored,
anchored, anchored, anchored, anchored,

a descent is a matter of time.

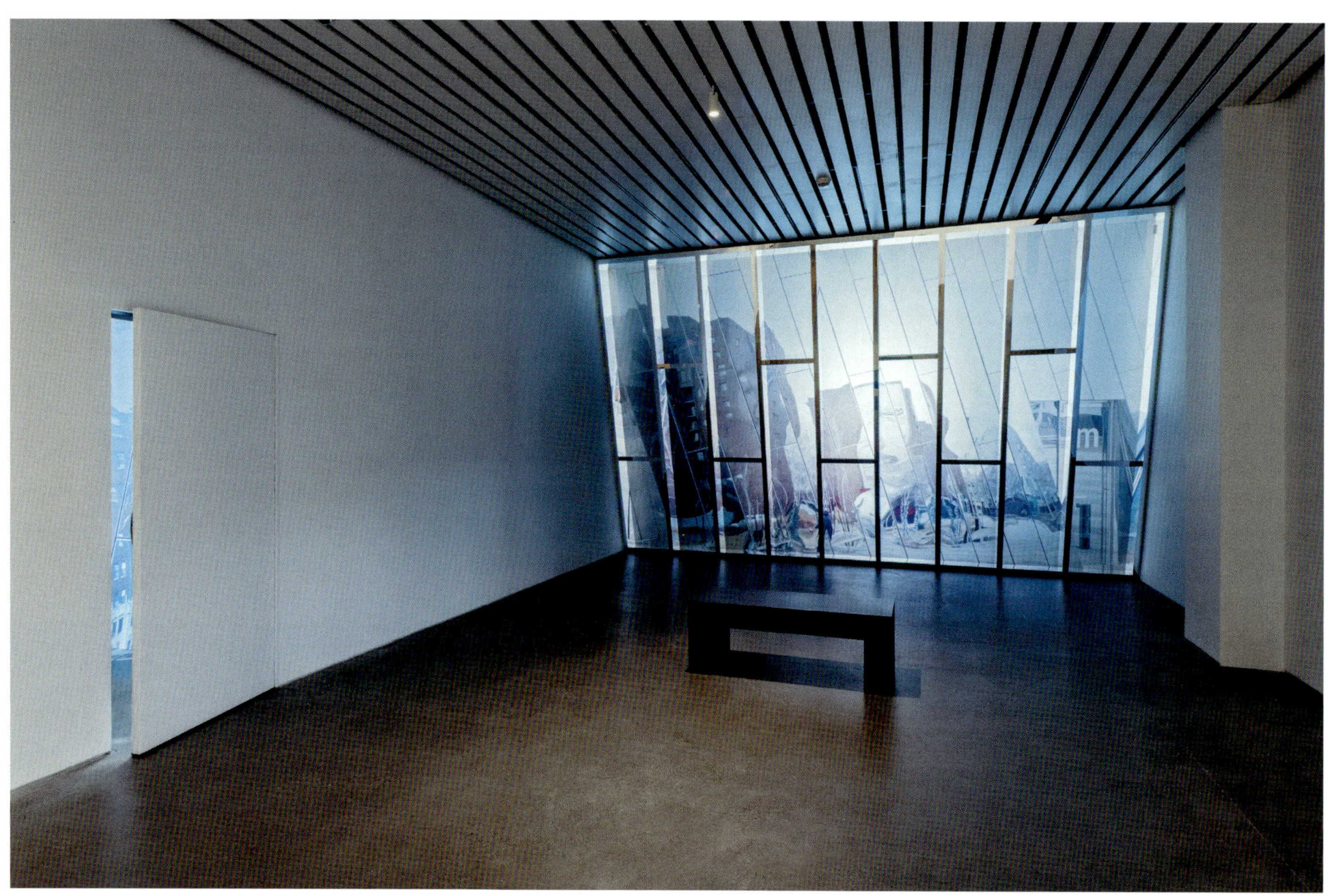

A descent into the terrible.
The terrible terror.
The terrible things.
The terrible things that happened.
The terrible things happening.
The terrible things that happened, here.

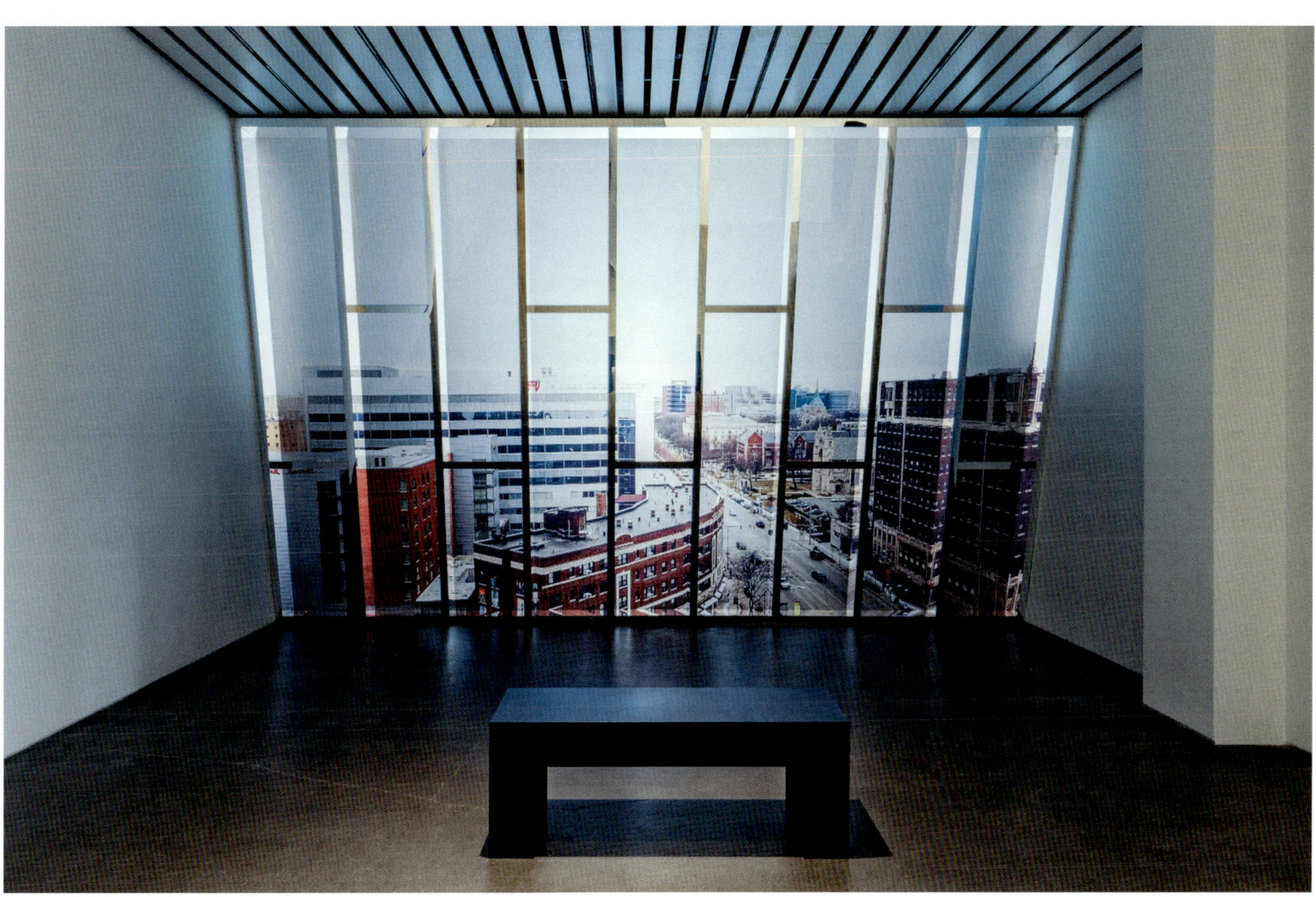

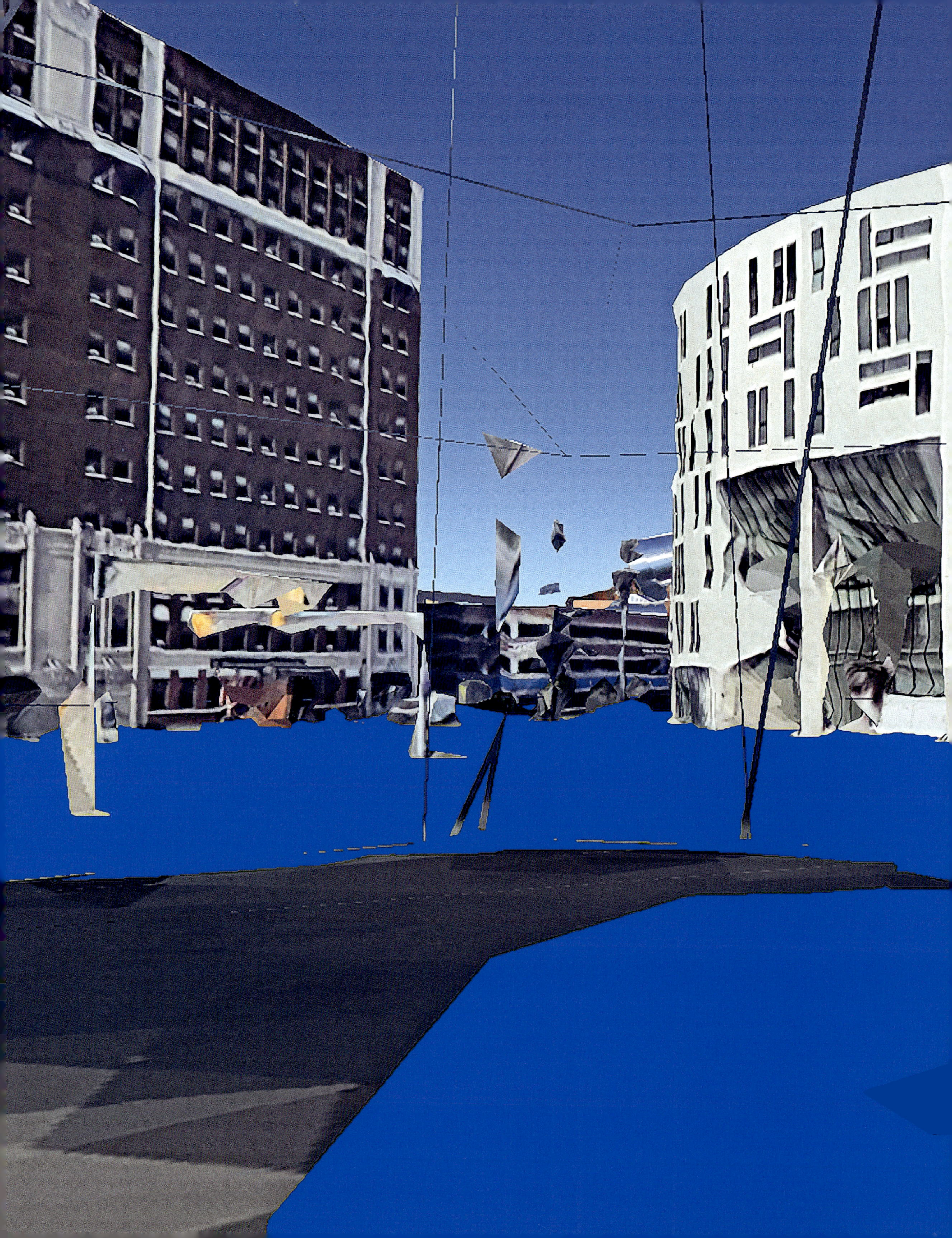

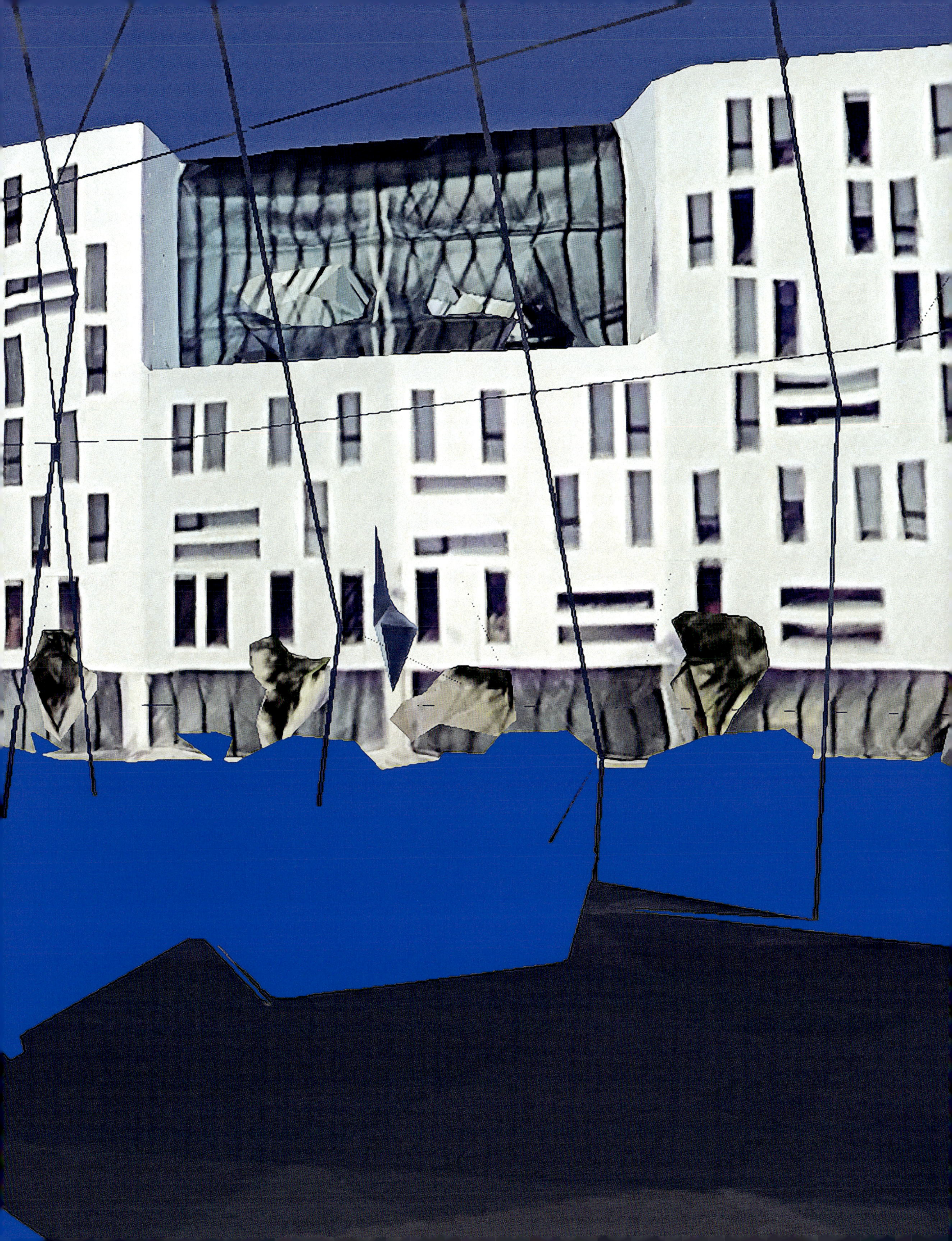

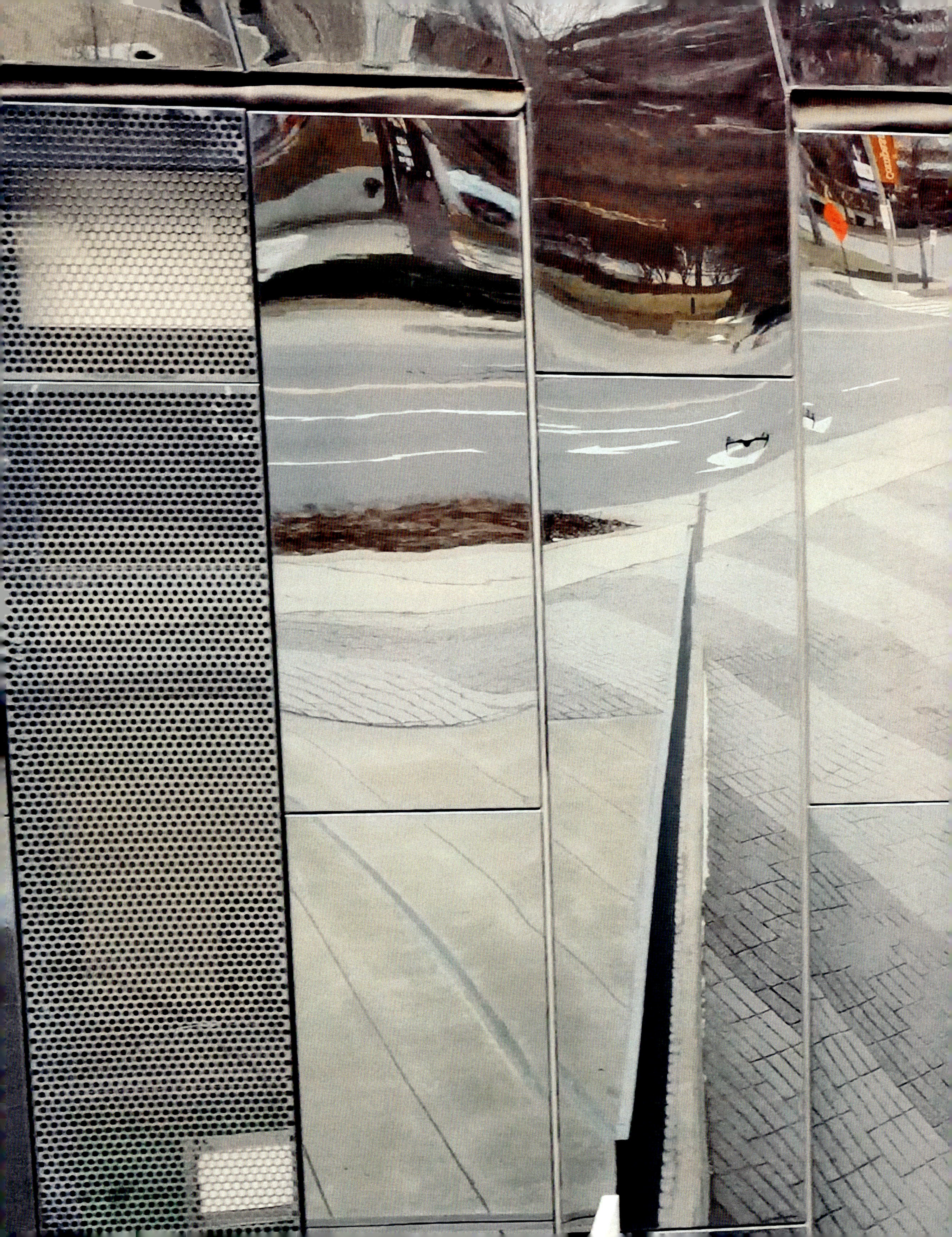

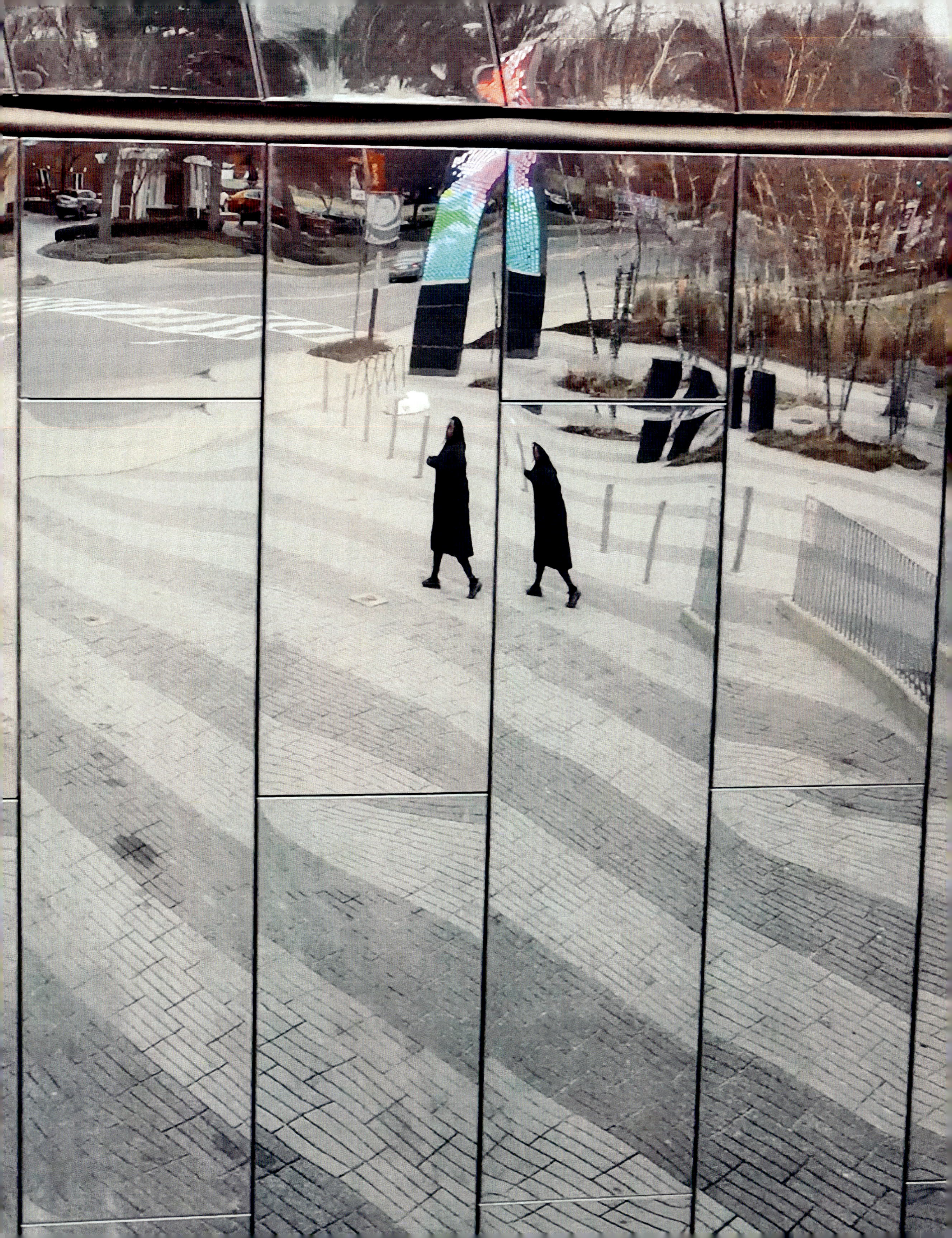

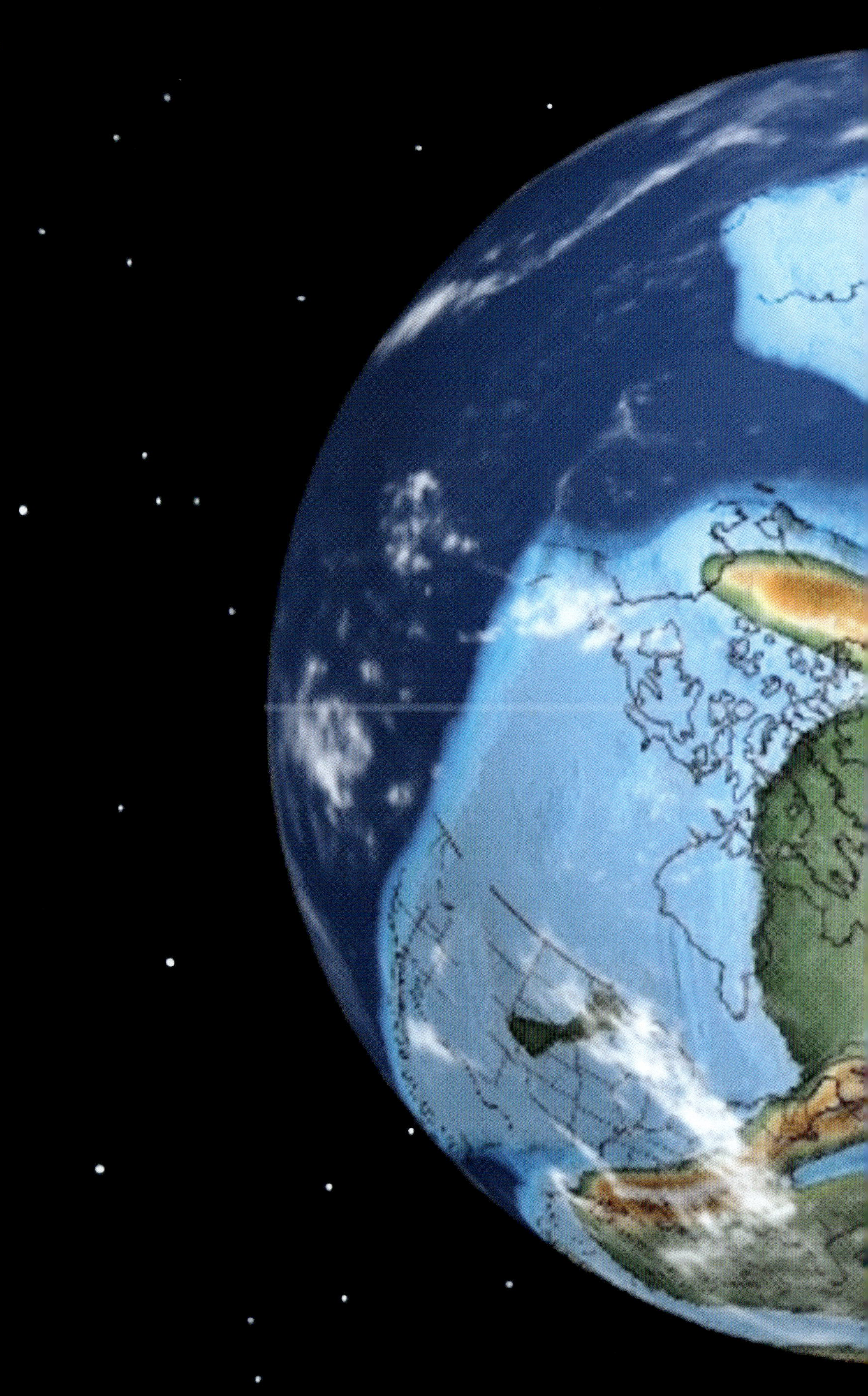

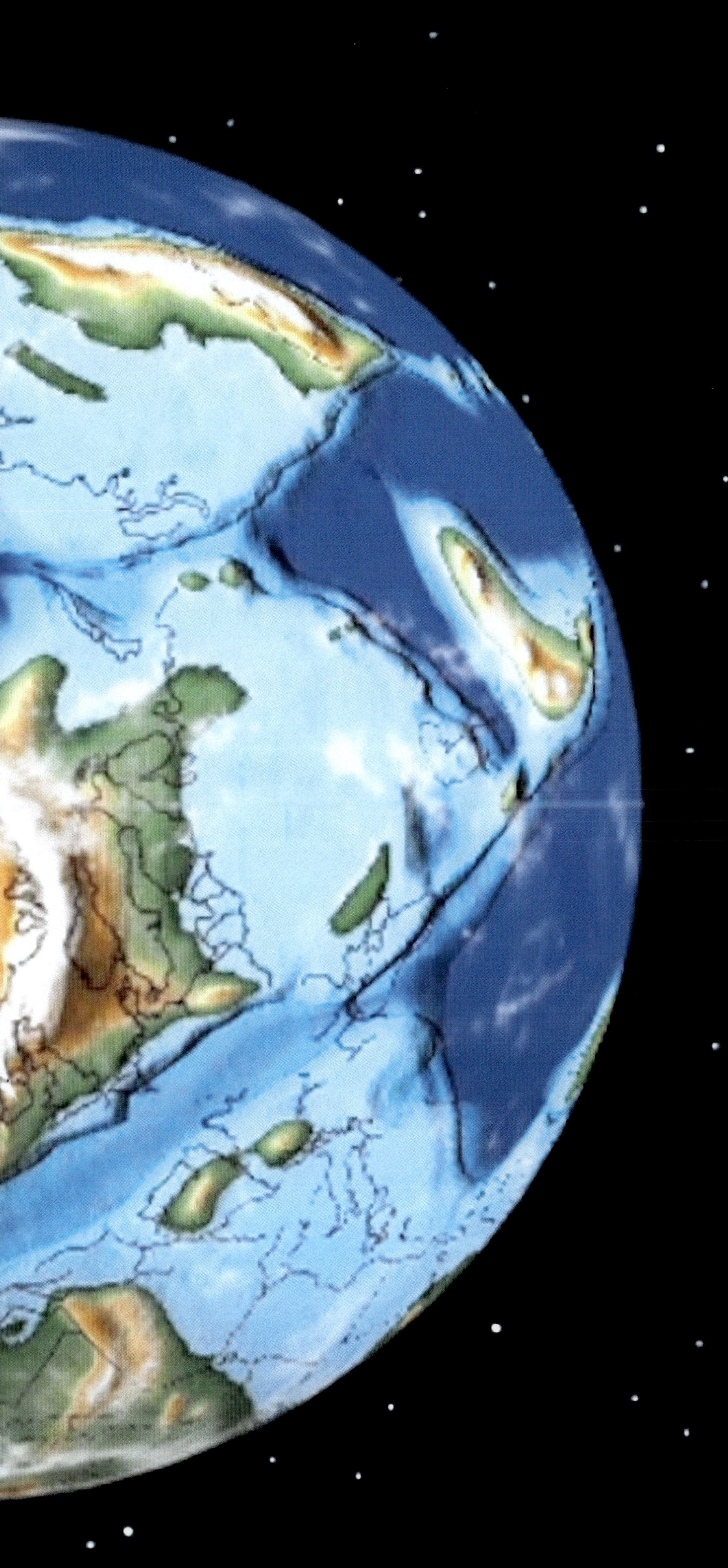

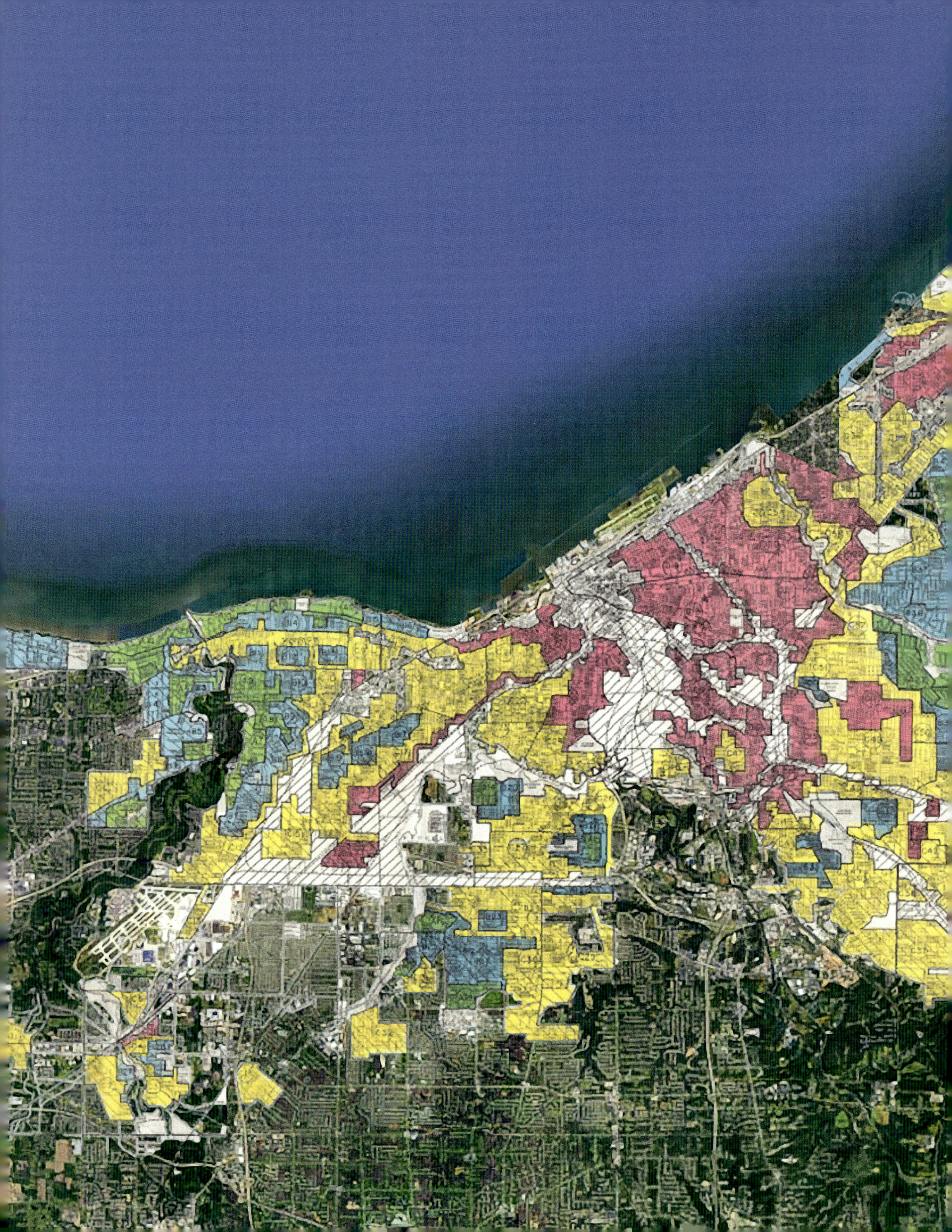

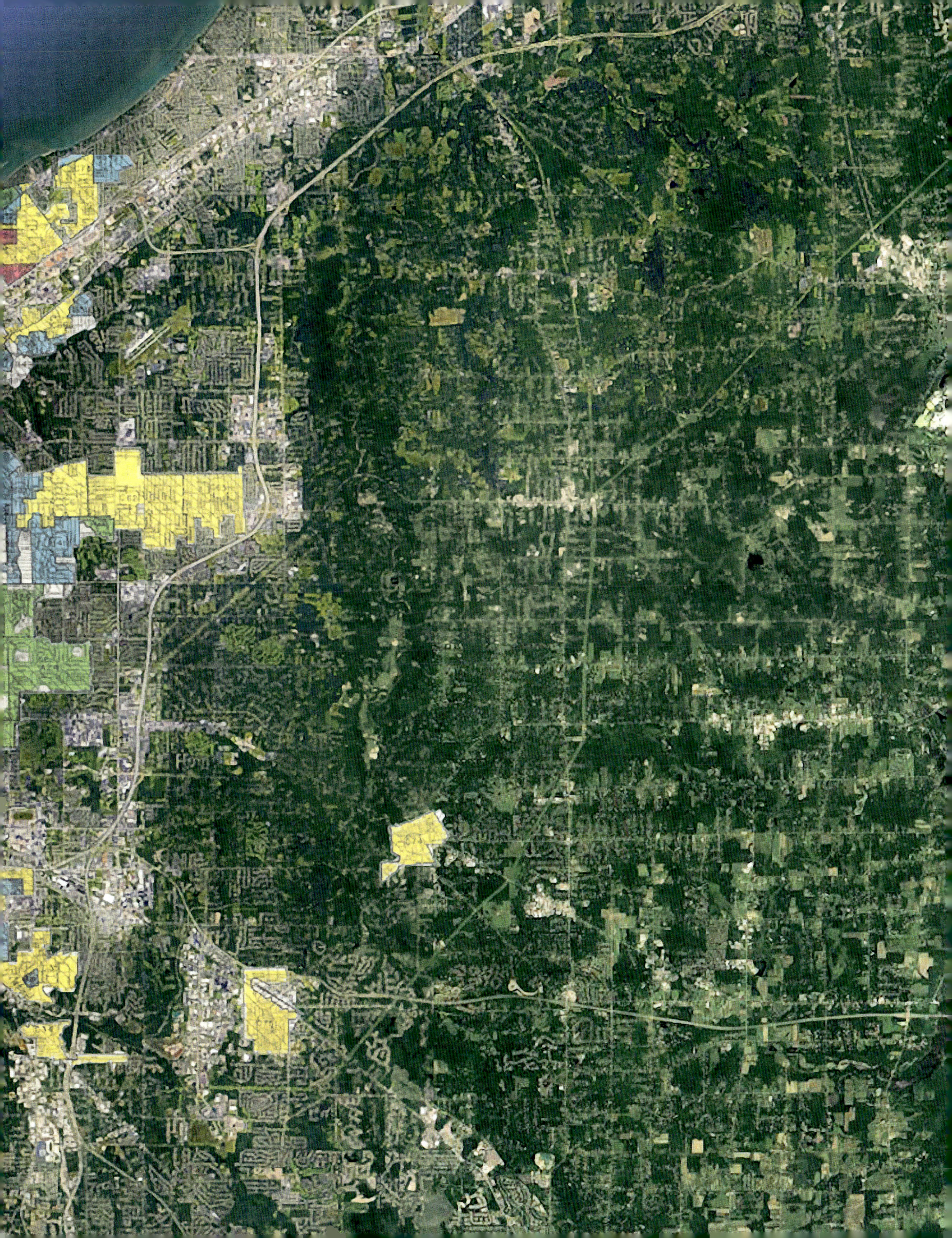

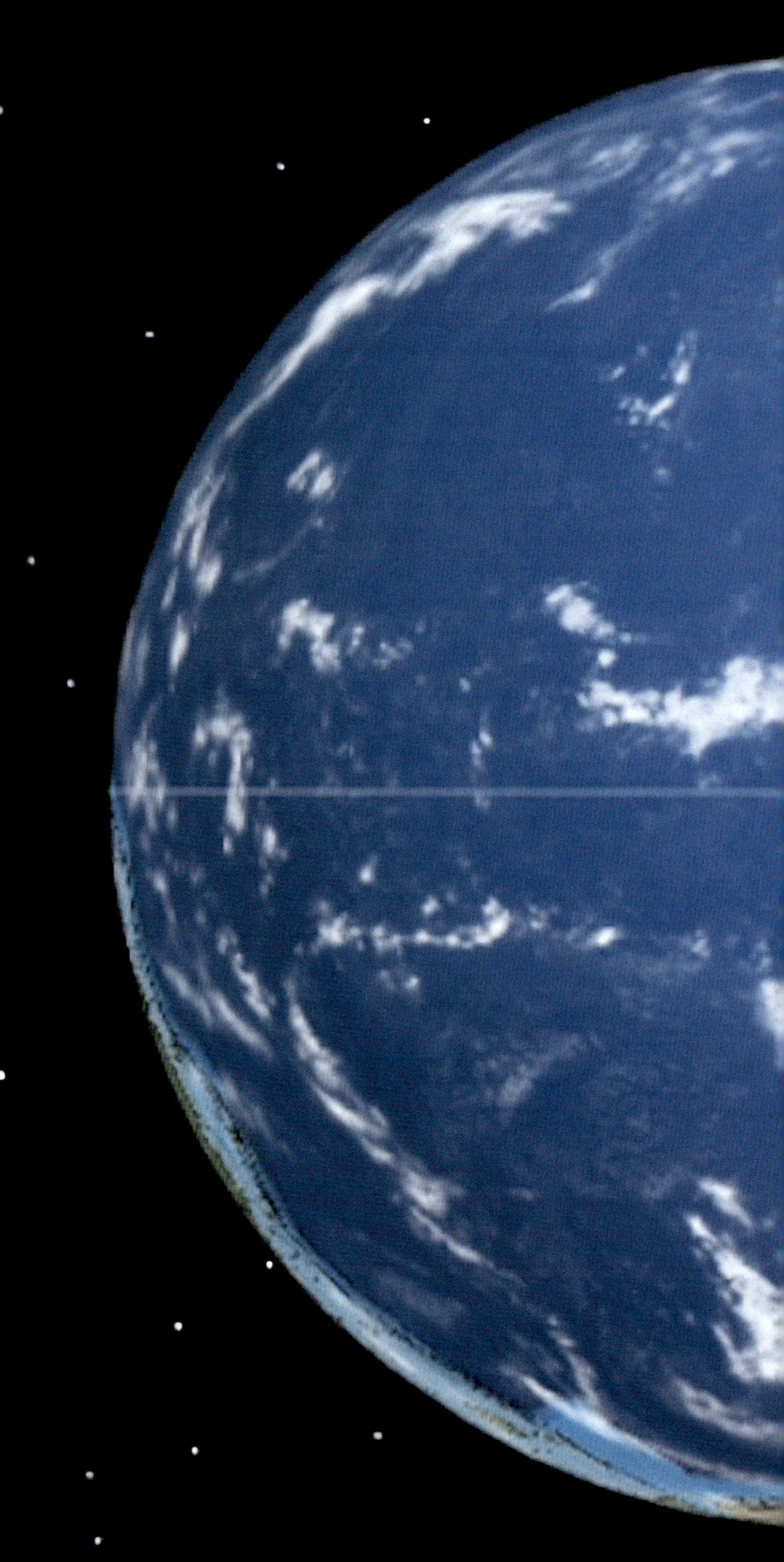

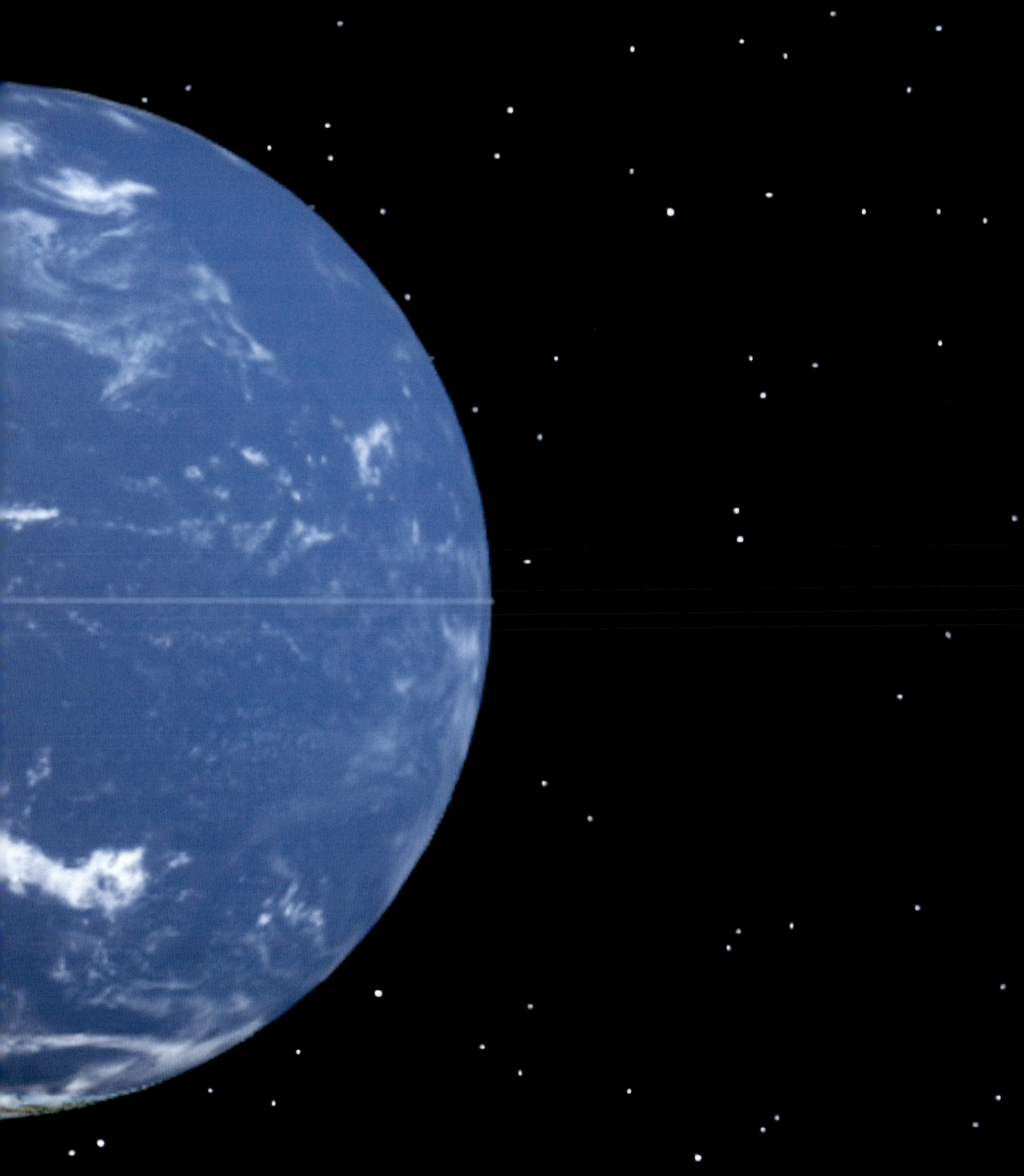

Here, between the soles of your feet and iron ore and the Cayuga and
Six Nations of the Iroquois. And panels of ColourTex Black Mirror and
the blast furnaces and the Jazz Temple on the Mayfield Triangle. The
Kirwan Institute for the Study of Race and Ethnicity engaged in research
on the Home Owners' Loan Corporation HOLC created in 1933 as a
government-sponsored corporation to help refinance homes at risk of
foreclosure in the wake of the Great Depression.

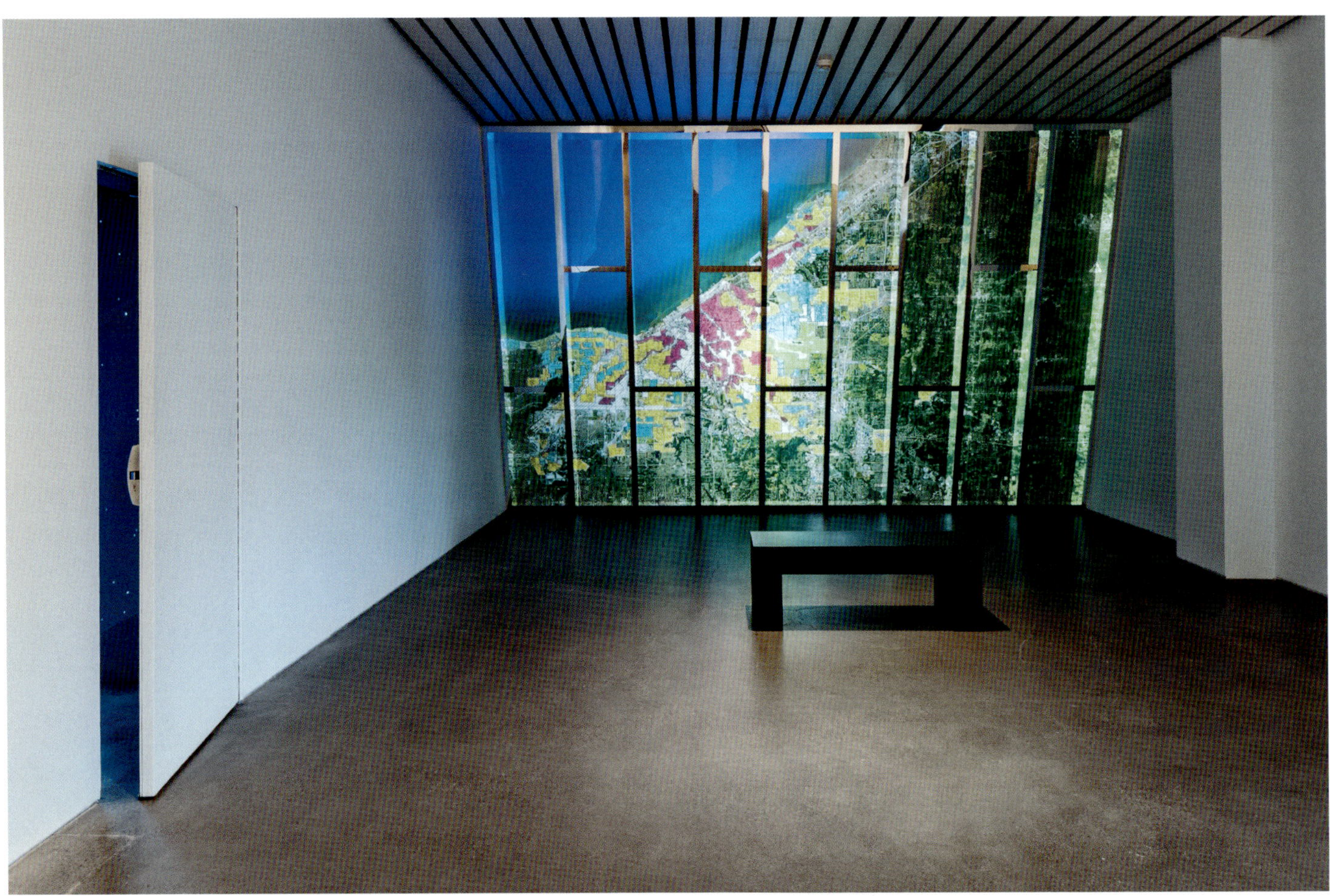

The HOLC created residential security maps or redlining maps
to lead investment in cities across the country.

Grades A through D were assigned to neighborhoods to indicate their investment desirability. Black and immigrant neighborhoods were often given grades of C or D, resulting in little or no access to mortgage insurance or credit for decades.

moCa, us, we live on Mayfield Triangle a neighborhood that was assigned a D rating.

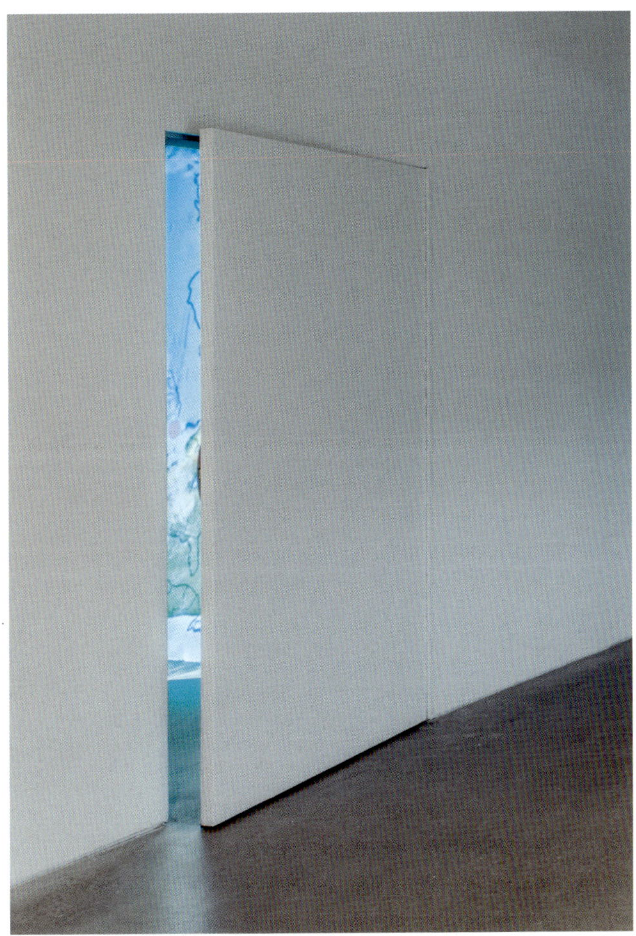

What a difference a day makes,

a song popularized by Dinah Washington, a singer and pianist who once performed at the Jazz Temple, a coffee house jazz club that lives, lived here, where we, moCa, exist. We survived several attempted bombings but fell in 1963 after an explosion that demolished the building.

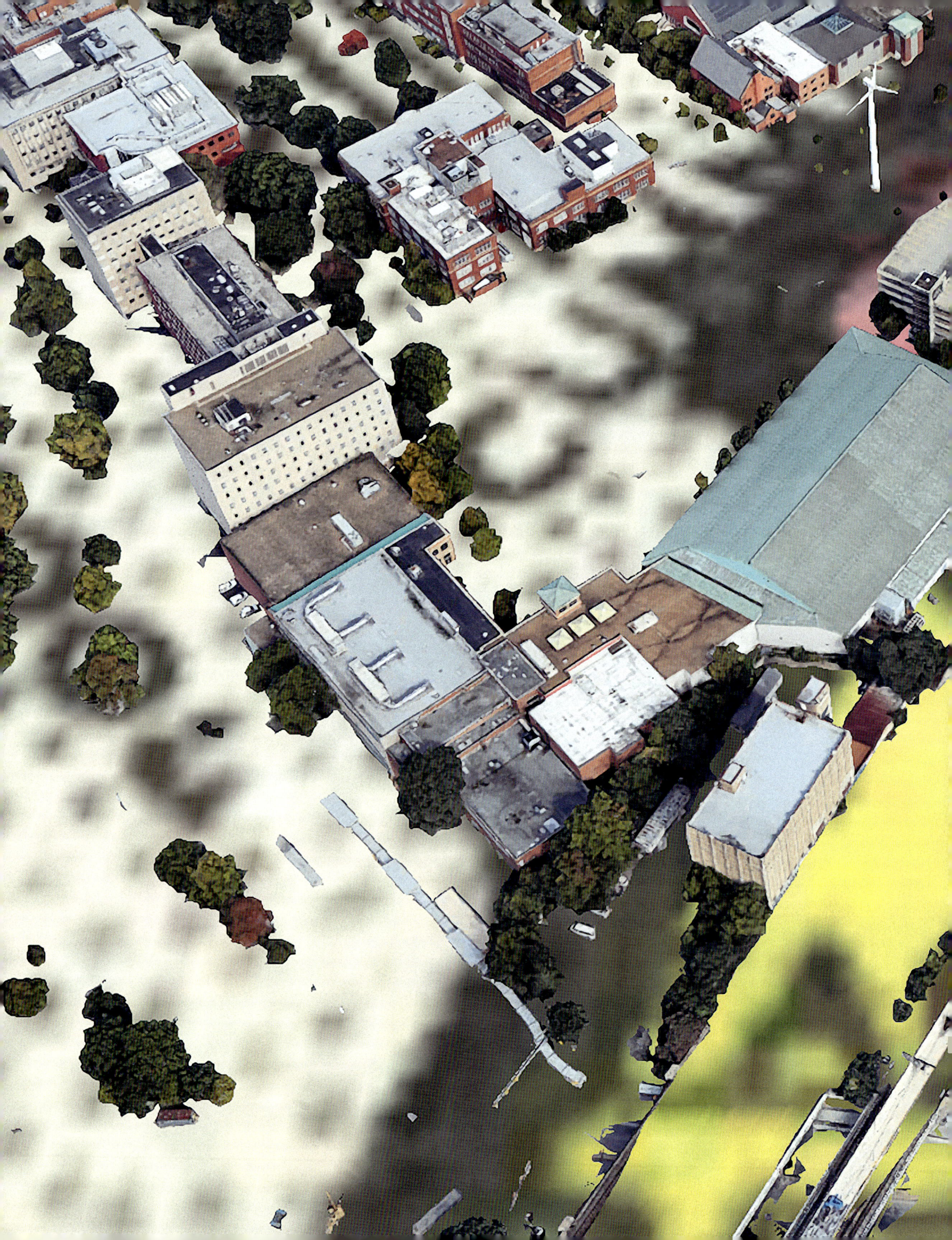

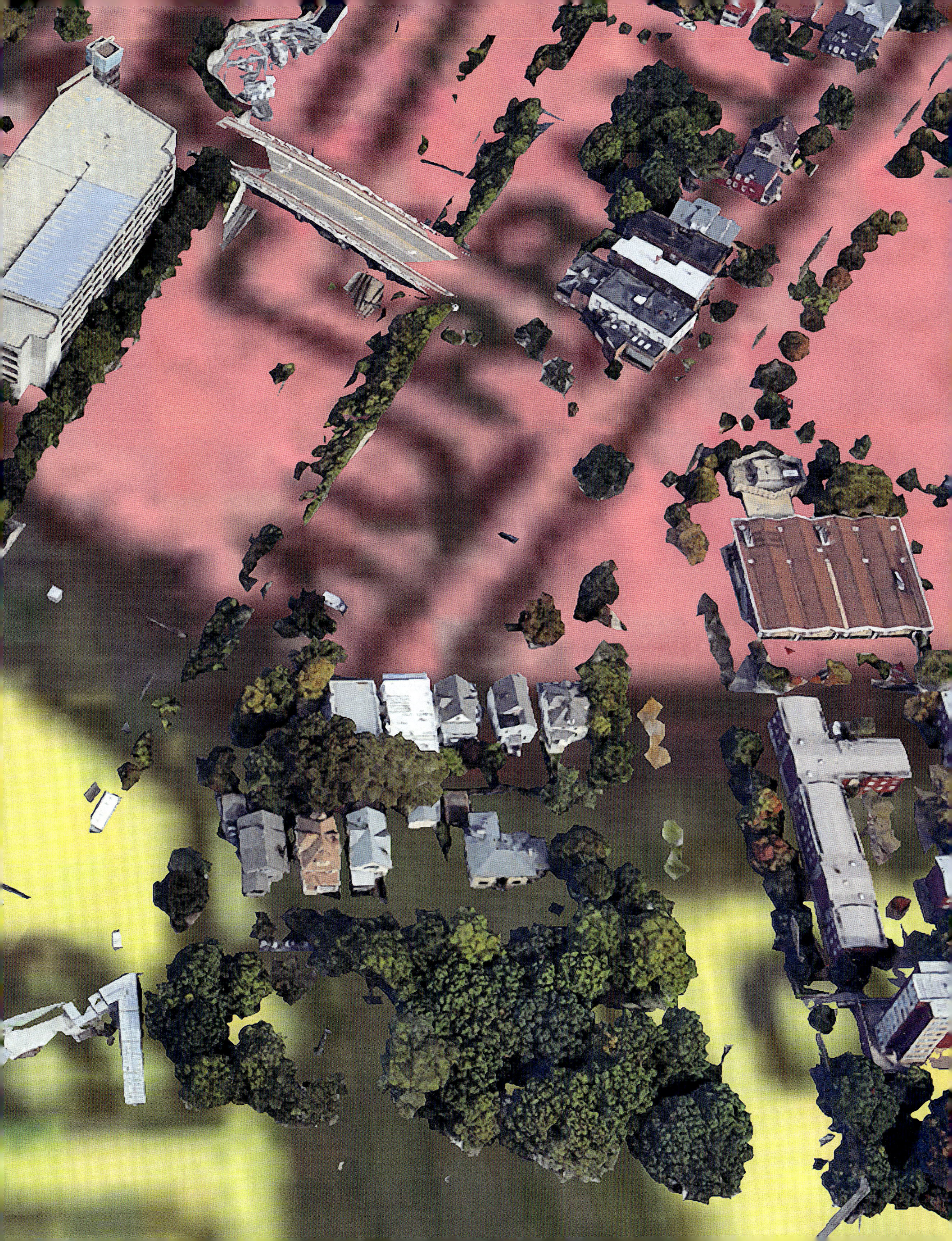

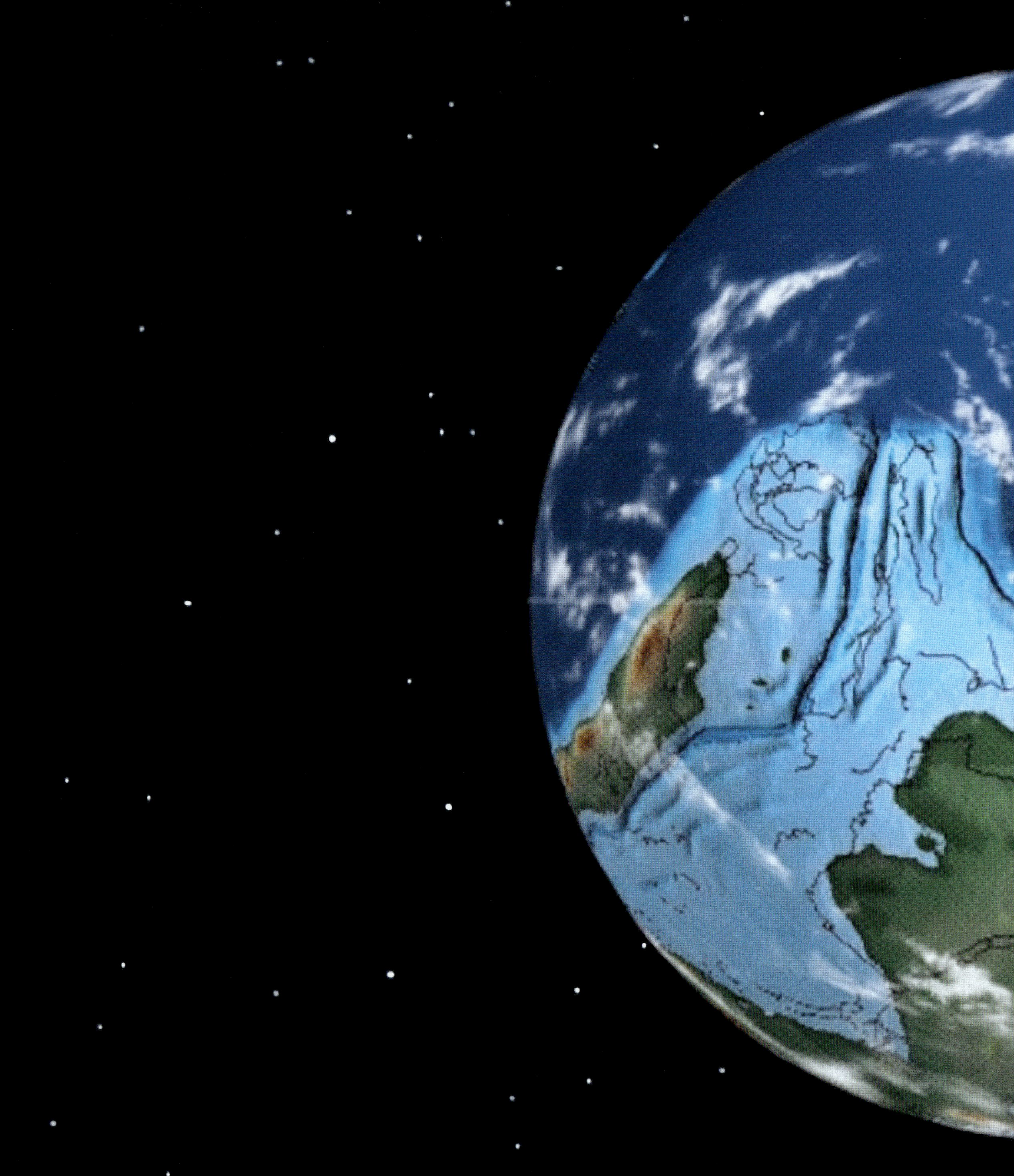

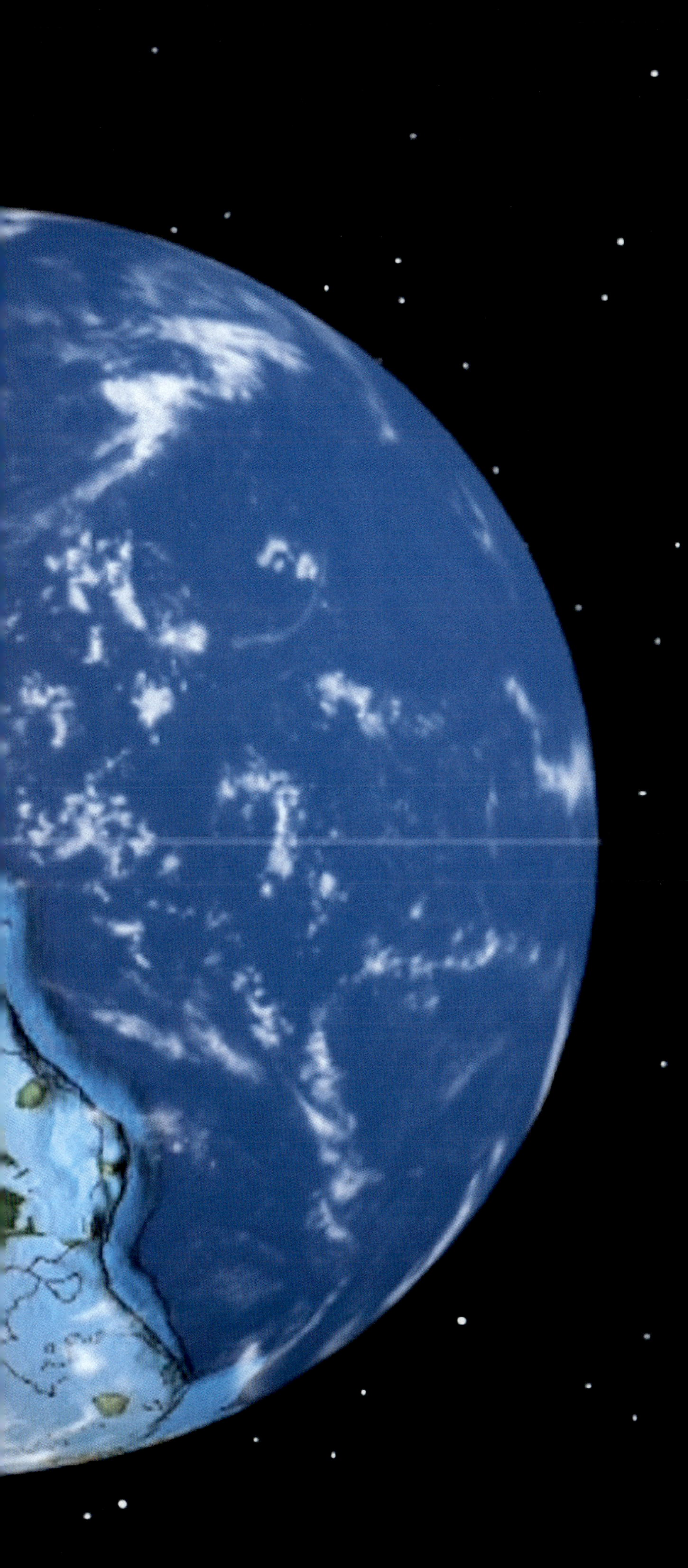

...ber from Portug...
war stings — hun...
shreds. Jellyfish sti...
first Bahamas-to-F...
two weeks ago afte...

About dawn yest...
cleared jellyfish fro...
using bang sticks ...
ward off sharks. She...
Sunday by a small jell...

Miss Nyad said the...
lost 10 or 12 of the 13...
she weighed when she...
into the water a few ...
past 8 a.m. EDT Sunday.

Therap

Willis'

By Joseph D. Rice

The Ohio Industrial Commissio... is planning a rehabilitation cente... on the south side of Euclid Ave. between E. 106th and E. 107th streets, that would probably require demolishing the buildings that house Winston Willis' business empire.

William O. French, chief of the real estate section of the Ohio De-

State lac

By Thomas K. Diemer
Plain Dealer Bureau

COLUMBUS — Ohio faces an $80 million cash flow problem over the next four to five months that could force a temporary cut in school subsidy payments, it was disclosed yesterday.

But Gov. James A. Rhodes' administration maintained the gap between incoming revenue and

Man says
Shak...

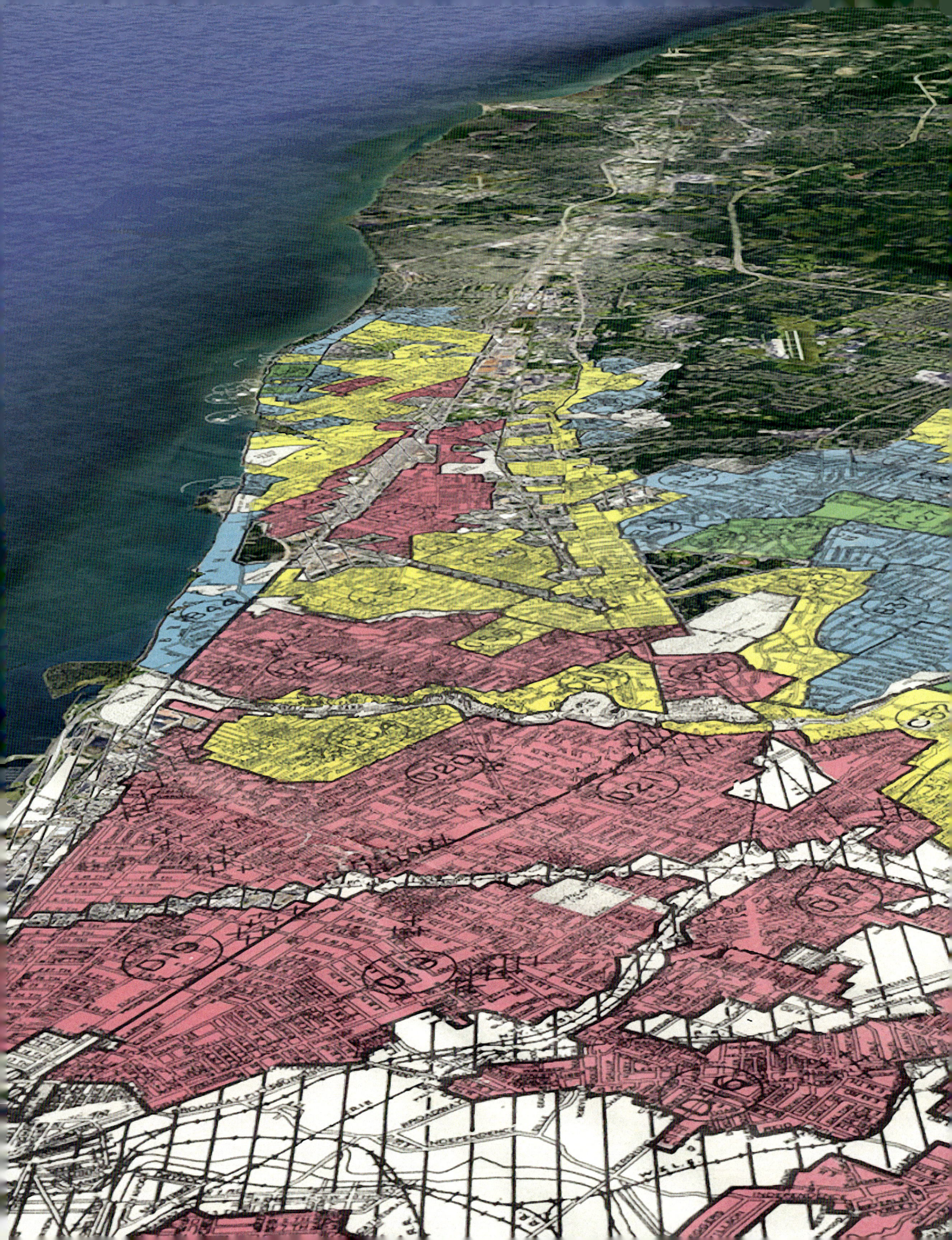

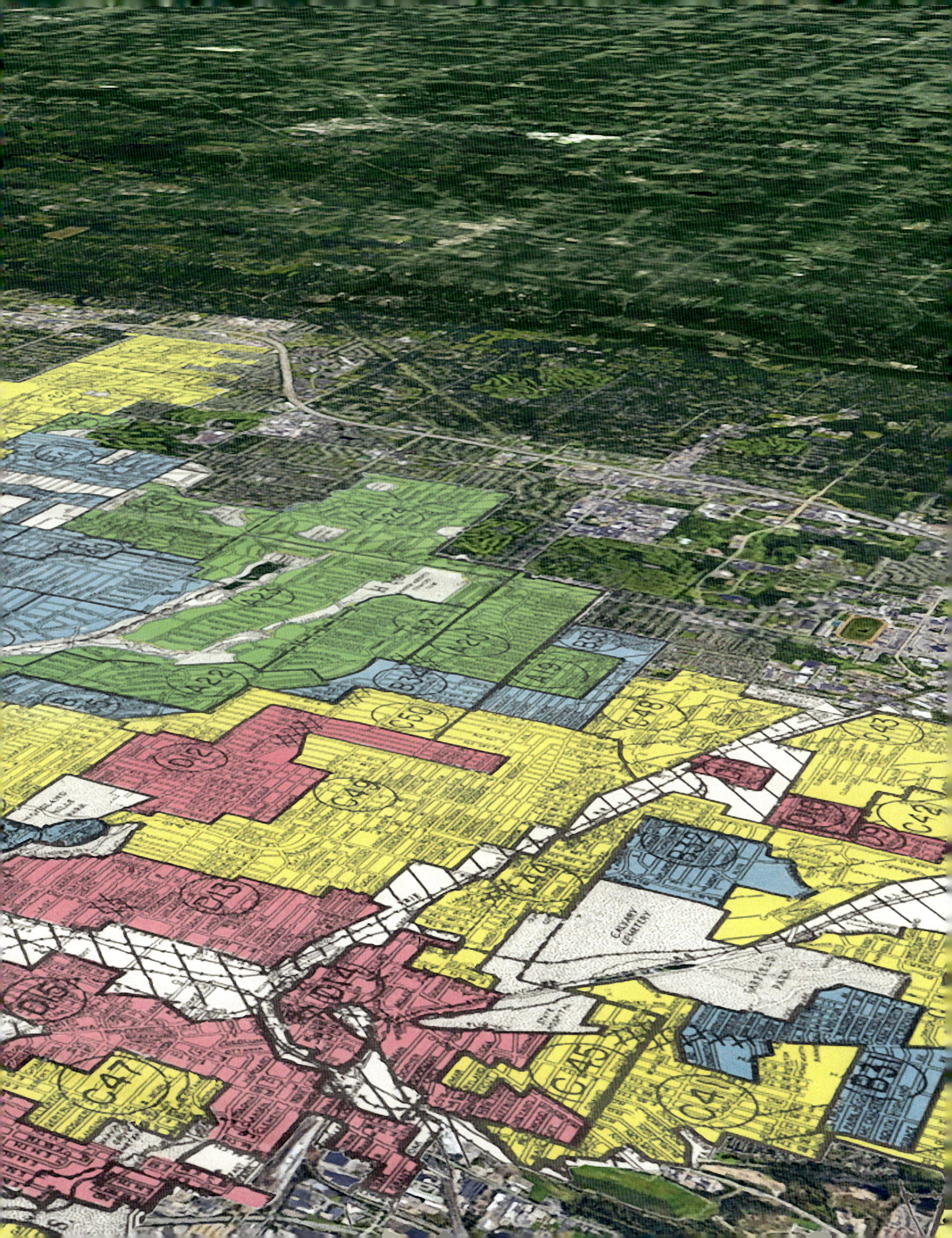

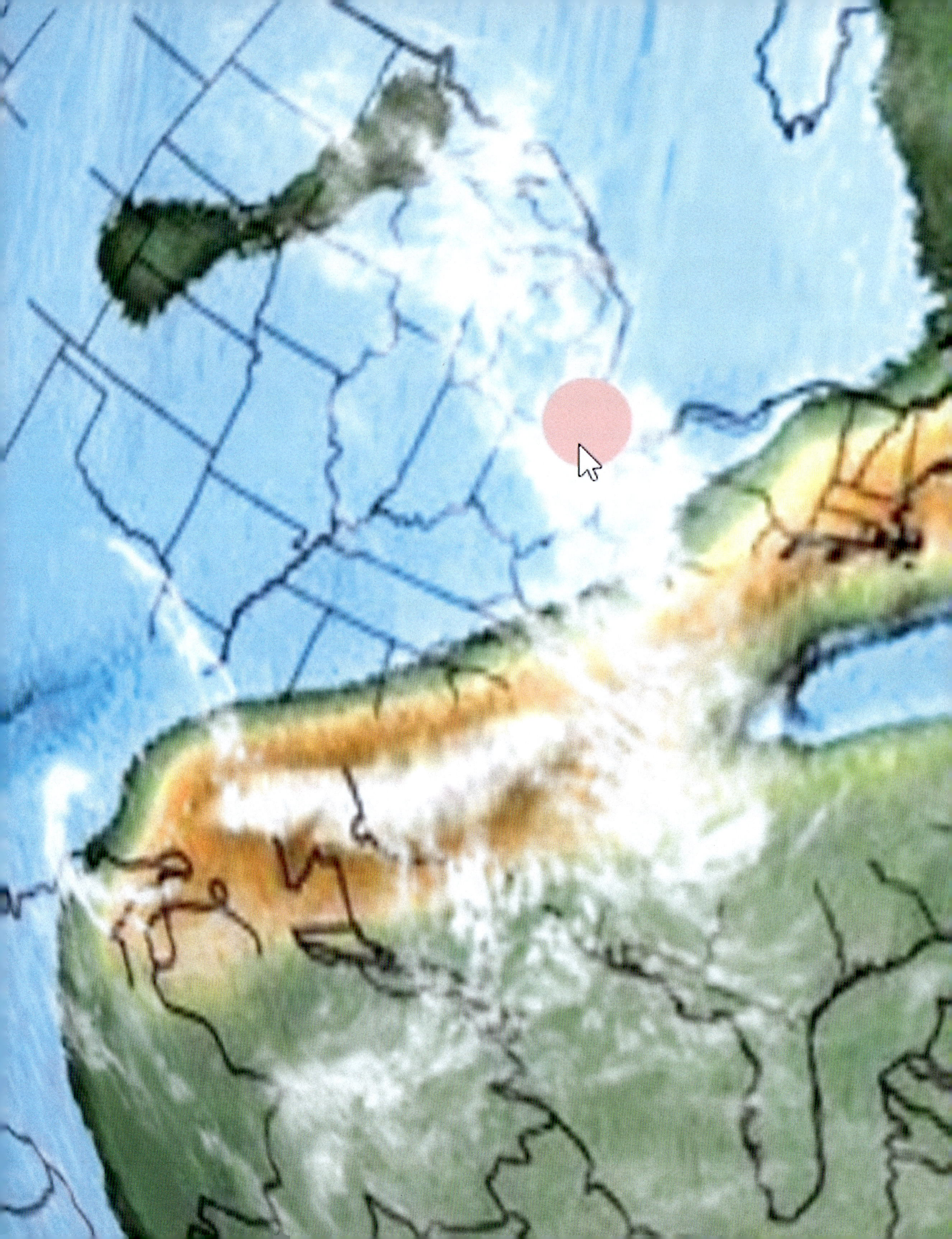

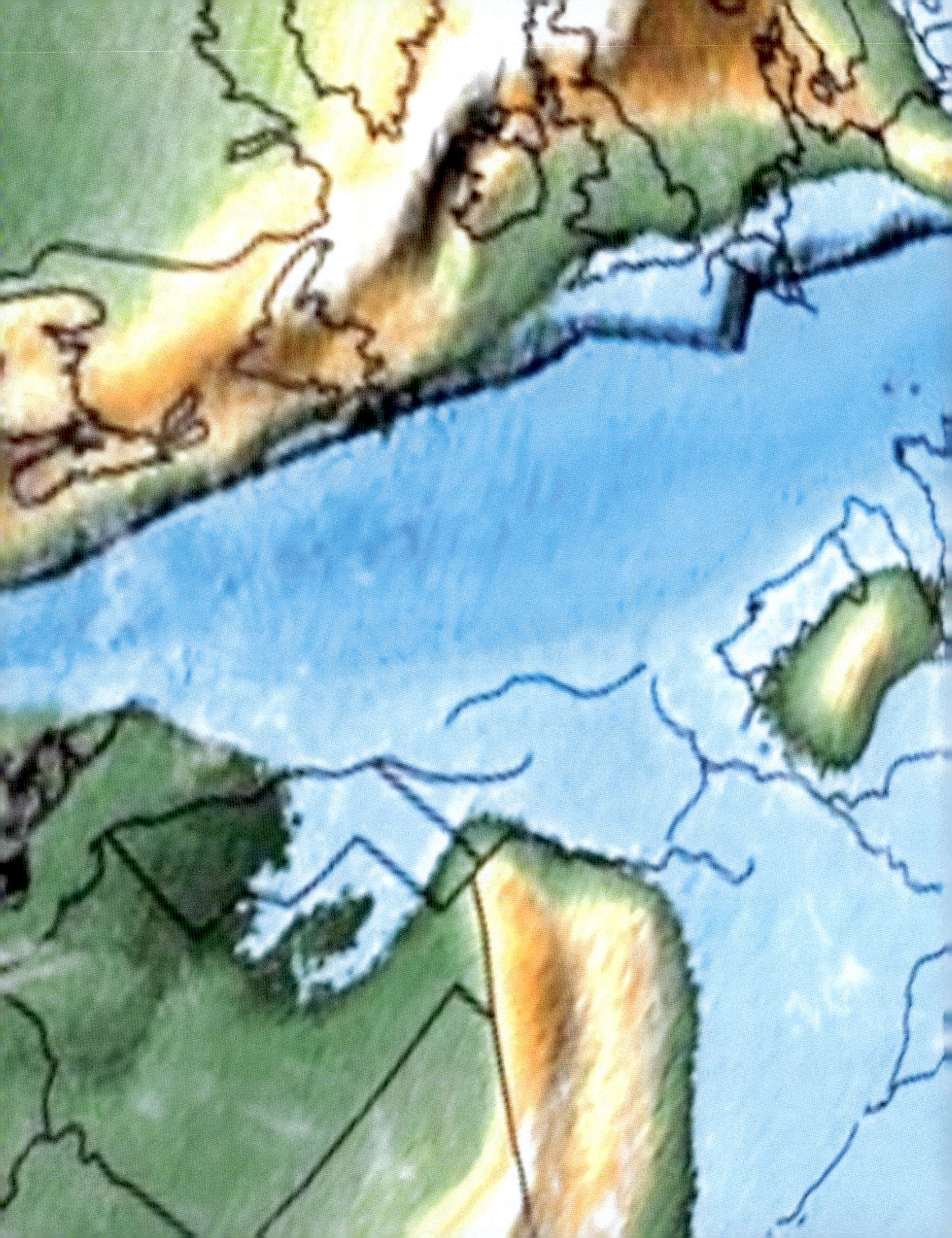

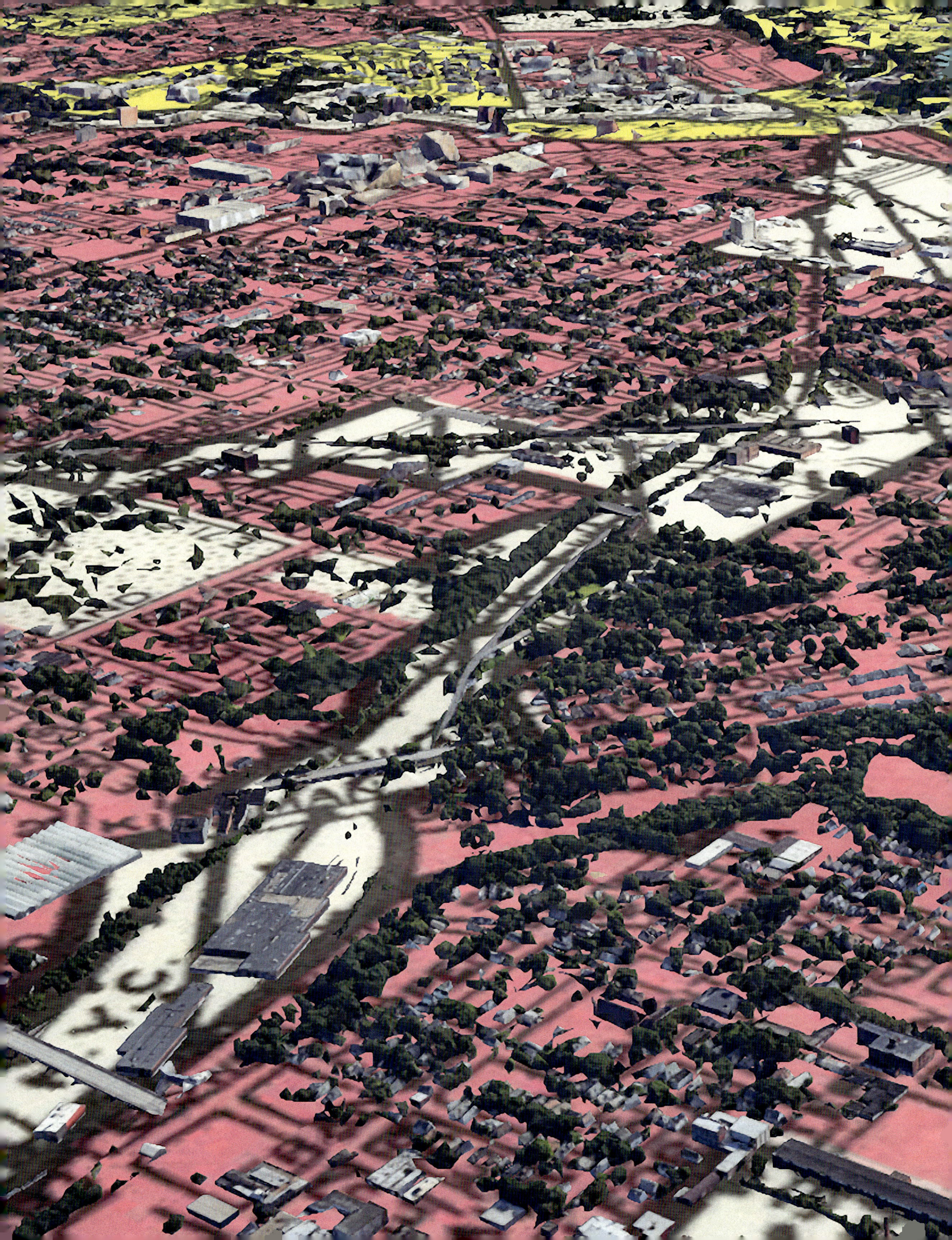

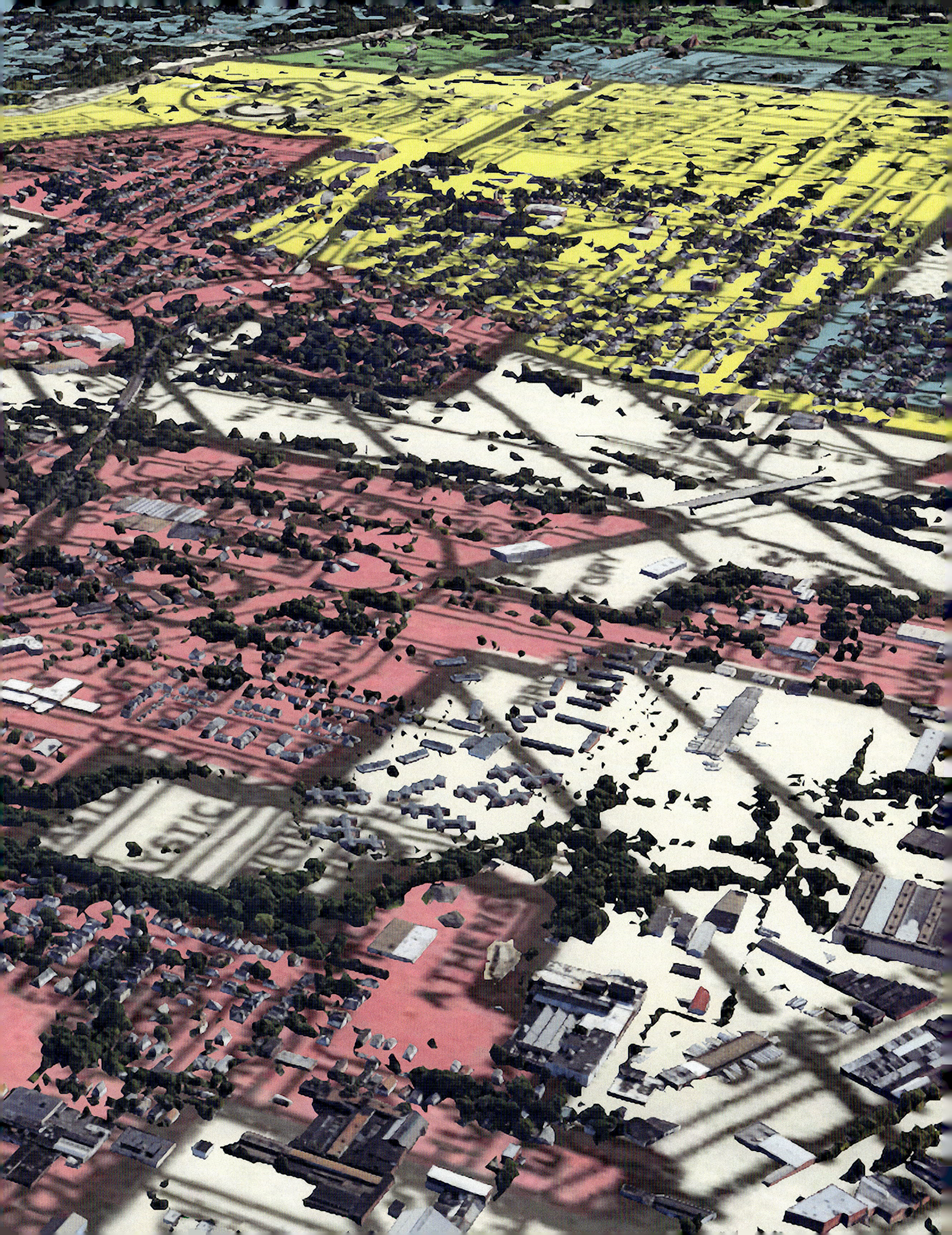

ATHENS

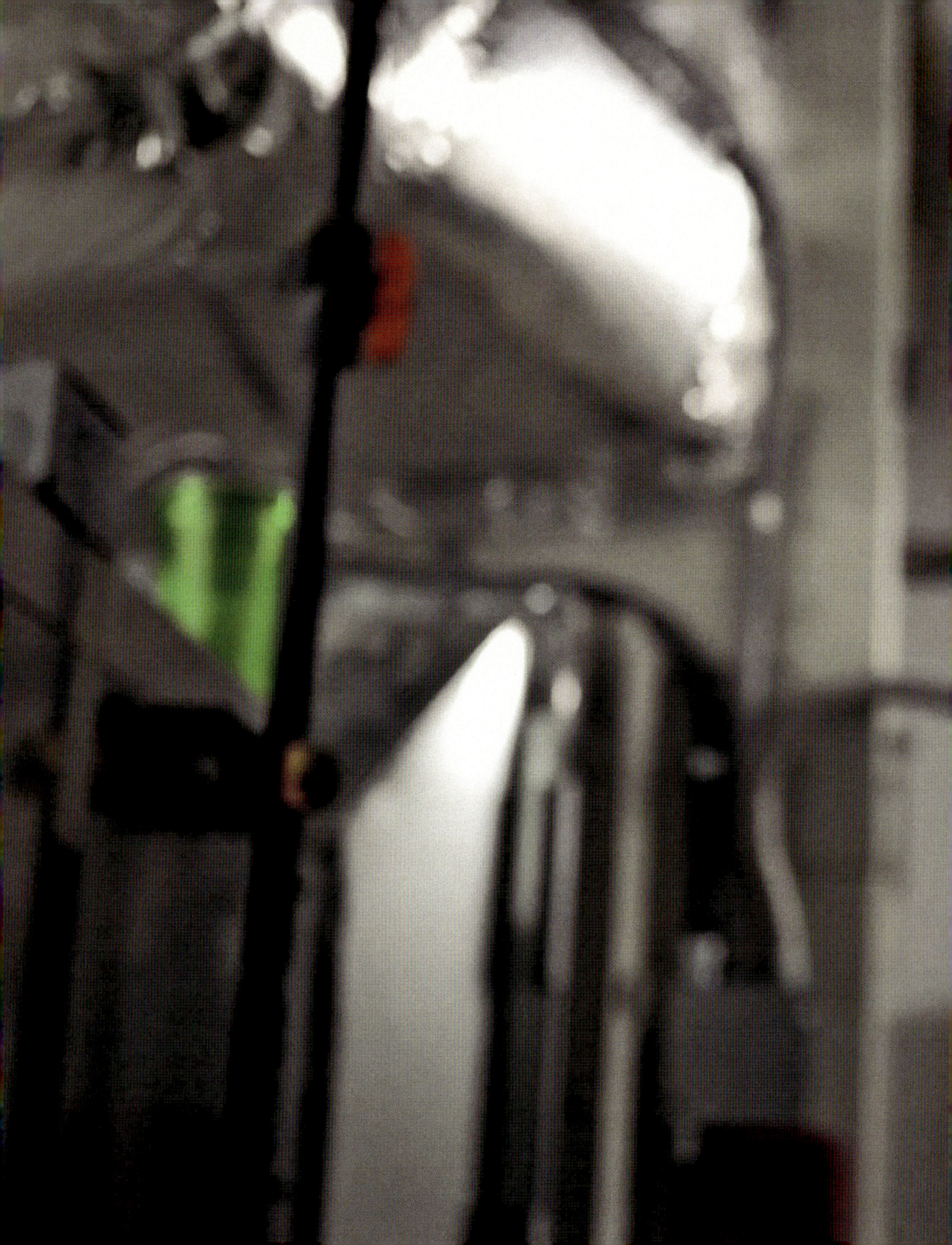

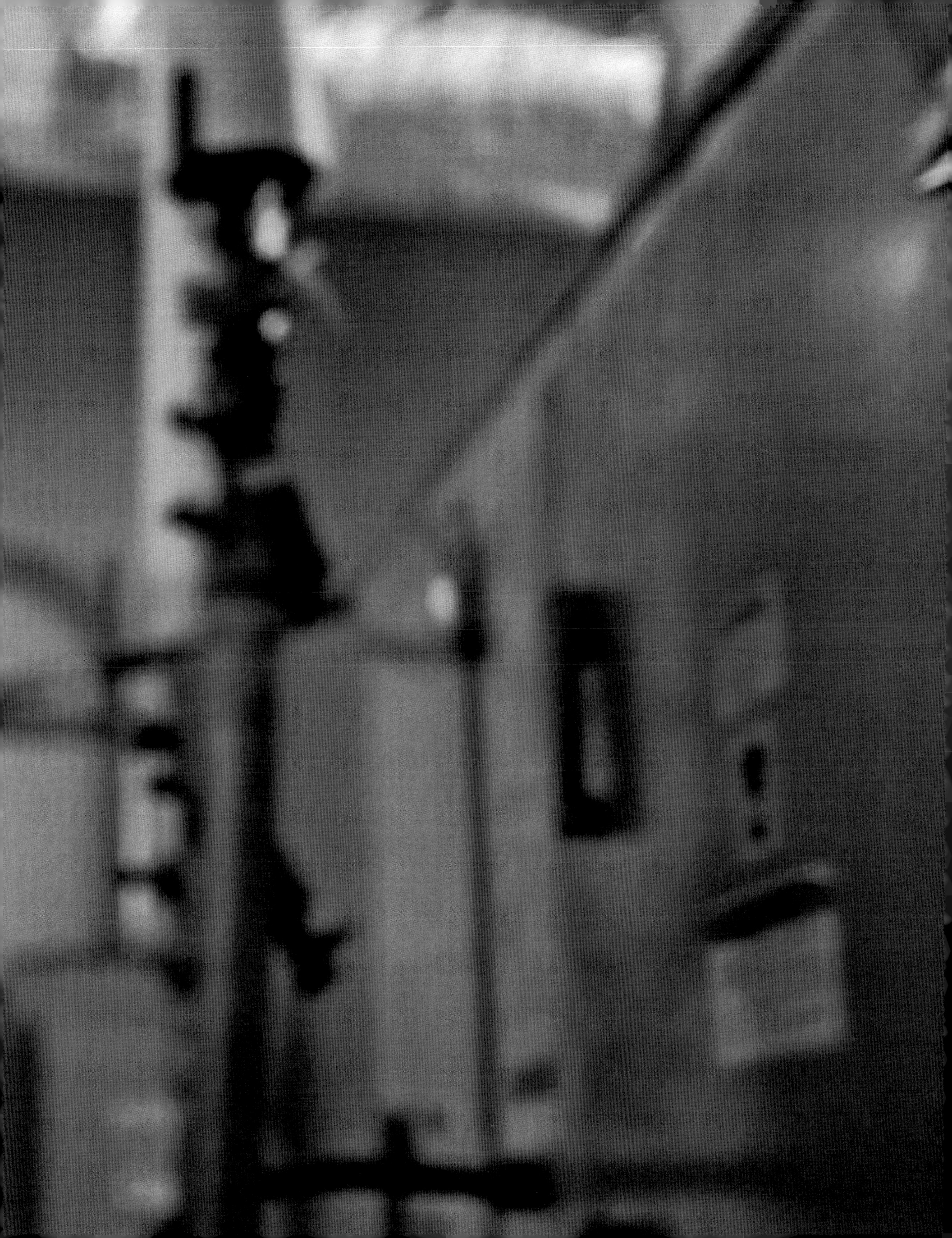

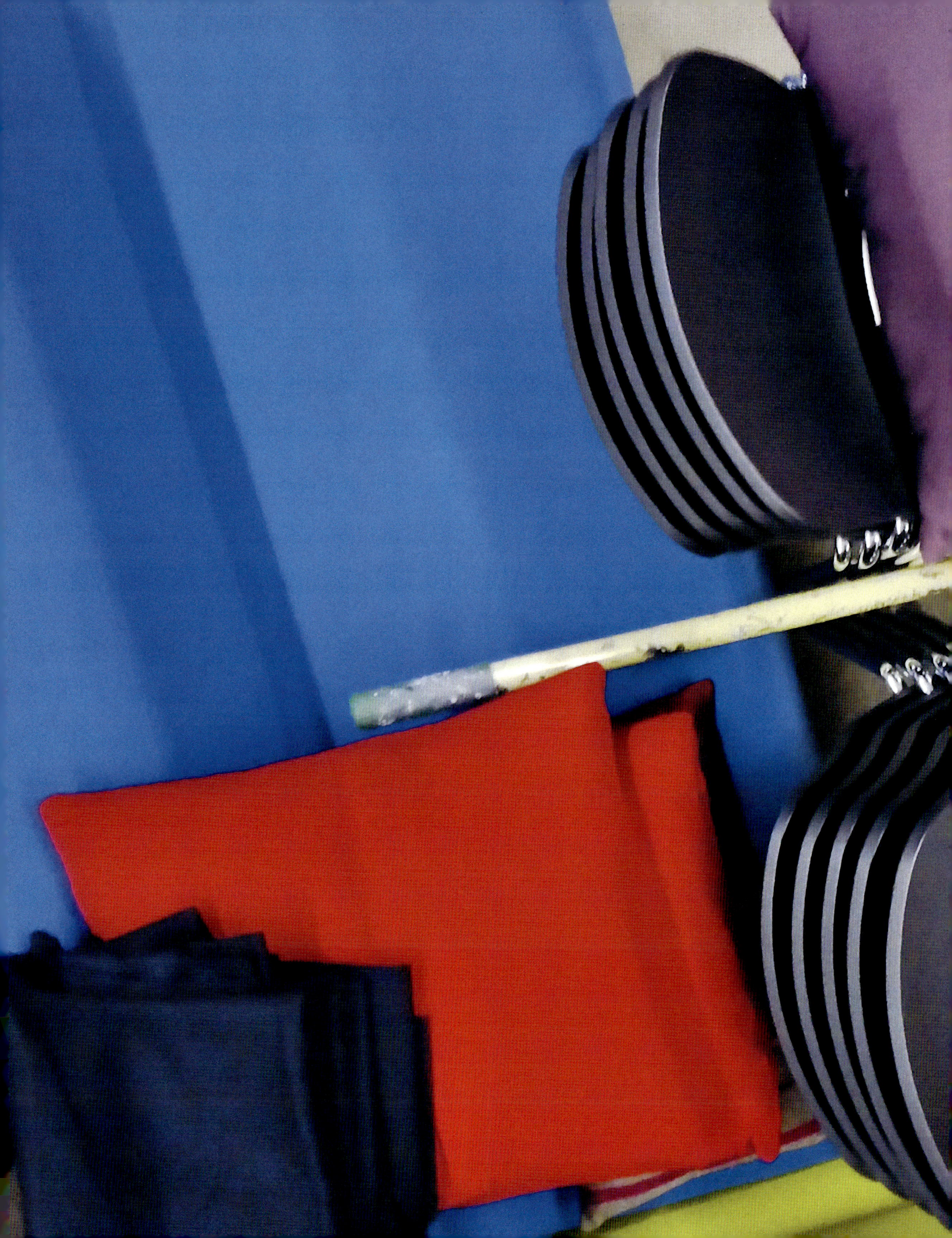

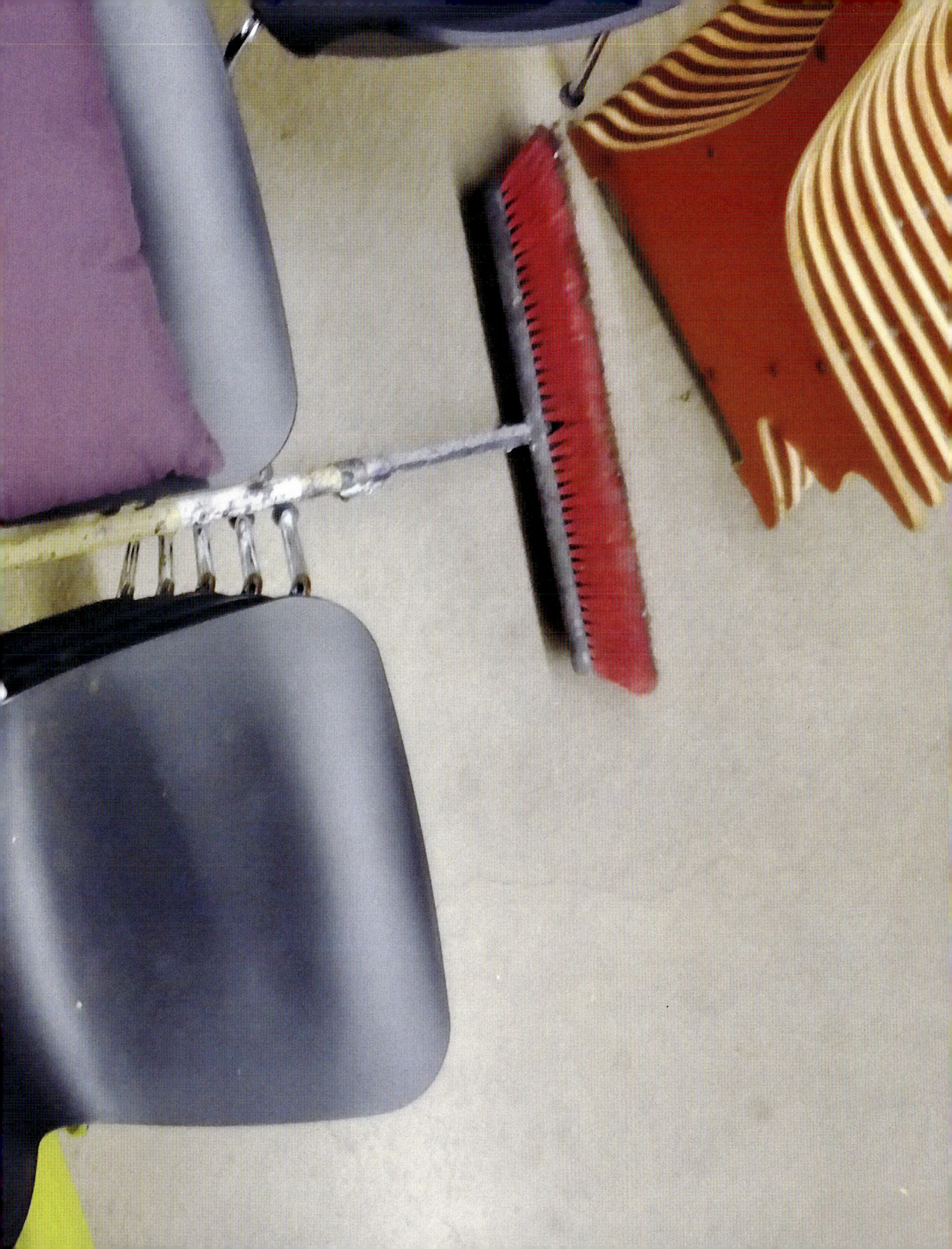

- A safe workplace.

- Raise a safety or health concern with
  your employer or OSHA, or report a work-
  related injury or illness, without being
  retaliated against.

- Receive information and training on
  job hazards, including all hazardous
  substances in your workplace.

- Request an OSHA inspection of your
  workplace if you believe there are unsafe
  or unhealthy conditions. OSHA will keep
  your name confidential. You have the
  right to have a representative contact
  OSHA on your behalf.

- Participate (or have your representative
  participate) in an OSHA inspection and
  speak in private to the inspector.

- File a complaint with OSHA within
  30 days (by phone, online or by mail)
  if you have been retaliated against for
  using your rights.

- See any OSHA citations issued to
  your employer.

- Request copies of your medical
  records, tests that measure hazards
  in the workplace, and the workplace
  injury and illness log.

... recognized hazards. It is illegal to retaliate
against an employee for using any of their
rights under the law, including raising a
health and safety concern with you or
with OSHA, or reporting a work-related
injury or illness.

- Comply with all applicable OSHA standards.

- Report to OSHA all work-related
  fatalities within 8 hours, and all inpatient
  hospitalizations, amputations and losses
  of an eye within 24 hours.

- Provide required training to all workers
  in a language and vocabulary they can
  understand.

- Prominently display this poster in the
  workplace.

- Post OSHA citations at or near the
  place of the alleged violations.

FREE ASSISTANCE to identify and correct
hazards is available to small and medium-
sized employers, without citation or penalty,
through OSHA-supported consultation
programs in every state.

This poster is available free from OSHA.

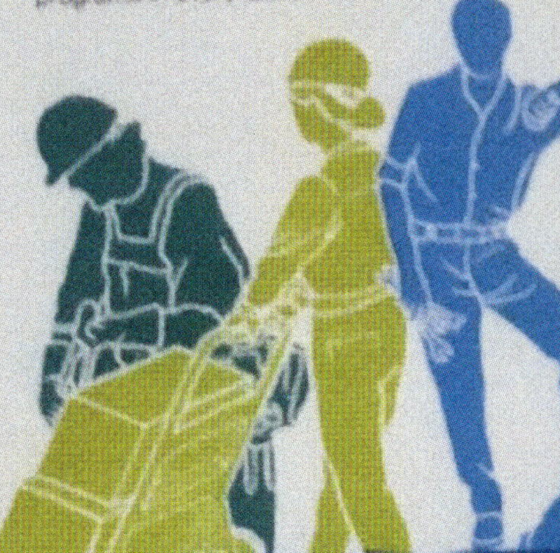

FOR USE BY PRIVATE SECTOR AND STATE GOVERNMENT EMPLOYERS

USERRA
Uniformed Services Employment and Reemployment Rights Act

Your Rights Under USERRA

USERRA protects the job rights of individuals who voluntarily or involuntarily
leave employment positions to undertake military service or certain types of service
in the National Disaster Medical System. USERRA also prohibits employers from
discriminating against past and present members of the uniformed services, and
applicants to the uniformed services.

REEMPLOYMENT RIGHTS

You have the right to be reemployed in your civilian
job if you leave that job to perform service in the
uniformed service and:

- You ensure that your employer receives advance
  written or verbal notice of your service;

- You have five years or less of cumulative service
  in the uniformed services while with that
  particular employer;

HEALTH INSURANCE PROTECTION

- If you leave your job to perform military service,
  you have the right to elect to continue your
  existing employer-based health plan coverage for
  you and your dependents for up to 24 months
  while in the military.

- Even if you don't elect to continue coverage
  during your military service, you have the right
  to be reinstated in your employer's health plan
  when you are reemployed, generally without any

NOTICE TO EMPLOYEES

THIS EMPLOYER PROVIDES UNEMPLOYMENT COMPENSATION COVERAGE FOR EMPLOYEES

Employees who become unemployed (or are working less than full time) may be eligible for unemployment compensation benefits.

Apply by phone at 1-877-644-6562 (OHIO-JOB) or at your local Department of Job and Family Services office with the following:

Social Security Card

Driver license or two other forms of identification (such as credit cards, insurance cards)

Birth dates of all dependent children

Employer's identification notice (pay stubs or W2 form)

Name and address of all other employers for whom work was performed during the past 18 months

APPLY FOR WORK AT YOUR NEAREST DEPARTMENT OF JOB AND FAMILY SERVICES OFFICE

Bob Taft
Governor

Jacqueline Romer-Sensky
Director

Ohio — Bureau of Workers' Compensation

Certificate of Ohio Workers' Compensation

This certifies that the employer listed below participates in the Ohio State Insurance Fund. Therefore, the employer is entitled to the rights and benefits of the fund for the period shown. It is only valid if premiums and assessments, including installments, are paid by the employer. To verify coverage, visit www.bwc.ohio.gov or call 1-800-644-6292.

This certificate must be conspicuously posted.

Policy number and employer:
09449557

MUSEUM OF CONTEMPORARY ART CLEVELAND
11400 EUCLID AVE STE 100
CLEVELAND, OH 44106-5823

www.bwc.ohio.gov
Issued by: BWC

Ohio Bureau of Workers' Compensation

Required Posting

Effective Oct. 13, 2004, Section 4123.54 of the Ohio Revised Code requires notice of rebuttable presumption. Rebuttable presumption means an employee may dispute or prove the presumption (or belief) that alcohol or a controlled substance not prescribed by the employee's physician is the proximate cause (main reason) of the work-related injury.

The burden of proof is on the employee to prove that alcohol or a controlled substance was not the proximate cause of the work-related injury. An employee who tests positive or refuses to submit to chemical testing may be disqualified from compensation and benefits under the Workers' Compensation Act.

Ohio — Bureau of Workers' Compensation

You must post this employer notice with the Certificate of Coverage.

DP-29 BWC-1639 (Rev. July 1, 2015)

RIGHTS AND RESPONSIBILITIES UNDER THE FAMILY AND MEDICAL LEAVE ACT

FMLA requires covered employers to provide up to 12 weeks of unpaid, job-protected leave to eligible employees for the following reasons:

- for incapacity due to pregnancy, prenatal medical care or child birth;
- to care for the employee's child after birth, or placement for adoption or foster care;
- to care for the employee's spouse, son or daughter, or parent who has a serious health condition or condition that makes the employee unable to perform the functions of the employee's job.

Entitlements

Eligible employees may take up to 12 weeks of leave for a spouse, son, daughter, or parent on active duty status in the National Guard or Reserves in support of a contingency operation may use their 12-week leave entitlement to address certain qualifying exigencies. Qualifying exigencies may include attending certain military events, arranging for alternative childcare, addressing certain financial and legal arrangements, attending certain counseling sessions, and attending post-deployment reintegration briefings.

FMLA also includes a special leave entitlement that permits eligible employees to take up to 26 weeks of leave to care for a covered servicemember during a single 12-month period. A covered servicemember is a current member of the Armed Forces, including a member of the National Guard or Reserves, who is undergoing medical treatment, recuperation, or therapy, is otherwise in outpatient status, or is on the temporary disability retired list, for a serious injury or illness.

Benefits and Protections

During FMLA leave, the employer must maintain the employee's health coverage under any "group health plan" on the same terms as if the employee had continued to work. Upon return from FMLA leave, most employees must be restored to their original or equivalent positions with equivalent pay, benefits, and other employment terms.

Use of FMLA leave cannot result in the loss of any employment benefit that accrued prior to the start of an employee's leave.

Eligibility Requirements

Employees are eligible if they have worked for a covered employer for at least one year, for 1,250 hours over the previous 12 months, and if at least 50 employees are employed by the employer within 75 miles.

Definition of Serious Health Condition

A serious health condition is an illness, injury, impairment, or physical or mental condition that involves either an overnight stay in a medical care facility, or continuing treatment by a health care provider for a condition that either prevents the employee from performing the functions of the employee's job, or prevents the qualified family member from participating in school or other daily activities.

Subject to certain conditions, the continuing treatment requirement may be met by a period of incapacity of more than 3 consecutive calendar days combined with at least two visits to a health care provider or one visit and a regimen of continuing treatment, or incapacity due to pregnancy, or incapacity due to a chronic condition. Other conditions may meet the definition of continuing treatment.

Use of Leave

An employee does not need to use this leave entitlement in one block. Leave can be taken intermittently or on a reduced leave schedule when medically necessary. Employees must make reasonable efforts to schedule leave for planned medical treatment so as not to unduly disrupt the employer's operations. Leave due to qualifying exigencies may also be taken on an intermittent basis.

Substitution of Paid Leave for Unpaid Leave

Employees may choose or employers may require use of accrued paid leave while taking FMLA leave. In order to use paid leave for FMLA leave, employees must comply with the employer's normal paid leave policies.

Employee Responsibilities

Employees must provide 30 days advance notice of the need to take FMLA leave when the need is foreseeable. When 30 days notice is not possible, the employee must provide notice as soon as practicable and generally must comply with an employer's normal call-in procedures.

Employees must provide sufficient information for the employer to determine if the leave may qualify for FMLA protection and the anticipated timing and duration of the leave. Sufficient information may include that the employee is unable to perform job functions, the family member is unable to perform daily activities, the need for hospitalization or continuing treatment by a health care provider, or circumstances supporting the need for military family leave. Employees also must inform the employer if the requested leave is for a reason for which FMLA leave was previously taken or certified. Employees also may be required to provide a certification and periodic recertification supporting the need for leave.

Employer Responsibilities

Covered employers must inform employees requesting leave whether they are eligible under FMLA. If they are, the notice must specify any additional information required as well as the employees' rights and responsibilities. If they are not eligible, the employer must provide a reason for the ineligibility.

Covered employers must inform employees if leave will be designated as FMLA-protected and the amount of leave counted against the employee's leave entitlement. If the employer determines that the leave is not FMLA-protected, the employer must notify the employee.

Unlawful Acts by Employers

FMLA makes it unlawful for any employer to:

- interfere with, restrain, or deny the exercise of any right provided under FMLA;
- Discharge or discriminate against any person for opposing any practice made unlawful by FMLA or for involvement in any proceeding under or relating to FMLA.

Enforcement

An employee may file a complaint with the U.S. Department of Labor or may bring a private lawsuit against an employer.

FMLA does not affect any Federal or State law prohibiting discrimination, or supersede any State or local law or collective bargaining agreement which provides greater family or medical leave rights.

FMLA section 109 (29 U.S.C. § 2619) requires FMLA covered employers to post the text of this notice. Regulations 29 C.F.R. § 825.300(a) may require additional disclosures.

For Additional Information:
1-866-4US-WAGE (1-866-487-9243) TTY: 1-877-889-5627
WWW.WAGEHOUR.DOL.GOV

U.S. Department of Labor
Employment Standards Administration
Wage and Hour Division

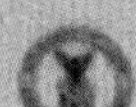

OHIO PUBLIC EMPLOYMENT RISK REDUCTION PROGRAM

SAFETY PROTECTION

THE PUBLIC EMPLOYMENT RISK REDUCTION PROGRAM IS DESIGNED TO PROVIDE SAFE AND HEALTHFUL WORKING CONDITIONS FOR OHIO'S PUBLIC EMPLOYEES

Employer Duties: Each public employer must furnish to each of its employees employment and a place of employment free from recognized hazards.

Employee Duties: Each public employee shall comply with all occupational safety and health standards.

Enforcement: The division of safety and hygiene:

1. Inspects job sites upon receipt of a complaint from an employee, public employee representative, or other official;

2. Issues citations requiring correction of violations.

Refusal to Work: Any public employee

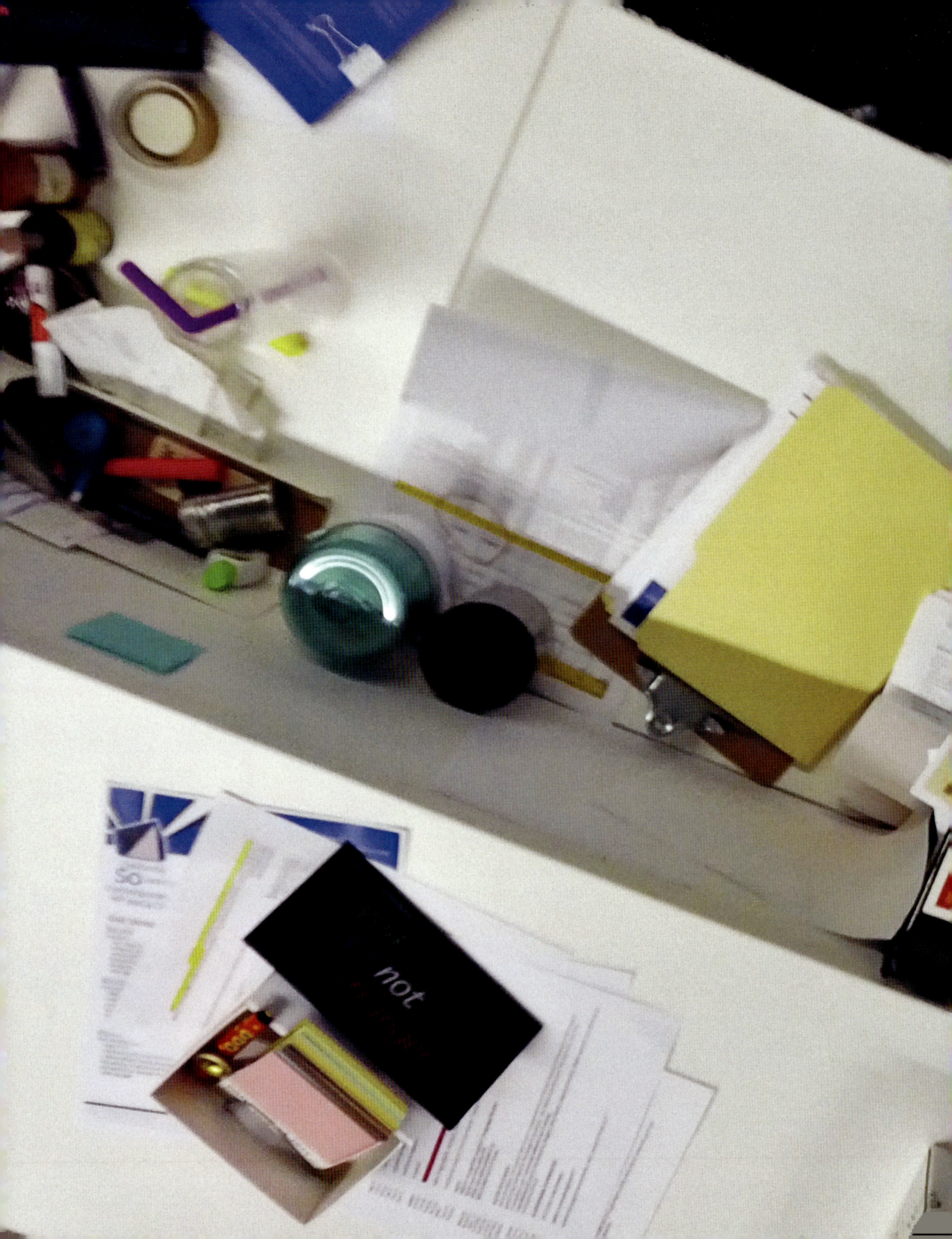
not

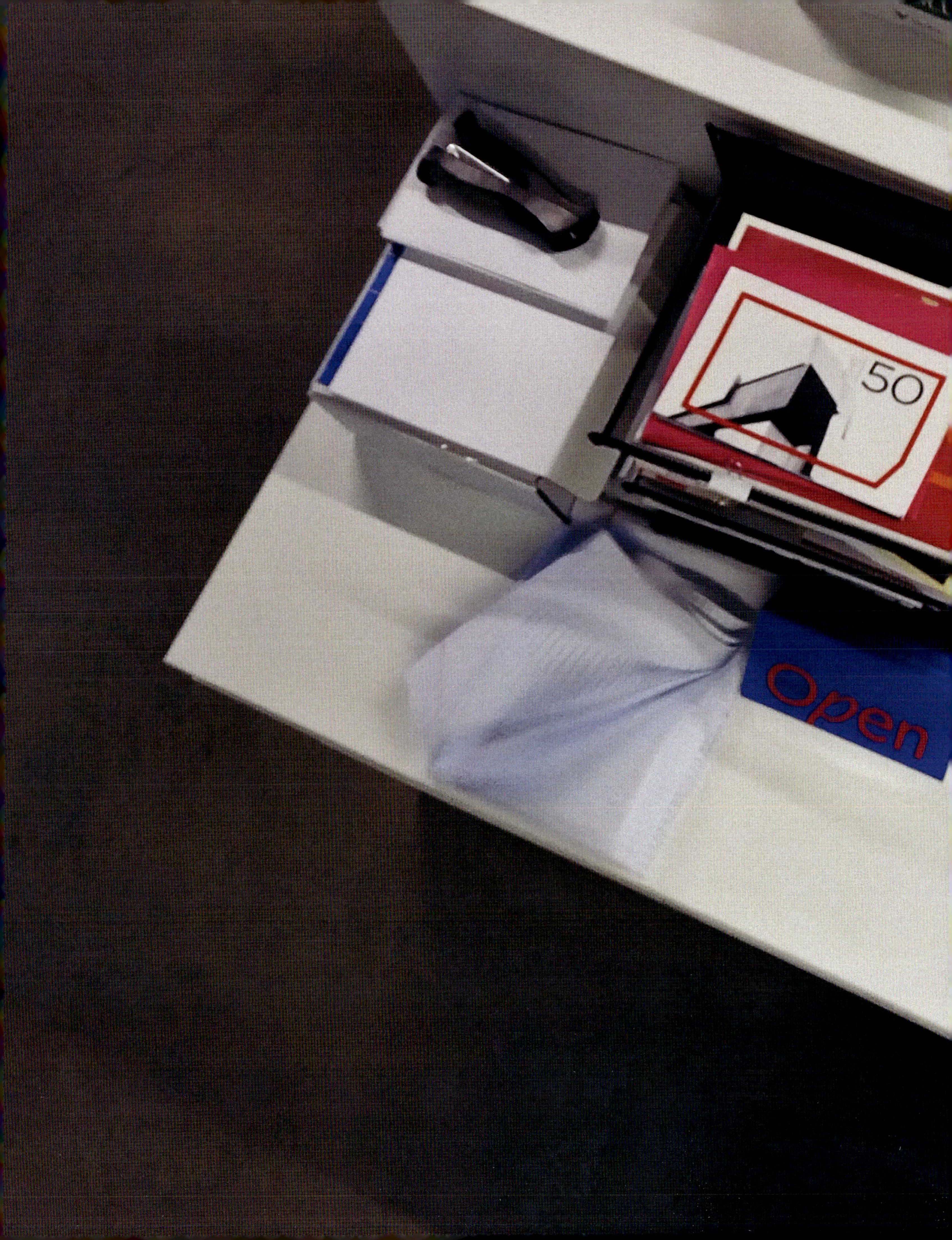
50
Open

They treat us like children. They think we won't be able to carry the weight, the knowing, the trauma. But we see everything. We hear it all, too! We are rooted six hundred feet into the ground!

> A building that is an anchor, anchor, anchor, anchor,
> anchor, anchor, anchor, anchor

is bound to descend into terror.

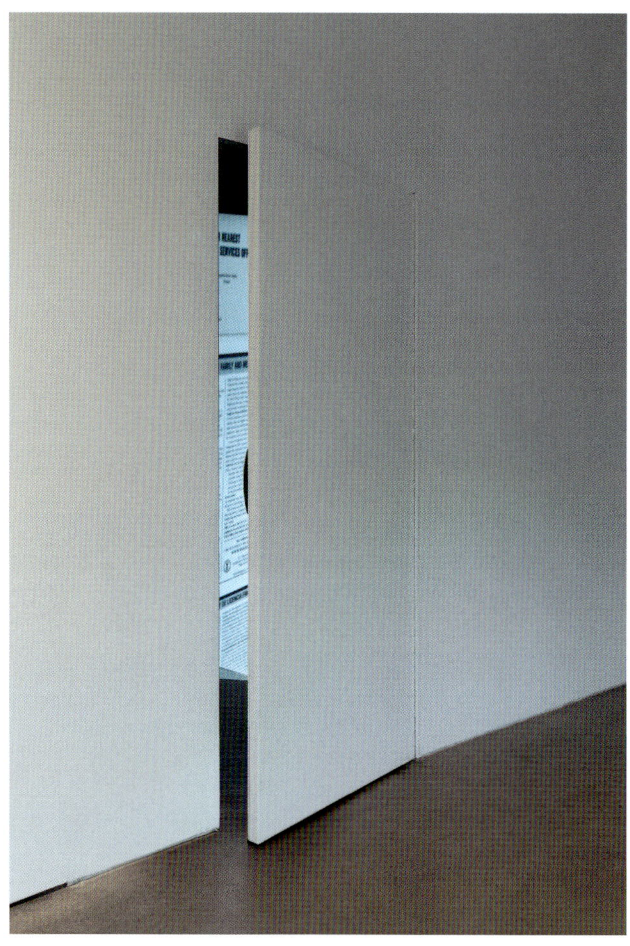

The terrible.
The terror.
The terrible terror.
The terrible things.
The terrible things that happened.
The terrible things happening.
The terrible things that happened here.

Here, between the soles of your feet and the revolving door and the glass, all the glass, and the humming of bodies and heartbeats, and the shafts of light that plague the concrete on sun-filled days.

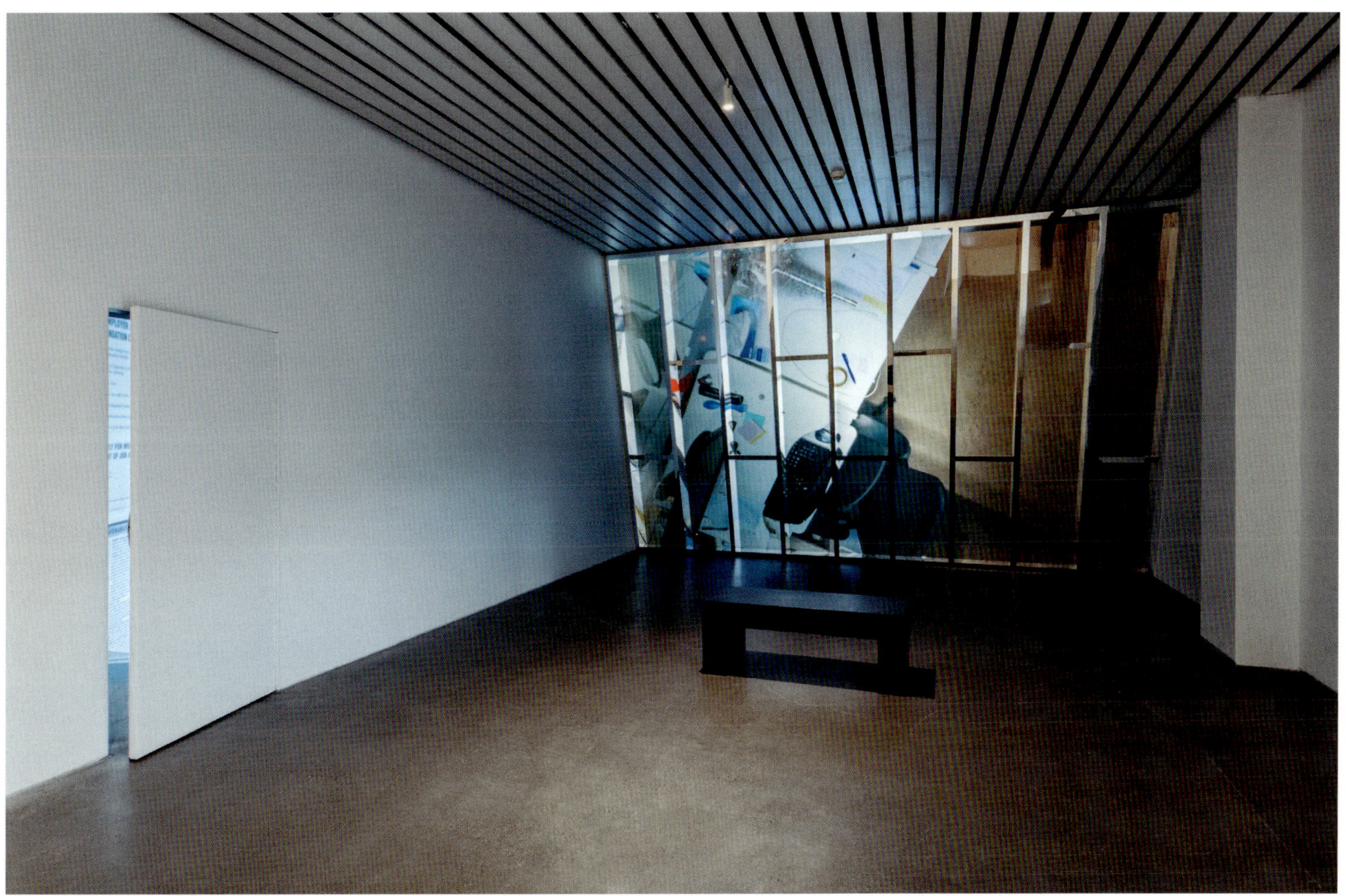

Doctors Alison Hirst and Christina Schwabenland published a paper called "Doing Gender in the 'New Office,'" investigating how gender is performed in the context of an open office workspace in November of 2017.

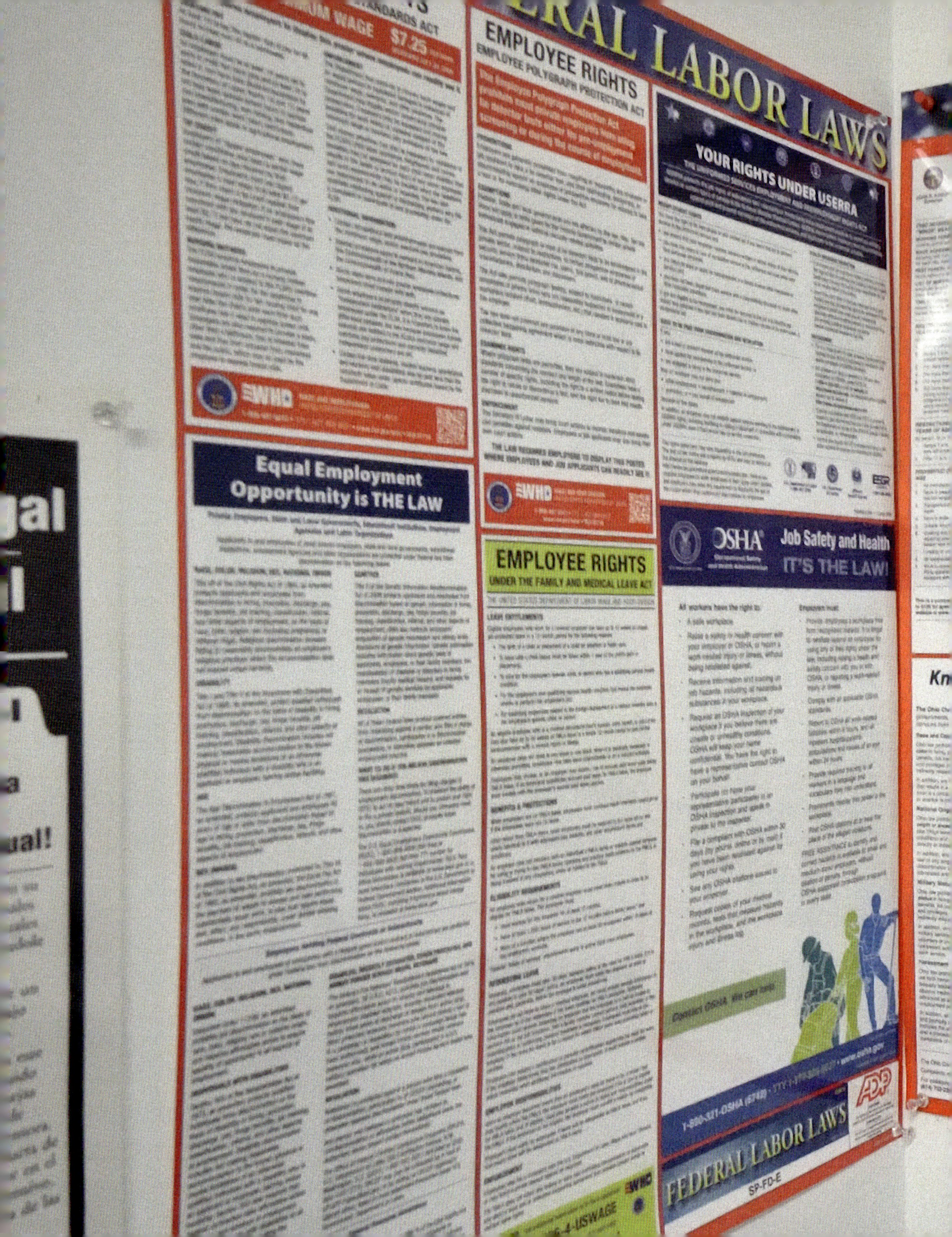

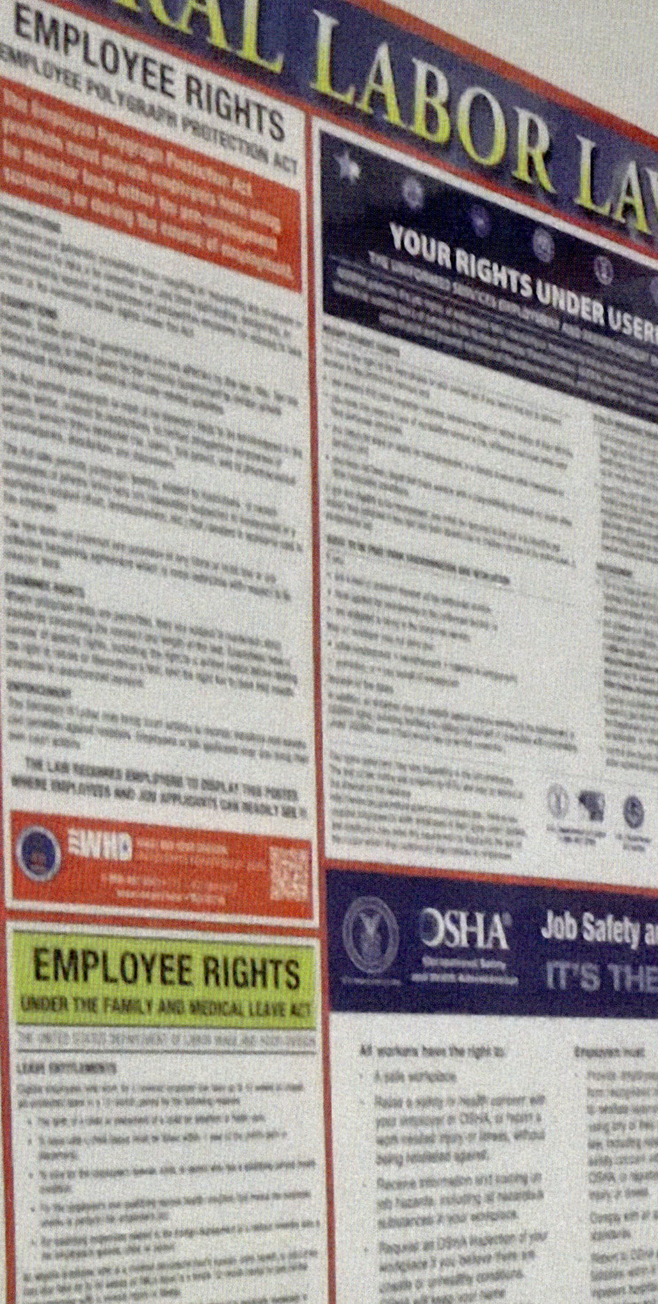

FEDERAL LABOR LAWS
EMPLOYEE RIGHTS
EMPLOYEE POLYGRAPH PROTECTION ACT
YOUR RIGHTS UNDER USERRA
MINIMUM WAGE $7.25
Equal Employment Opportunity is THE LAW
EMPLOYEE RIGHTS
UNDER THE FAMILY AND MEDICAL LEAVE ACT
OSHA
Job Safety and Health
IT'S THE LAW
All workers have the right to:
Employers must:
Contact OSHA. We can help.
1-800-321-OSHA (6742)
www.osha.gov
FEDERAL LABOR LAWS
SP-FD-E
1-866-4-USWAGE

OHIO

STATE OF OHIO
2019 MINIMUM WAGE
www.com.ohio.gov

Ohio | Department of Commerce

NON-TIPPED EMPLOYEES
A Minimum Wage of
$8.55 per hour

TIPPED EMPLOYEES
A Minimum Wage of
$4.30 per hour **PLUS TIPS**

INDIVIDUALS EXEMPT FROM MINIMUM WAGE

POST IN A CONSPICUOUS PLACE

WORKERS' COMPENSATION
Notice to Employers / Employees

This Posting is for Informational Purposes Only

NOTICE TO EMPLOYEES

THIS EMPLOYER PROVIDES UNEMPLOYMENT INSURANCE COVERAGE FOR EMPLOYEES

APPLY FOR WORK AT YOUR NEAREST OHIOMEANSJOBS CENTER

John R. Kasich
Governor

Cynthia C. Dungey
Director

Ohio | Department of Job and Family Services

OHIO

130 131 133 134 135
SP-OH-E

C0119

ADP

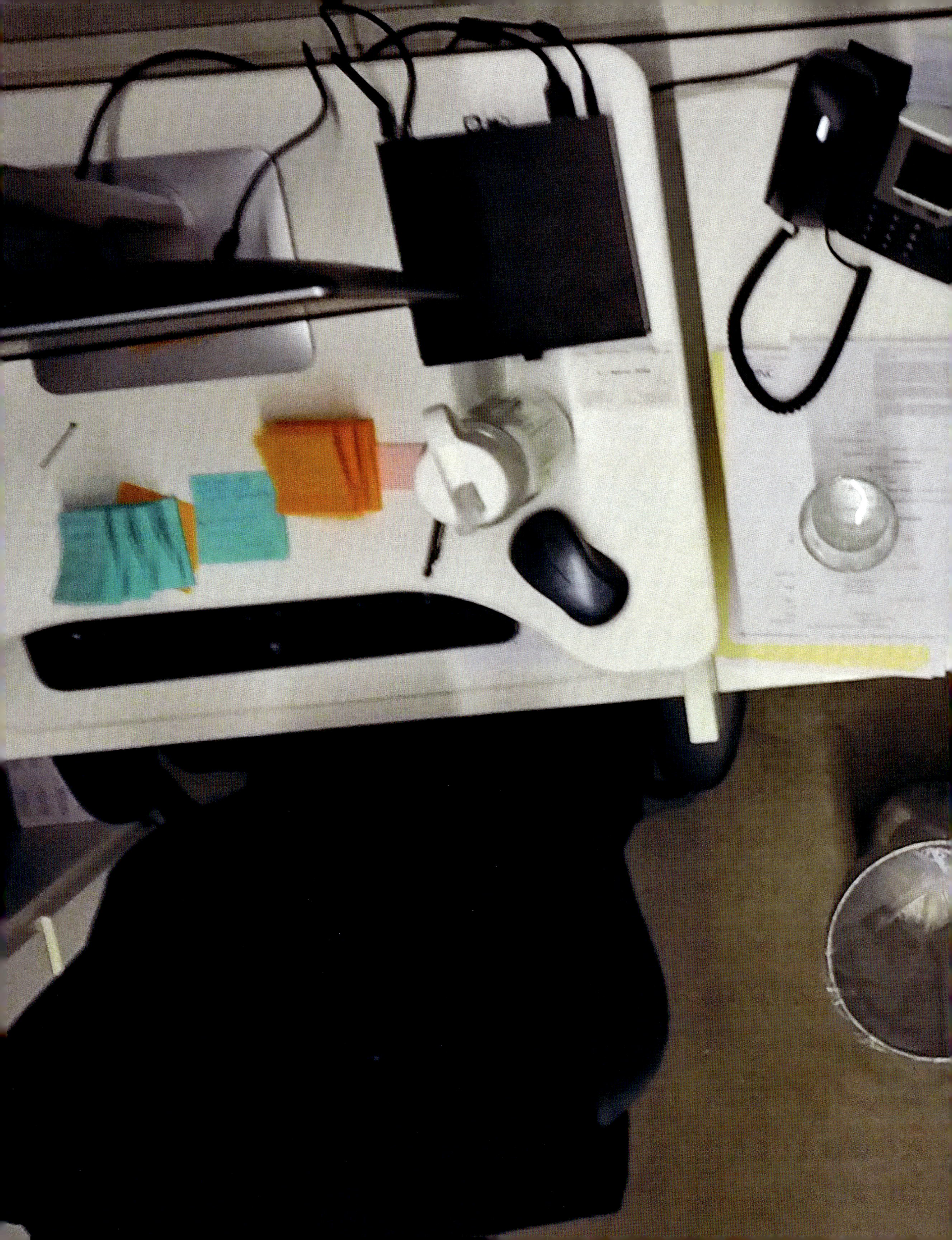

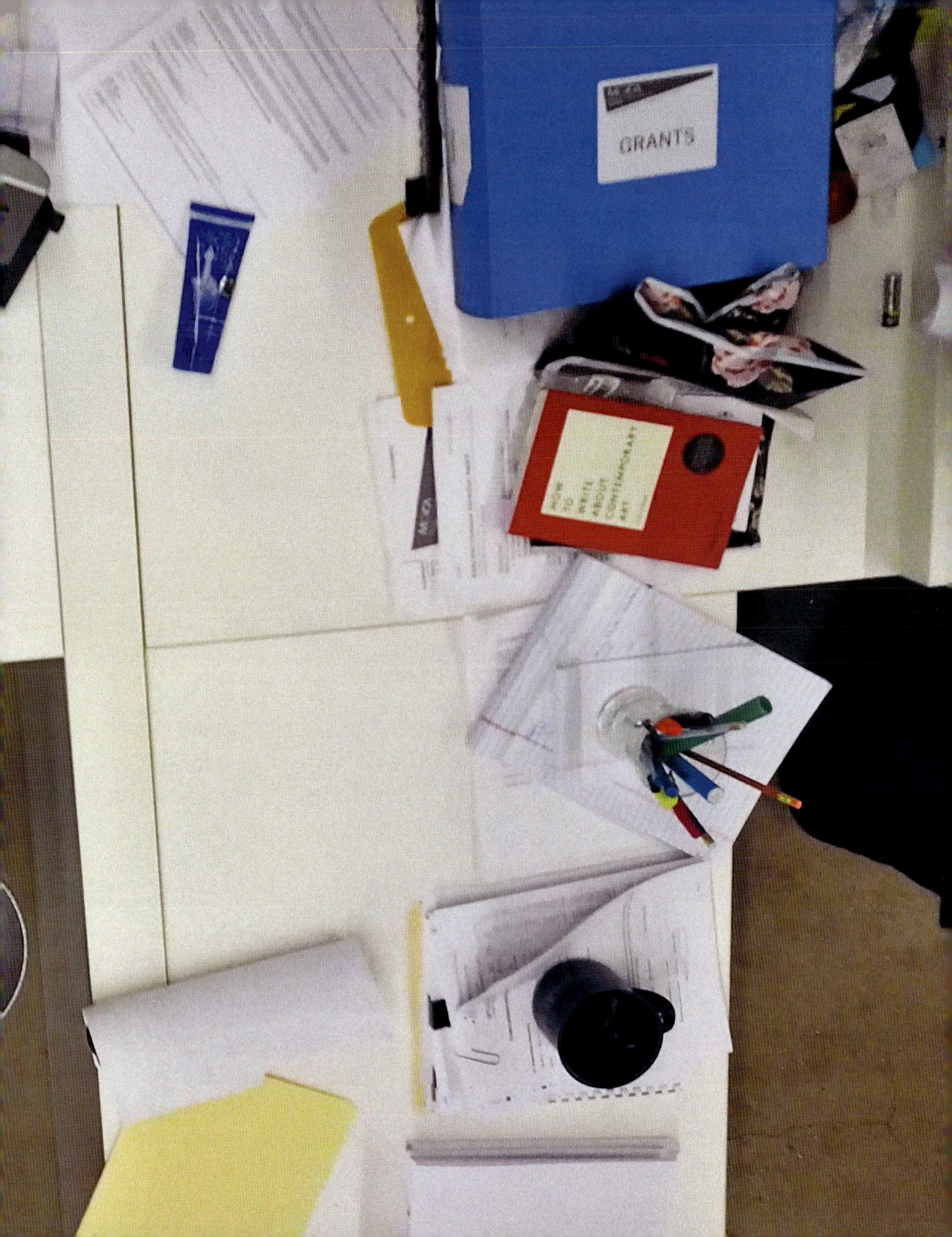

GRANTS
HOW TO WRITE ABOUT CONTEMPORARY ART

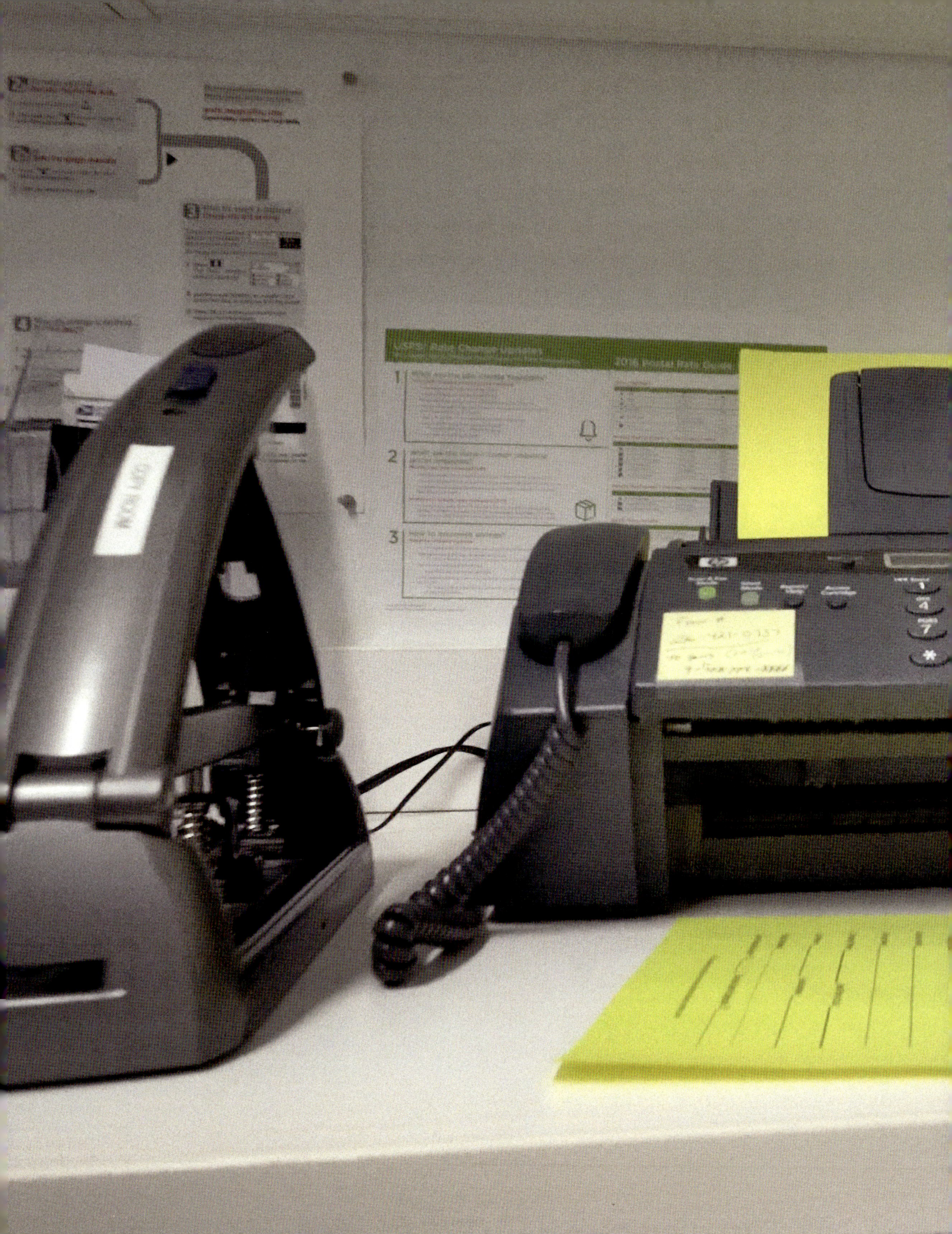

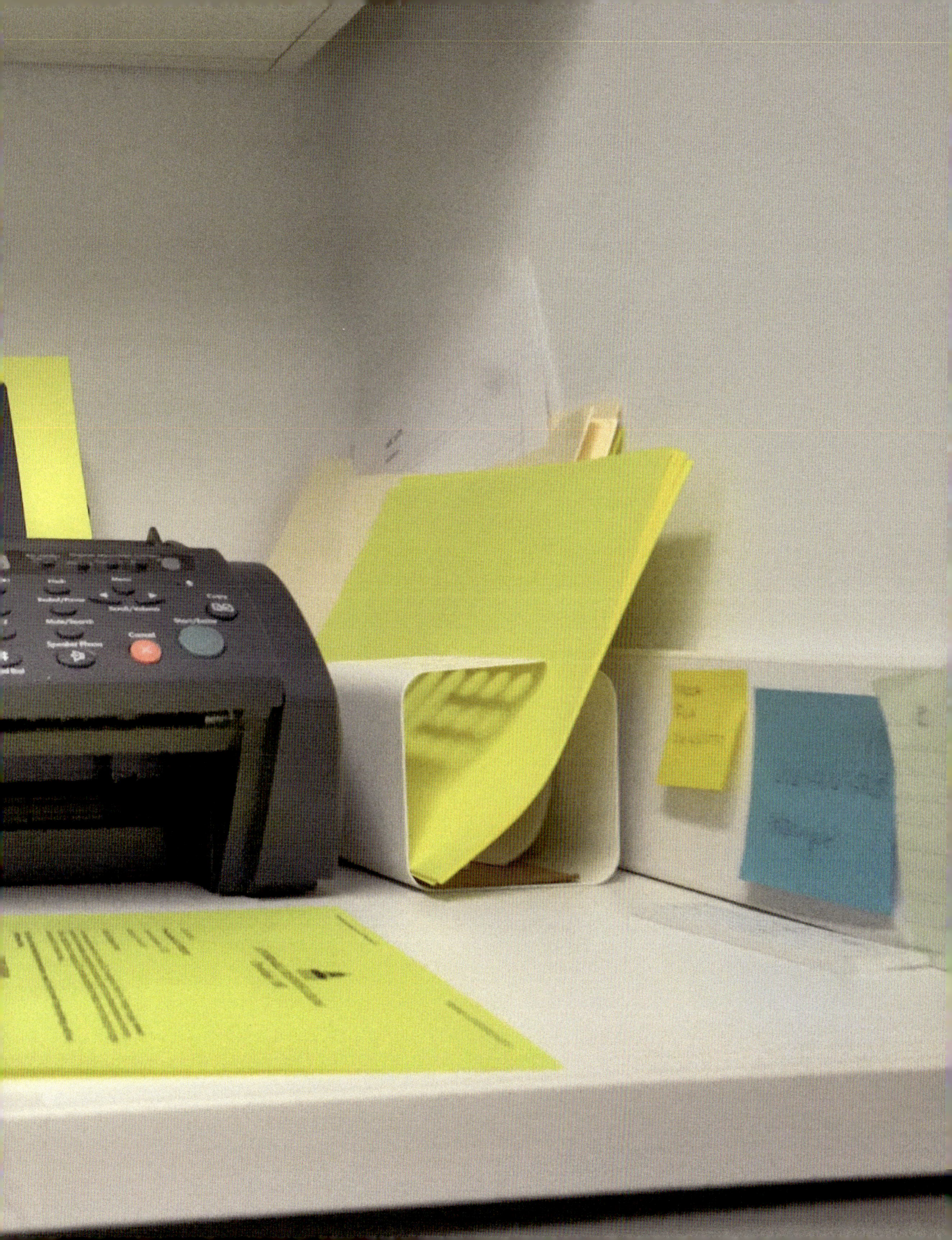

In an interview with eurekaalert.org, lead author Doctor Alison Hirst said "When changing from a more closed, compartmentalized office space to a new open-plan, transparent, and fluid working space, office workers were more conscious of their visibility and often found this unsettling rather than liberating.

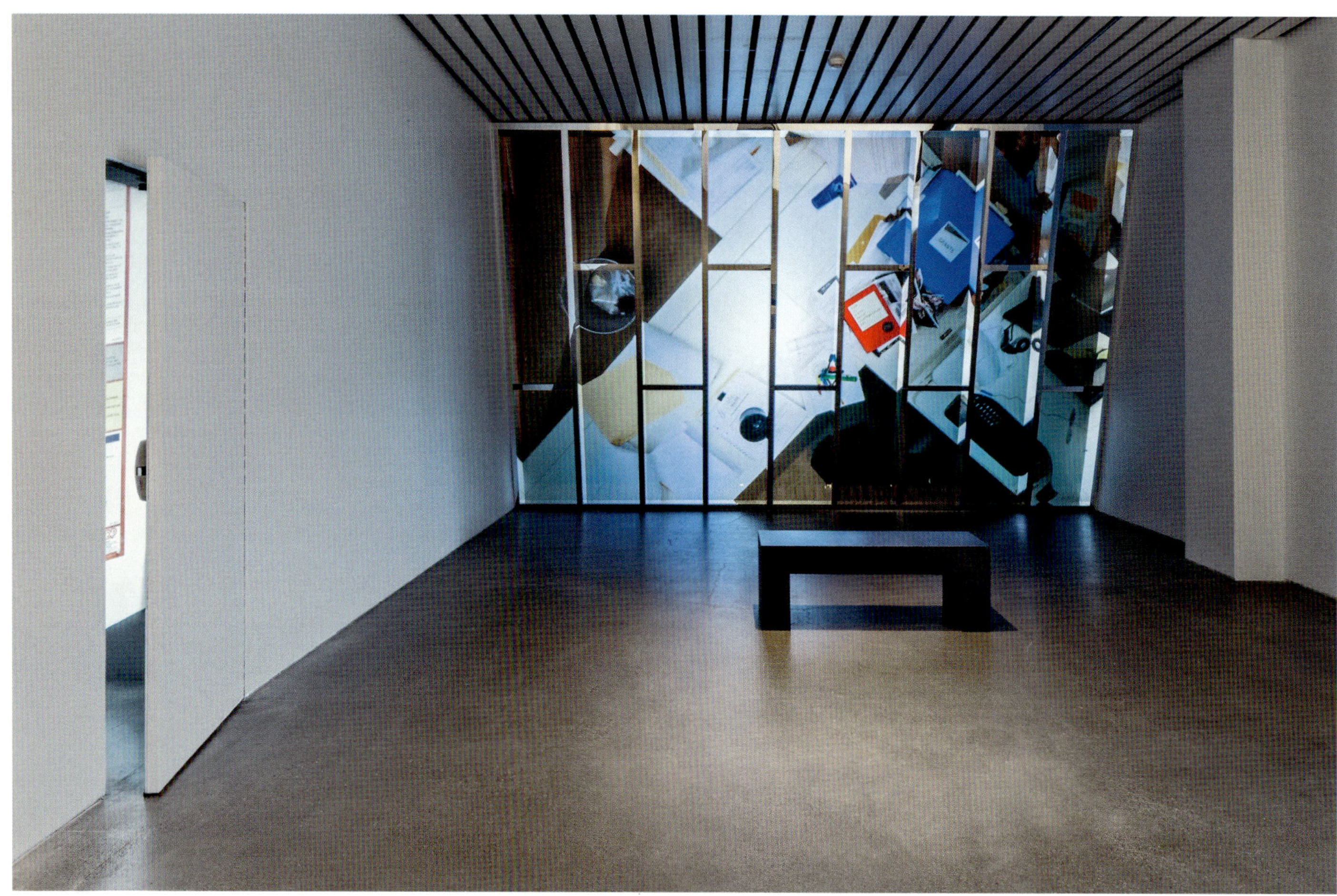

Women in particular felt anxious about the idea of being constantly watched, and felt they had to dress in a certain way. However, there was also evidence that workers felt more equal as everybody was more approachable in an open space. It was also seen by some as a chance to dress more smartly and fulfill a new identity."

Is this true? Is this what it feels like to be inside of us?
Fortunately, bodies are strange and do not always acquiesce to attempts
to regulate them.

We are highly   When we are anchored, anchored, anchored, anchored,
visible, and we   anchored, anchored, anchored, anchored, anchored,
have sight.   anchored, anchored, anchored, anchored, anchored
We are alive.   to a space, descent is a matter of time.

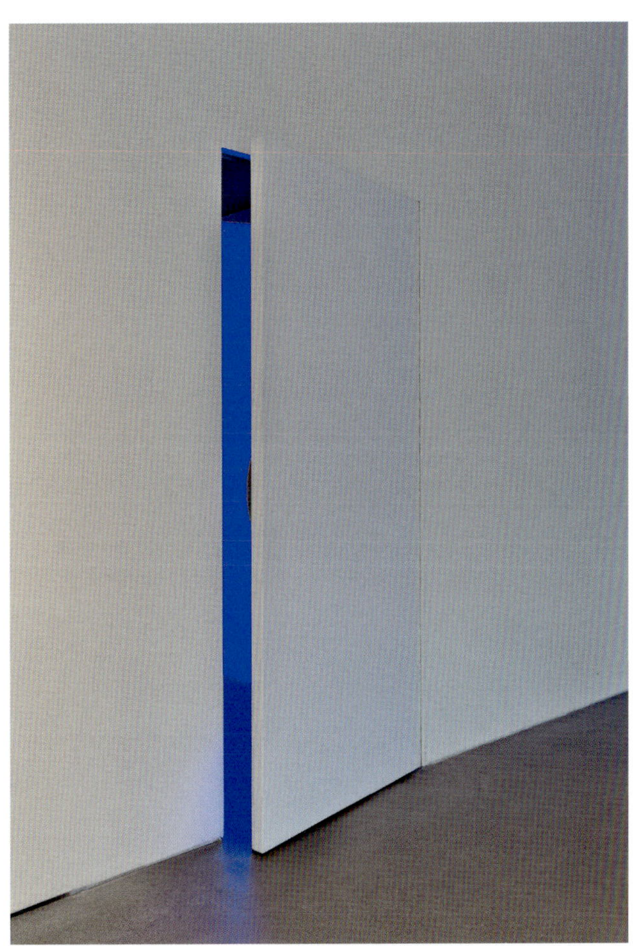

A descent into the glorious.

The terrible terror.
The glorious things.
The terribly glorious things we conjure.
The glorious things that happened.
The glorious things that happened, here.

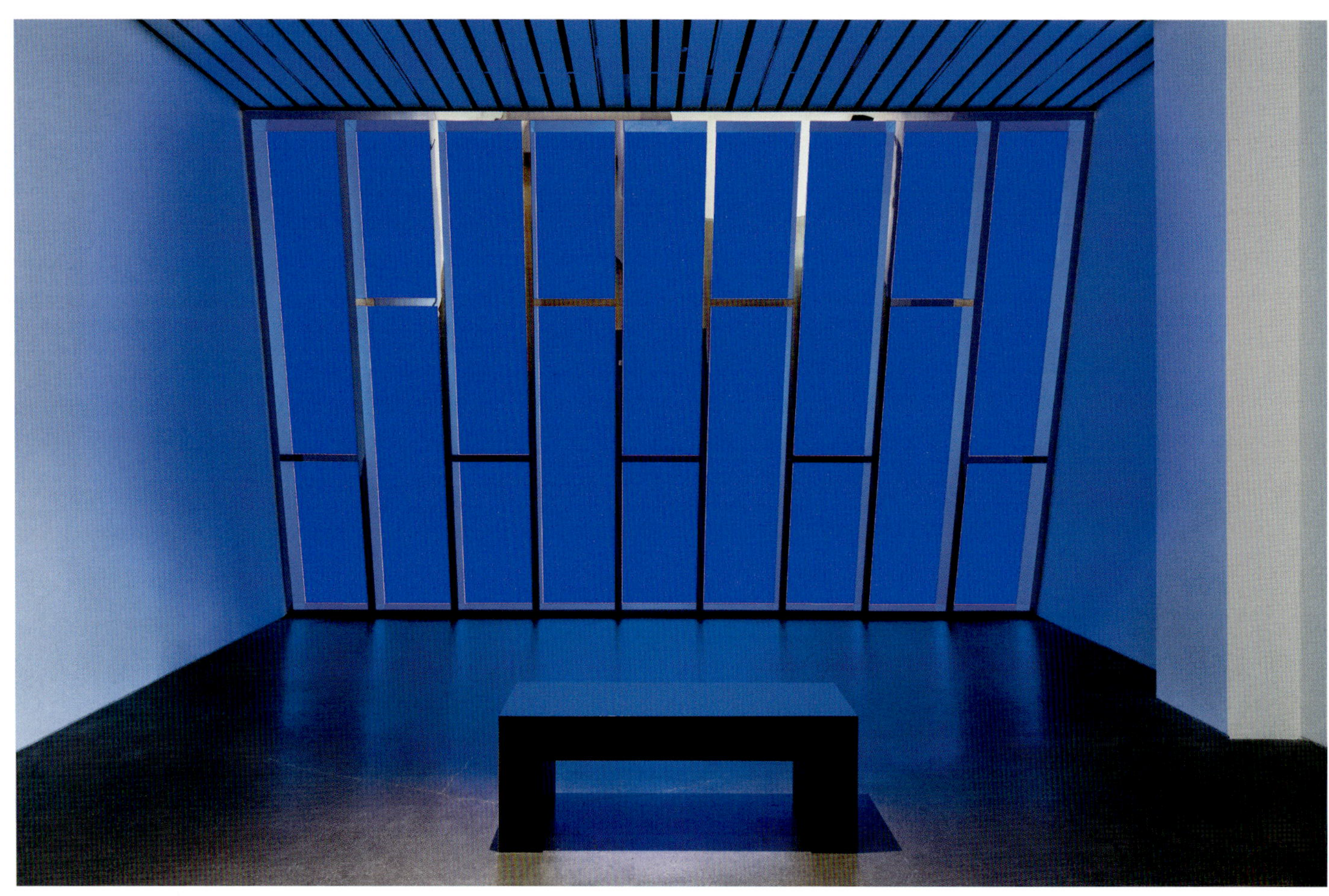

MARIO GOODEN

SCANNING MODERNITY: SONDRA PERRY AND THE DARK SIDE OF PROGRESS

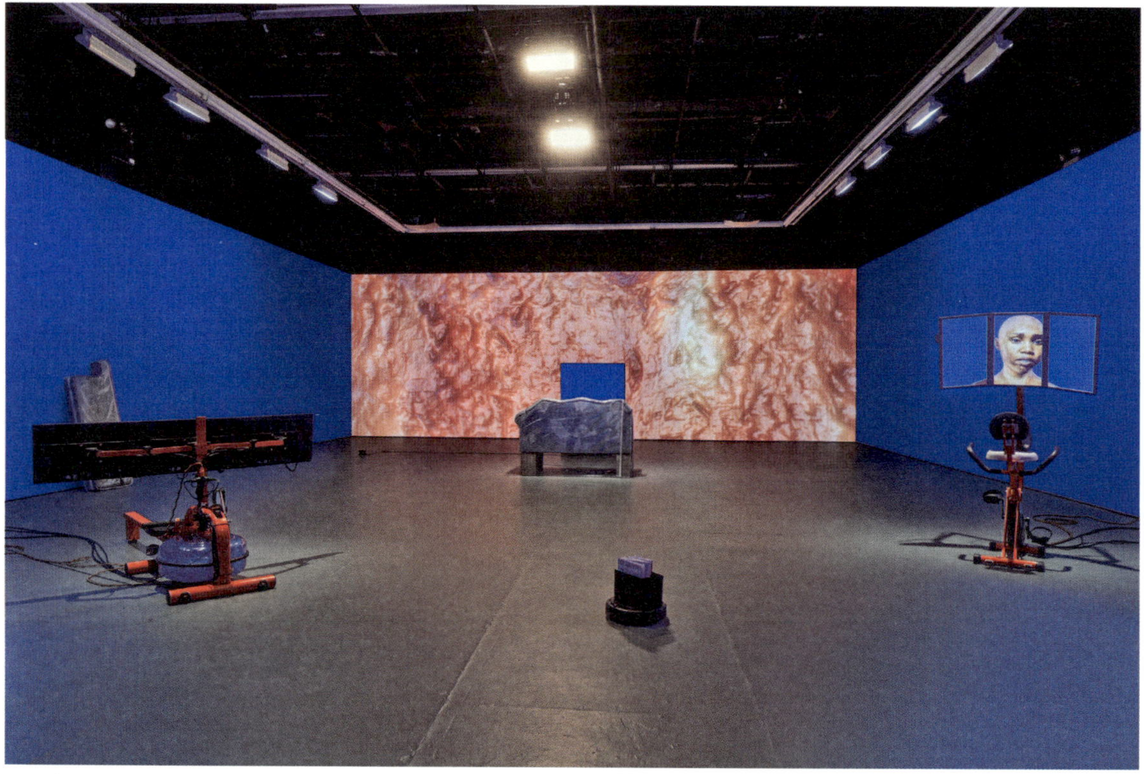

Installation view: Sondra Perry, *Resident Evil*, 2016. The Kitchen, New York. Photo: Jason Mandella

"'The invisible of a visible field is not generally anything whatever outside and foreign to the visible defined by that field' but rather, the 'invisible is defined by the visible as its invisible, its forbidden vision.'" —Hortense Spillers, "The Idea of Black Culture," *New Centennial Review*, 2006[1]

In the wake of Italian Renaissance painting and the historical split between reason and religion emerged a new, radical way of seeing and being in the world. Renaissance painting developed with the emergence of one-point-perspective drawing, which shifted the point of view from the all-seeing omniscience of God— evidenced in medieval painting through the "above is beyond" representation of depth and space—to the all-seeing omniscience of Man, for which the mathematical construction of depth and space is predicated upon the point of view of an ideal subject. That ideal subject is epitomized by Leonardo da Vinci's drawing *L'uomo Vitruvio* (ca. 1490), otherwise known as *Vitruvian Man*. The drawing depicting a man in two superimposed positions, inscribed within a circle and overlaid with a square, is based upon the writings of the Roman architect and military engineer Marcus Vitruvius Pollio in his 30–15 BC treatise *De architetura*, published as *Ten Books on Architecture*. In Book III, under the topic "On Symmetry: In Temples and in the Human Body," Vitruvius extolls the virtues of symmetry and proportions, equating the design of temples with the design of the human body, and thereby implicates architecture and the conception of space with the notion of an ideal male European body:

Without symmetry and proportion there can be no principles in the design of any temple; that is, if there is no precise relation between its members, as in the case of those of a well-shaped man.

Mario Gooden

For the human body is so designed by nature that the face, from the chin to the top of the forehead and the lowest roots of the hair, is a tenth part of the whole height; the open hand from the wrist to the tip of the middle finger is just the same; the head from the chin to the crown is an eighth, and with the neck and shoulder from the top of the breast to the lowest roots of the hair is a sixth; from the middle of the breast to the summit of the crown is a fourth.[2]

While the navel exists at the center point of the circle, the eyes in da Vinci's drawing exist along the vertical centerline of the circle and square, and near the top of the square are emphasized by heavy eyebrows. In perspectival construction, the cone of vision as well as the line of sight emanate from centerline at the height of the eyes. From this position, the square in da Vinci's drawing becomes both the rectangle of the projected vertical picture plane as well as the organizing geometry for the all-expansive, universal horizontal grid that locates an object in space relative to a vanishing point along the ideal subject's line of sight.

Contemporary to da Vinci's drawing of *Vitruvian Man*, Pietro Perugino's *Delivery of the Keys* (1482) is considered one of the earlier examples of Italian Renaissance perspective painting and represents the literal handing of spiritual power from Christ to earthly man, formerly known in the Bible as Simon Peter. The painting also represents the celestial transference of knowledge that comes with sight to the human, making it an early predecessor to European humanism, early modern epistemology, and the birth of the humanist subject, which was never ideal nor universal but was exclusively European and male.

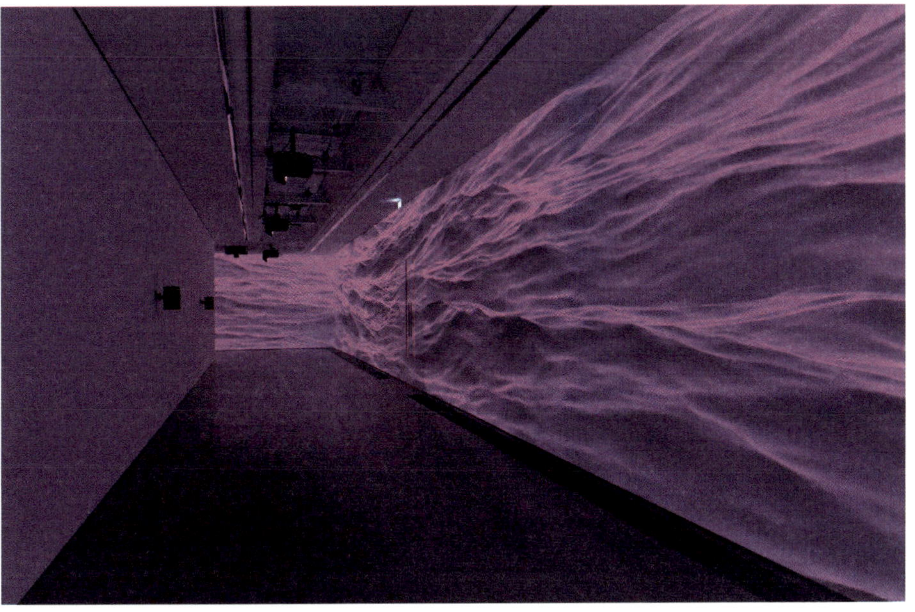

Installation view: Sondra Perry, *Typhoon coming on*, 2018. Serpentine Galleries, London. Photo: Mike Din

"In this here place, we flesh; flesh that weeps, laughs; flesh that dances on bare feet in grass. Love it. Love it hard. Yonder they do not love your flesh. They despise it. They don't love your eyes; they'd just as soon pick em out. No more do they love the skin on your back. Yonder they flay it.... And O my people, out yonder, hear me, they do not love your neck unnoosed and straight. So love your neck; put a hand on it, grace it, stroke it and hold it up. And all your inside parts that they'd just as soon slop for hogs, you got to love them. The dark, dark liver— love it, love it, and the beat and beating heart, love that too. More than eyes or feet. More than lungs that have yet to draw free air. More than your life—holding womb and your life—giving private parts, hear me now, love your heart. For this is the prize." —Baby Suggs's sermon in Toni Morrison, *Beloved*, 1998

It is no coincidence that the relationships between sight, power, and the mathematical construction of space through perspectival techniques emerged simultaneous to the beginning of European colonization of the rest of the world. This new way of seeing became an instrument of colonization as evidenced by fifteenth- and sixteenth-century European *mapa Descobrimentos* (discovery maps), indicating mathematical triangulations and projections between locations of colonial sea-faring exploitations. In his article "Coloniality: The Darker Side of Modernity," Walter D. Mignolo puts forth the basic thesis of his decades-long research that "coloniality" is the darker side of Western modernity, which is a complex matrix of power that has been created and controlled by Western men and institutions from the Renaissance through the late twentieth century and the dictates of neoliberalism. Mignolo states that the root of this darker side of modernity is the European Renaissance's double colonization of time and space:

> Colonisation of time was created by the simultaneous invention of the Middle Age in the process of conceptualising the Renaissance; the colonisation of space by the colonisation and conquest of the New World. In the colonisation of space, modernity encounters its darker side, coloniality. During the time span 1500 to 2000 three cumulative (and not successive) faces of modernity are discernable: the first is the Iberian and Catholic face led by Spain and Portugal (1500–1750, approximately); the second, the "heart of Europe" (Hegel) face lead by England, France and Germany (1750–1945); and finally the US American face lead by the United States (1945–2000). Since then, a new global order began to unfold: a polycentric world interconnected by the same type of economy.[3]

However, Mignolo goes on to argue that this cycle of "coloniality" is coming to an end due, principally, to two main forces that challenge Western leadership in the early twenty-first century. The first of these is de-Westernization and an irreversible shift to Asia and the struggle with the West over economics as well as knowledge and politics. The second force is "decoloniality" and the global resistance to Western dominance. Mignolo explains that "decoloniality" requires delinking from the colonial matrix of power underlying Western modernity to imagine and build global futures in which human beings and the natural world are no longer exploited in the relentless quest for wealth accumulation.

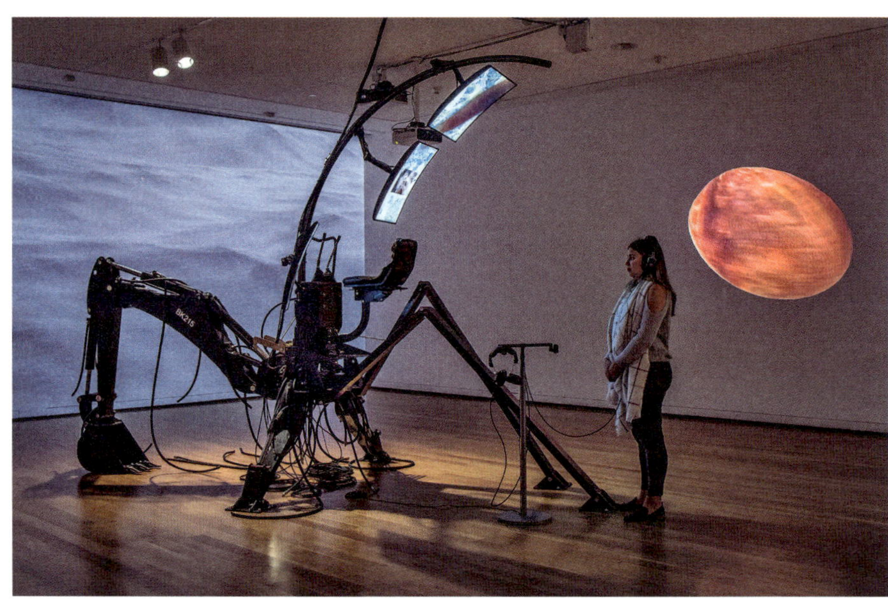

Installation view: Sondra Perry, *Eclogue for [in]HABITABILITY*, 2018. Seattle Art Museum. Photo: Natali Wiseman

Mario Gooden

The paradox of Mignolo's argument is that, semantically, "decoloniality" is predicated upon undoing "coloniality," which occupies the first position. It must also be acknowledged that "coloniality" is not only the product of a complex network but that the residues of "coloniality" are also entanglements that ensnare time and space in four dimensions and are infrastructural in terms of the political, social, economic, and environmental. The cynical view of this disorder suggests that, as a process, "decoloniality" is not necessarily futile but it is never-ending at best. For, as Frantz Fanon explains in his exposition of "decolonial" processes in *The Wretched of the Earth*, "The colonist and the colonized are old acquaintances. And consequently, the colonist is right when he says he 'knows' them. It is the colonist who fabricated and continues to fabricate the colonized subject. The colonist derives his validity, i.e., his wealth, from the colonial system."[4] Furthermore, holding to this point of view suggests that agency, sight, and independence are limited, restricted, and not self-actualized under this condition.

Yet, the work of Sondra Perry demonstrates that the very opposite is true. Perry does not sublimate entanglements, nor does she make attempts to unravel the entanglements as one might expect. Rather, the artist exposes the "spookiness" of entanglement while transforming its strangeness into multidisciplinary art across time and space that demands a new way of thinking, seeing, and speaking critical discourse. The work does not easily fit into the European enlightenment epistemology. As a matter of fact, its aim is to challenge, discomfort, and confound that epistemology by defamiliarizing and disassociating the colonized from the colonist. Hence, this is much more than a process of "decoloniality"; it is a practice of "anti-coloniality."

In one of Perry's earliest, critical works, her single-channel video performance *Black Girl As A Landscape* (2010), she reveals her strategy of disassociation. In the first part of the black-and-white video, the camera, as though the eye of surveillance from an aerial view, pans slowly across the silhouette of a horizontal female figure. The figure's subtle movements are barely noticeable; yet, this portion of the video establishes the familiarity of the black female body under the gaze of the overseer. Furthermore, the characteristics and shapes of the silhouette recall the "Young Negress" from Kara Walker's silhouettes of antebellum slave and plantation cut-outs. Within the realm of familiarity, viewers may recall the tropes of the black female body that Hortense Spillers seeks to undermine through her distinction between "body" and "flesh" in "Mama's Baby, Papa's Maybe: An American Grammar Book," where she writes:

> But I would make a distinction in this case between "body" and "flesh" and impose that distinction as the central one between captive and liberated subject-positions. In that sense, before the "body," there is the "flesh," that zero degree of social conceptualization that does not escape concealment under the brush of discourse, or the reflexes of iconography. Even though the European hegemonies stole bodies—some of them female—out of West African communities in concert with the African "middleman," we regard this human and social irreparability as high crimes against the *flesh*, as the person of African females and African males registered the wounding. If we think of the "flesh" as a primary narrative, then we mean it's seared, divided, ripped-apartness, riveted to the ship's hole, fallen or "escaped" overboard.[5]

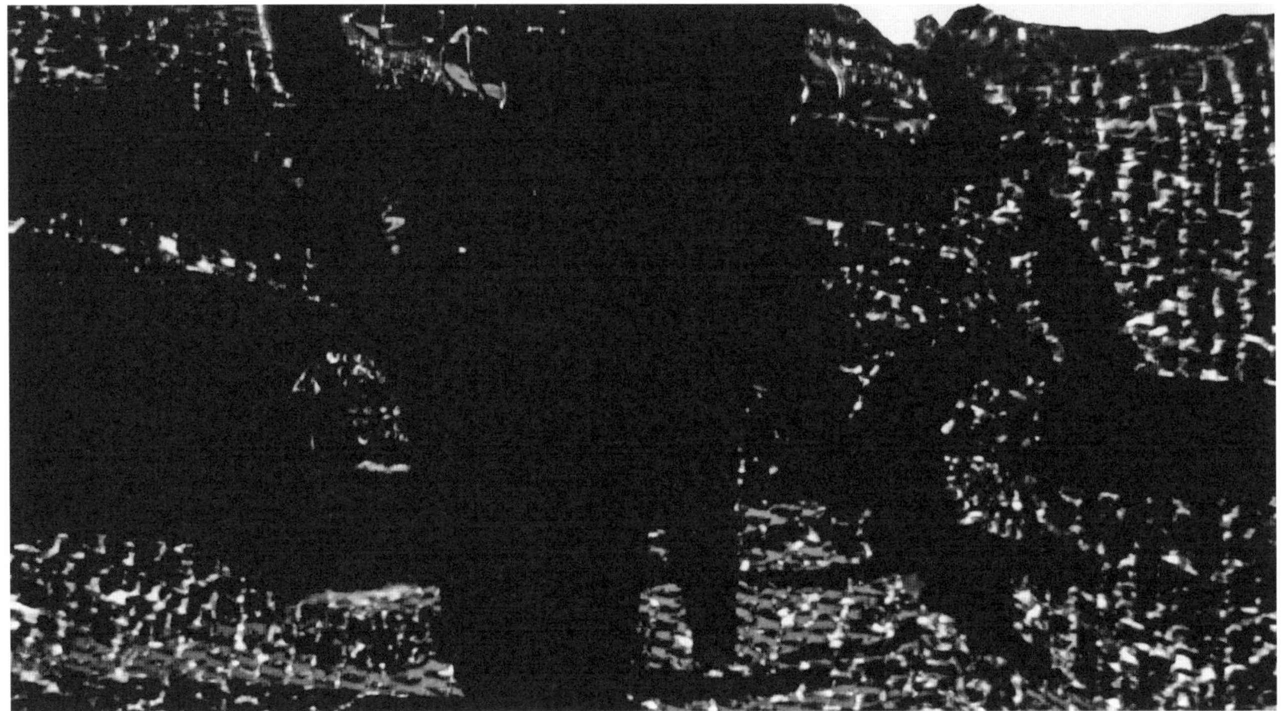

Sondra Perry, *Black Girl As A Landscape*, 2010. Single-channel HD video, color, silent; 10:04 min. Performed by Dionne Lee. Courtesy the artist and Bridget Donahue, New York

The second part of the video begins with a fade-in from black and shifts in scale as the camera scans across the other-worldly topography of super-black but varying surfaces in high contrast to the absence of color. The different textures of this alien landscape exhibit geological characteristics that are bedazzling yet mysterious in their origin. The imagery takes on the quality of some kind of landscape X-ray. The final part of the video reveals the landscape to be the body and dress of the female figure as the camera scans horizontally back and forth. The video concludes with close-up scenes of the female figure's eyes in sharp, eerie, white contrast to the blackness of her face, while calling into question the viewer's gaze and the inability to familiarize the presence in the video.

From this earliest work to Perry's *A Terrible Thing* (2019), the artist deploys the technological gaze of the aerial or bird's-eye view scanning across a terrain to dislocate the presumed ideal Western subject from his position of familiarity and authority. In *A Terrible Thing*, a site-specific, two-channel video and installation-based work at the Museum of Contemporary Art Cleveland, Perry explores the entanglements of "coloniality" in the four dimensions of space and time as well as the sensory dimension of smell. These entanglements include networks and systems of power extending from the 1796 dispossession of land from the Haudenosaunee by Moses Cleaveland, the Western Reserve of the Connecticut Land Company (an extension of colonial power from New England); to early urban development patterns in Cleveland as well as early technologies of telecommunications and transportation; to the 1939 Federal Home Loan Bank Board/Home Owners' Loan Corporation (HOLC) redline map of Cleveland and Cuyahoga County that detailed, by color code (red, yellow, blue, and green), the spatialization of racist home mortgage lending policies; to the forced erasure of black businesses and jazz clubs in what would later become known as Cleveland's Euclid Avenue Corridor; and finally to the institutional structures of labor within moCa itself as well as the systems of construction labor and materials in the building of the museum, which, not so ironically, sits on the site of the former Jazz Temple that was fire-bombed and destroyed in 1964.

Mario Gooden

A Terrible Thing conducts an archeological inquiry of its terrain at multiple scales of perception and spatial experience. For one part of the gallery installation, Perry constructs a false curtain wall that mirrors the exterior façade of the museum and projects a video onto the wall from its opposite side, giving viewers a sense of seeing directly through a window to the exterior of the building. In the video, the artist begins with satellite imagery of Cleveland and its environs and then overlays that imagery with the 1939 HOLC redline map. As the video zooms in from satellite to bird's-eye surveillance, various elements of Geographic Information System data, including three-dimensional-modeled landscape and building aspects, come into view. However, as the camera scans and robotically moves about this geography, its overlay with the HOLC redline map gives the strange illusion that the city has been flooded by Lake Erie, where streets and parks become rivers, lakes, and ponds of red, yellow, blue, and green.

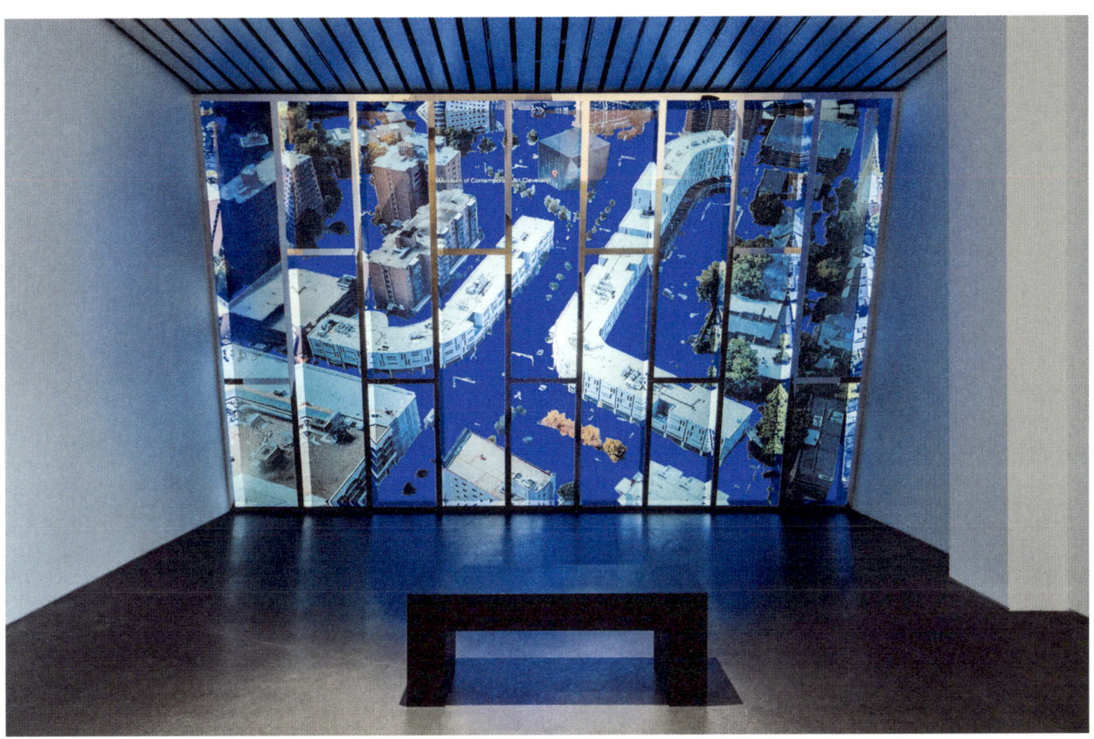

Installation view: Sondra Perry, *A Terrible Thing*, 2019. Museum of Contemporary Art Cleveland. Photo: Field Studio

The uncanny juxtapositions of data and digital imagery subtly but unmistakably allude to the region's fourteen-thousand-year-old Pleistocene Era history when the Wisconsinan glacier melted its way through the geological formations of Northeast Ohio, leaving lakes, rivers, streams, and, eventually, forming Lake Erie. As another portion of the video—taken from the point of view of a CCTV camera mounted high up on the exterior of moCa's building—surveils the site below, viewers are confronted by the ongoing gentrification of Cleveland's Uptown district and the museum's central position within this condition. Finally, using drone technology, Perry scans the office environment of hidden labor within the museum building.

The design of the open office area is predicated upon the modernist architectural concept of the "free plan." As formulated in the 1920s by renowned Swiss architect Le Corbusier, "The plan is a slave of the bearing walls. Reinforced concrete in the house brings about the free plan! The floors no longer superimpose rooms of the same size. They are free. A great economy of constructed volume, a rigorous use of each centimeter. A great financial economy. The easy rationalism of the new plan!"[6] Yet, what the drone video imagery captures is not the openness of the workspace but rather its cluttered, messy condition, thereby calling into question the modernist ethos of rationality and efficiency. The second video of the installation offers a more intimate view of the office workspace through a glimpse into what appears to be a supply closet constructed by Perry in the gallery, thus presenting viewers with a sense of voyeurism into a private, back-of-house space in the museum.

Finally, Perry adds the sensory condition of smell through the emission of a somewhat sweet but perhaps ominous scent to the gallery. The scent relates to the idea of the chemical reaction that occurs when human skin comes into contact with metal and recalls the skilled laborers who construct buildings and infrastructure. The scent adds to the atmosphere of the installation, juxtaposing the familiar with the unfamiliar in order to render what is uncanny, strange, and eerie. At times barely perceptible, it suggests the chloroform condition of "progress." For, as Mignolo states, progress is the rhetoric of modernity and, in turn, the rhetoric of coloniality.

Modernity, in general, is synonymous with the evolution of society and with ideas of newness. From the Renaissance to the Enlightenment, European colonialists—principally Portuguese and Spanish powers—propagated the myth of colonialization through the spearhead of Christian theology and the rhetoric of salvation. In the seventeenth and eighteenth centuries, British and French imperial powers translated this myth as the goal of "civilizing" the non-European world and bringing to it Western ideas of modernity through forms of governance and the extraction of natural resources for the industrialization of the West. Furthermore, these concepts of "civilizing" were accompanied by the idea of "progress" and advancement. Following World War II, when the United States emerged as a world military and economic superpower, the concepts of salvation, newness, and progress took on a new vocabulary under the name of "development and modernization" and the project of "globalization."[7]

Hence, the entanglement that Perry's work seeks to expose and transform, at its epistemological basis, is the spookiness of "progress." Perry's practice ultimately questions how cultural production can be defined on its own terms as a liberatory practice of black ontological development.

NOTES

1 Hortense Spillers refers to Althusser and Balibar's *Reading Capital* to suggest that their argument regarding reading is also applicable to a larger field of consideration of structural relationships.

2 Marcus Vitruvius Pollio, "Book III: On Symmetry: In Temples and in the Human Body," in *Ten Books on Architecture*, trans. Morris Hicky Morgan (Cambridge: Harvard University Press, 1914), 72–73.

3 Walter D. Mignolo, "Coloniality: The Darker Side of Modernity," in *Modernologies: Contemporary Artists Researching Modernity and Modernism*, ed. Sabine Breitwieser, exh. cat. (Barcelona, Spain: Museu d'Art Contemporani, 2009), 41–42.

4 Frantz Fanon, "On Violence," in *The Wretched of the Earth*, trans. Richard Philcox (New York: Grove Press, 2004), 2.

5 Hortense Spillers, "Mama's Baby, Papa's Maybe: An American Grammar Book," *Diacritics* 17, no. 2 (1987): 67.

6 Le Corbusier, "Les Cinq Points d'une Architecture Nouvelle," in *Oeuvre complète* (Zurich: Edition Girsberger, 1929), 128.

7 Mignolo, "Coloniality: The Darker Side of Modernity," 43.

Mario Gooden

ALISON HIRST & CHRISTINA SCHWABENLAND

DOING GENDER IN THE "NEW OFFICE"

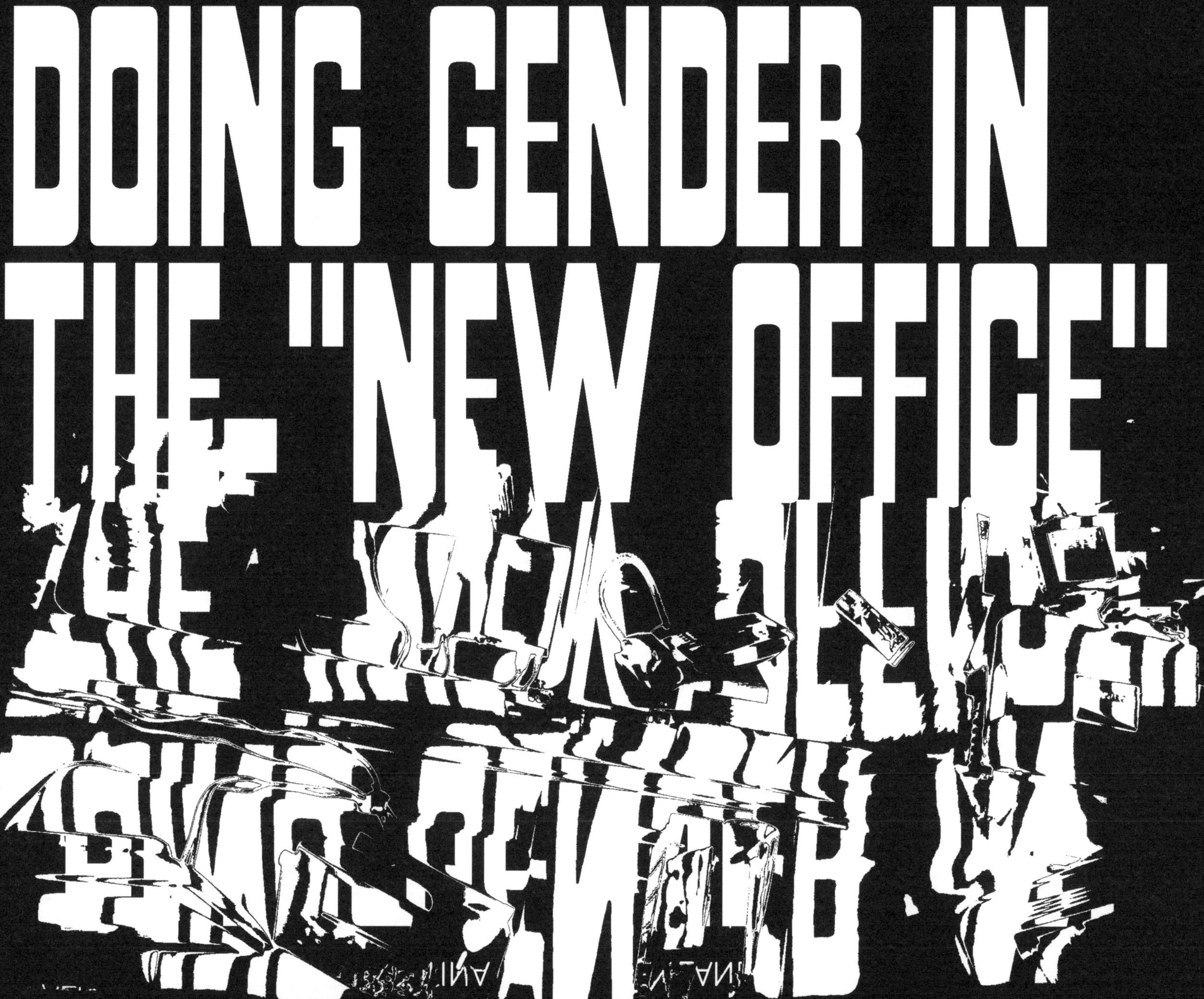

This paper investigates how gender is performed in the context of an office setting designed to promote intensive, fluid networking. We draw on an ethnographically oriented study of the move of staff into a new office building constructed primarily from glass, and incorporating open-plan offices, diverse collective areas, and walking routes. Although the designers aimed to invoke changes in the behavior of all staff, they conceptualized these changes in masculine terms. We, therefore, analyze the gender norms materialized by the workspaces of the "new office" and how women responded to these. We suggest that the new office encourages an image of the ideal worker, which brings together ways of acting and interacting that have been characterized as both masculine and feminine—active movement and spontaneous encounters, but also intensive face-to-face interaction and deep relationship building. Women are driven into this mode of working in an uncompromising, almost aggressive way, but a straightforward gender-based dynamic does not emerge in their responses, with conventional gender characteristics being reshuffled and recombined.

INTRODUCTION

There is a rich body of literature exploring the ways in which gender is socially constructed by and within organizations. Studies in this literature proceed from the assumption that women and men are not pre-given, natural categories, but

rather that gender is "done." Nentwich and Kelan's (2014) review of studies of "doing gender" distinguishes two overlapping research positions. The ethnomethodological approach originally proposed by West and Zimmerman (1987, 2009) suggests that gender is achieved in interaction, and involves "being *accountable* to current cultural conceptions of conduct becoming to—or compatible with the 'essential natures' of—a woman or a man" (West and Zimmerman, 2009, p. 14; original emphasis). The poststructuralist understanding subsequently developed by Butler (1990, 2004) stresses the notion of performativity, summarized by Nentwich and Kelan (2014) as "the process through which gendered subjects are constituted by regulatory norms that are restrictive and heterosexual" (p. 123). Summarizing the conclusions from both approaches, Nentwich and Kelan (2014) state that gender is "done" in response to specific situations, and its performative character means that it is unstable, and can be resisted, subverted, or ignored. Because being a man or a woman "should be seen as the outcome of a process rather than the starting point" (p. 124), the difficult challenge for empirical studies is the need to investigate the actual practices of constructing or performing gender, and the ways in which these can be consciously chosen or disrupted.

Our interest focuses specifically on these practices as constituted by the body within space. There is, so far, relatively little research on this nexus of

organizational space and the gendered body (Tyler and Cohen, 2010; Wasserman and Frenkel, 2015). According to Butler, the body "matters" because it is a "site of doing and being done to" (Hancock and Tyler, 2007, p. 520) as it becomes implicated in social processes, inscribed by norms, and evaluated. These embodied social processes are also spatially contingent. For example, gender is done differently by nurses based in a "large and fast" regional hospital from those in a district hospital that was "small and slow" (Halford and Leonard, 2006), and by female farmers as they move between the different spaces of a livestock auction (Pilgeram, 2007). In their study of women working in diverse roles in a university setting, Tyler and Cohen (2010) argue that workspaces are "a materialization of the cultural norms according to which particular gender performances are enacted" (p. 193) and that the construction of a gendered identity involves spatial responses to these norms. They show that women's and men's gender performances differ: women's accounts were characterized by spatial constraint (being fixed in place and having to remain accessible), "spillage," that is, encroachment of their space by male colleagues, and "bounded appropriation" of space in ways largely consistent with the gender norms of the organization and society more generally. Tyler and Cohen (2010) conclude that "in order to be perceived as feminine, women have to occupy space in a more tentative way than men" (p. 181). Wasserman

Alison Hirst & Christina Schwabenland

and Frenkel's (2015) study of the Israeli Ministry of Foreign Affairs shows that all the occupants of the hierarchically configured workspace experienced it as masculine, and that women reported their consciousness of the risk of being seen as "too feminine." As Tyler and Cohen (2010) recognize, "*Workspaces matter* to the myriad ways in which we continue to perform, practise and negotiate gender at work" (p. 195; original emphasis). They call for more work exploring gender materialization within a broader range of organizational settings.

Our analysis draws on a longitudinal ethnographic study of a UK local authority (Westshire County Council, or WCC[1]) in which approximately a thousand senior staff moved from six separate departmental buildings into a shared "new office" building (Duffy, 1997). The design of the office building, making extensive use of glass as a construction material and incorporating large open-plan offices and collective spaces, was aimed explicitly at eroding hierarchical and departmental boundaries and promoting fluid, informal networking. In Dale and Burrell's (2008) terms, it was designed to enchant rather than control overtly, and to encourage movement rather than fixity. What is distinctive about our study is that it analyzes how gender, body, and space act on each other in an organizational context where people *have* to create, re-create, challenge, and/or redraw boundaries. During the three years of the study, the building was purchased, employees moved into the new work environment, and work routines were re-established, modified, or created anew. Thus, the move into the strategic center can be seen as a kind of laboratory for the study, in that it is bounded in time (rather than ongoing observation of business as usual); and immersion in the new physical environment led to the establishment of new spatial norms, as members engaged in intensive interaction and exposure, provoking self-conscious reflection on theirs and others' roles and relationships. This opportunity also enabled us to observe and interpret the significance of gender within such boundary-defining activities, and the specific conceptualizations of gender that were reconstructed or changed.

We bring together two theoretical perspectives to analyze the gendered norms that were materialized in the workspace, and the various ways in which women maintained, resisted, and changed these norms. First, we draw on West and Zimmerman's (1987) conceptualization of gender as something that is "done," rather than ascribed. It is clear that if doing gender is "at once institutional and interactional" (p. 114), such cultural conceptions are mutable. Second, we consider Lefebvre's (1991) conceptualization of the production of space. Although Lefebvre's work does not engage explicitly with the relationship between social space and the construction of gendered bodies (Blum and Nast, 1996; Simonsen, 2005), as Blum and Nast (1996) show, gender is an implicit but recurrent theme throughout his theoretical framework. Consequently, they argue that, for Lefebvre, gender construction is "*the* fundamental social process through which alterity is achieved" (p. 559; original emphasis). In the study that follows, we draw specifically on his distinction between conceived space (the intended changes of behavior to be facilitated by the new design) and spatial practices (the actual responses made by women working in the new building) through which the collective norms become more available for co-option and/or contestation.

We have chosen to focus our analysis on women for two reasons. First, as Hassard *et al.* (2000) argue, the male body becomes invisible in organizations, and female bodies stand out as different and problematic; simultaneously, the male norm can be contested. Lewis (2008) also shows that the male is the norm against which women have to be evaluated. In this case (as we will show in our findings), when the male designers spoke of the behaviors they wanted the new building to change, they framed these using masculine metaphors, although both men and women were relocated to the new office. Second, there was a lack of evidence that men had responded in ways comparable to women (i.e., none commented on whether and how they had changed their style of dress, in contrast with women participants). Our argument is that although workspaces are presented as neutral, they are material expressions of cultural conceptions of the "ideal" worker, including how the worker "does" gender. Therefore, we pose two research questions: what are the *particular* gender norms materialized by the workspaces of the "new office"; and what types of spatial and embodied responses do women make?

Our paper is structured as follows. We begin with a more in-depth consideration of the construction of gender at work, before discussing how this literature intersects with Lefebvre's theorization of space. We then describe the design of the research study before presenting our findings. We uncover the changing expectations of gender performance held by the design team, and follow with an analysis of the ways in which women responded to these expectations. We conclude with a discussion of the ways in which gender characteristics are reshuffled and recombined in these new workspaces.

"DOING" GENDER AT WORK

The influential essay by West and Zimmerman (2009) established the ground for interest in gender as something that is "done" rather than ascribed. West and Zimmerman conceptualize "doing" gender as a process, involving the identification of "current cultural conceptions of conduct" (p. 114) at play within the workplace and the reciprocal dynamics of simultaneously responding to, and contributing to, these conceptualizations. Concomitantly, "undoing" gender implies "a change in the normative conceptions to which members of

particular sex categories are held accountable" (West and Zimmerman, 2009, p. 117). Such changes have to be granted by members of the collective as well as being taken up by the members of the category whose norm-orientation has changed. If this acceptance is not granted, or the changes not acknowledged, then the "undoing" of gender is not accomplished and the prevailing normative conceptions can reassert themselves. As such, gender is one of many forms of difference, such as race, class, or status, that may be accomplished simultaneously in interaction (West and Fenstermaker, 1995).

As we are concerned with inequality and oppression, the extent to which such culturally contingent norms can be influenced and even overturned seems to be the crux of the matter. Furthermore, would such challenging of traditional norms lead to greater homogenization and the absence of gender distinctiveness or to a re-interpretation of the content of gender norms (with the possibility that these new formulations will also be imbricated with power dynamics)? Risman (2009) suggests that "a criterion for identifying undoing gender might be when the essentialism of binary distinctions between people based on category is challenged" (p. 83), implying that it is not the content of those distinctions but their very existence that constitutes doing gender.

More recent theorizing sees femininity in the workplace as "reconfigured," incorporating both conventional masculine

and feminine aspirations and behaviors. Lewis (2014) suggests that new conceptualizations of management are emerging in which feminized behaviors and forms of relationship building are valorized with "the new ideal manager characterized by a feminine ethos manifest in a range of managerial attributes associated with femininity" (p. 1846). Hence, there is a greater range of "available bodily and relational performances" (p. 1853) in "doing" both gender and management; "Women *and* men can successfully mobilize femininity when doing management and business" (p. 1847; original emphasis). However, she argues that men are still more likely to reap economic advantage from more feminized behaviors while women's performances are "unrecognized and naturalized" (p. 1848). Lewis identifies a further underlying hierarchy in which not all forms of femininity are equally valued, with white, middle-class, and heteronormative modes being privileged. Nentwich and Kelan (2014) similarly argue that "doing gender means doing hierarchies and eventually leads to inequality" (p. 127). However, they conclude that the simultaneous doing of gender and hierarchy requires further empirical investigation. This is because, as West and Fenstermaker (1995) stress, "doing difference" is an ongoing interactional accomplishment, where accountability to gender and other norms is judged according to specific social circumstances.

Many studies of "doing" gender have taken up West and Zimmerman's (2009) suggestion that "the practices, props, bodily postures, and movements that go into producing a display of sex category incumbency" (p. 118) merit close attention. These studies have found that the ways in which working women manage, maintain, and present their bodies are not innocuous considerations but have material consequences for their careers (Brewis and Sinclair, 2000; Singh *et al.*, 2002; Trethewey, 1999; Wolf, 1990). Trethewey (1999) shows how women at work have to discipline their bodies and prevent their tendency to overflow via menstruation, pregnancy, and unruly clothing. During pregnancy and early motherhood, the gap between social norms of good motherhood and organizational bodily norms is particularly wide (Gatrell, 2013). Gatrell's (2013) study of working women managing their maternal bodies highlights the possibility of "leakage" of emotions and body fluids deemed organizationally inappropriate, and the risk of shame and "abjection"—the attribution of lower intellect to the women as she is subsumed by her body (Irigaray, cited in Gatrell, 2013). Some women managed their situation using "stoicism"—concealing leakage or ill health, but others were able to confront and challenge organizational norms.

As we now examine, embodied performances of gender are made in relation to particular spaces. We theorize the relationship between space and the embodied performance of gender by bringing together West and Zimmerman's understanding of "doing gender" with Lefebvre's

(1991) conceptualization of the social construction of space, which we consider next.

THE SPATIAL CONSTRUCTION OF GENDER NORMS

Lefebvre's (1991) influential book, *The Production of Space*, established the idea that space is simultaneously material and social, both produced through embodied social relations and producing them. As well as analyzing the processes by which space is constructed, Lefebvre provides a broad chronology of Western space, which he claims has been fashioned through a series of spatial transformations, each reflecting the specific power relations in play. His work has become prominent in organization studies (e.g., Dale and Burrell, 2008; Taylor and Spicer, 2007). Our focus in this paper is on both the embodied process that Lefebvre describes and on the persistent but implicit gendered-ness of his account, as Blum and Nast's (1996) critique identifies.

Lefebvre (1991, p. 39) proposes that space is produced through the interaction of three analytic dimensions: the material environment itself, designed and built to achieve particular social outcomes (which he terms "conceived spaces"); the everyday routines of embodied action that emerge through them ("spatial practices"); and the meanings and interpretations that inhabitants attribute to them ("lived" spaces). For Lefebvre, conceived spaces (such as offices) are materializations of the force of capitalism and are

the dominant dimension. They fulfill a dual role, being simultaneously material constructions and are "conceived of not just as structures but as projects embedded in a spatial context which set up enduring sets of relations" (p. 42).

According to Lefebvre, each conceived space instigates particular spatial practices, the everyday, and often taken-for-granted routines of inhabiting space—such as the routes we take through a building, where and how we sit, the selection and arrangement of artifacts on a desk, and our dress, gestures, and manners. Lived space refers to how spaces are construed, interpreted, and imagined by people occupying and using them. The body occupies a central role in the construction of space, because "bodies with their opacity and solidity, their warmth, their life and their death" (Lefebvre, 1991, p. 7) mediate between these three analytic dimensions. The body responds to the materiality of space and the cultural norms it represents, and it is also "generative," possessing agency of its own arising from its "spatial qualities (symmetries, asymmetries) and energetic properties (discharges, economics, waste)" (p. 61). Embodied spatial practices are experienced directly before they are conceptualized as interpretations or "lived" spaces. The idea that the body is a source of knowledge is developed by Harquail and King (2010), who show that "embodied cognition" is derived from sensory engagement with the workplace. The embodied practices and understandings that construct space are also "definitions of selfhood internalized within the body" (Simonsen, 2005, p. 5). Lefebvre (1991), thus, sees personhood as the emergent outcome of a dialectic between the dominant spatial norms and practices within a society, and the generative body that participates in and produces it. Both lived space and spatial practices can be sources of resistance and creativity.

However, Lefebvre also attributes gendered characteristics to the spatial configurations he discusses. For instance, industrial capitalism is facilitated by and grounded in "abstract space" (Lefebvre, 1991, p. 285–87)—the workspaces, transport routes, and spaces for consumption and living that we now take for granted—and Lefebvre identifies a masculine, phallic "formant" that powerfully shapes them. This phallic dimension refers to the power and intentionality of professional space designers, such as architects and managers, who recognize that space has agency and deploy their know-how in pursuit of specific social outcomes. Consequently, conceived spaces are frequently geometrically configured and highly visual, so that individuals can be located and their position plotted. For Lefebvre, the phallic formant is masculine: as he writes, "Metaphorically, [abstract space] symbolizes force, male fertility, masculine violence" (p. 287). Leonard (2002) characterizes the phallic dimension as the capacity to design spaces in ways that flatten out religion, fantasy, and the body

to create "public, hierarchical and 'mappable' space, which men naturally occupy" (p. 63). It is through the intentionality behind these designs that control is attempted and individuals are scripted into place (Blum and Nast, 1996). However, Lefebvre notes that such attempts at control are not always overt; rather, successful capitalist relations are reliant on people moving through and appropriating space, so that they become consumers of the space itself. According to Blum and Nast (1996), this variation of abstract space, which we can see exemplified in new offices designed to "enchant" their occupants as they roam through, complicates the gender relations at play. As "consumers" of these spaces, people "increasingly think about what utopic place *they* will penetrate and inhabit for the sake of pleasure" (p. 574; original emphasis).

Blum and Nast (1996) seek to extend the liberatory potential that Lefebvre offers by questioning the gendered metaphors that pervade his writing—such as the "phallic" dimension of contemporary conceived spaces. As Blum and Nast (1996) state, Lefebvre persistently equates the masculine with "activity, movement, agency, force, history," while the feminine is "passive, immobile, subject to force and history" (p. 577), and fails to recognize that this understanding is itself socially constructed. The active–passive binary, they argue, is most problematic, because it has rendered women's socio-spatial agency invisible. We can see the social effects of this

pervasive assumption in, for example, Tyler and Cohen's (2010) finding that women's occupation of space is "more tentative" (p. 181) than men's.

Bringing together Lefebvre (1991), Blum and Nast (1996), and West and Zimmerman (2009) enables us to conceptualize doing and undoing gender as spatial and embodied processes. Doing and undoing are brought about through the "practices, props, bodily postures, and movements" (West and Zimmerman, 2009, p. 118) that we all use to express a gendered identity, in relation to the dominant spatial norms of a particular place. The spatial practices people adopt may variously observe and reproduce the kinds of spatial practice regarded as appropriate, or they may challenge them. We need to be alert to the possibility that "the more mutable and 'feminized' socio-spatial practices and struggles" (Blum and Nast, 1996, p. 577) may be less easy to recognize, and seek out more subtle challenges to dominant norms. But, as West and Zimmerman (2009) remind us, such "undoing" can only take place if modified practices are collectively accepted and embedded as new norms.

Our investigation of these processes takes place in a building that is part of the widespread trend toward "new offices," specifically a "club" office design intended to promote information sharing and creativity (Duffy, 1997). These designs incorporate open-plan office areas, liminal spaces without clearly defined purposes, and choices of walking

Alison Hirst & Christina Schwabenland

routes, all aiming to encourage movement and flow, and enable interaction between occupants irrespective of formal level or specialism. Desks, computers, and other essential artifacts are standardized rather than reflecting status through size or quality. The sensual experiences of occupants are carefully designed, using light, artwork, and color, in order to "'capture hearts and minds': ... to encourage individuals to *identify* themselves with the organisation" (Dale and Burrell, 2008, p. 99; original emphasis). New offices often incorporate features that have traditionally belonged to non-work social domains (Dale and Burrell, 2008), such as kitchen facilities and informal areas for relaxation, eating and drinking, or play. In Blum and Nast's (1996) terms, new offices can be thought of as spaces for consumption as well as production. In light of the complexity of these workspaces, we need to examine the particular gender norms they channel and communicate, and the spatial and embodied responses they might provoke.

RESEARCH DESIGN

Empirical Setting

Our analysis draws on a wider longitudinal, inductive, and exploratory case study of the spatial reconfiguration of WCC. This reconfiguration began with the acquisition of Enterprise House, a new office building designed to provide a "strategic center" by housing elected councillors, senior managers, and supporting staff. About 1100 staff moved into Enterprise House from the "old campus"—a collection of six buildings of different ages, each accommodating a single directorate. Enterprise House exemplified the trends in office design discussed above. It reflected Duffy's (1997) design logic for a "club"-type office, aiming to support knowledge work performed by autonomous networkers requiring high degrees of interaction.

To support these new working practices, the new building was constructed predominantly from reinforced glass and was almost entirely transparent. The visibility of the workspace meant that merely by being present, employees were participating in interaction. Apart from discreet "ladies" and "gents" signs labeling the toilets, material and symbolic indications of difference were absent. All office space was open plan, the desks and other artifacts that employees used were identical, and large areas were left available for collective activity, mostly undefined. Thus, the new design entailed physical proximity, allowed movement and opportunities for spontaneous interaction, and implied a lack of differentiation between roles— although differentiation might happen in the context of particular projects, structures could dissolve and re-form easily.

Fieldwork

Research access to Enterprise House was granted by the Chief Executive shortly after it was first occupied. The first author (Alison) had sole responsibility for data collection, which included participant-observation, semi-structured interviews, and reviewing a wide range of official and unofficial documents. Fieldwork was conducted throughout a three-year period, with two phases of intensive participant-observation and interviewing, and further fieldwork visits between them. Participant-observation in Enterprise House involved attending formal and informal meetings, administrative work relating to the research project, and lunch and coffee breaks with organizational members. This direct involvement enabled Alison to observe the spatial practices members used (e.g., ways of dressing, walking, and interacting) and to perform them in broadly similar ways. In doing so, she could construct aspects of the embodied knowledge (Harquail and King, 2010) that occupants similarly derived from their sensory engagement with the workspace. As Gregson and Rose (2000) recognize, participant-observation entails not only "interpreting discursive accounts...but also observing and interpreting the visual, aural, olfactory space...and participating in its production" (p. 435).

Forty-six semi-structured interviews ranging from fifty-five minutes to two hours were conducted, with forty employees (twenty-seven women and thirteen men). The interview schedule was semi-open-ended, and, in the spirit of ethnographic interviewing, allowed interviewees to shape the questions being asked and develop the focus of the research (Heyl, 2001). Interviews were recorded and professionally transcribed, and the length of transcripts ranged from 7500 to 12,000 words. Key informants in phase 1 were all men. They were the Chief Executive (James), Marcus, the Director of the Project Board (the team of eight senior staff specially created to finalize the building design and orchestrate staff moves), the lead Architect (Rory), and the Project Consultant (Simon). We classified members of this group as "organization designers," concerned with the simultaneous redesign of the physical environment and the social life of the organization. Interviewees in the second phase of fieldwork included both men and women, and occupied a much wider range of roles and statuses, ranging from Directors of Service to temporary project workers. Questions were open-ended and focused on: informants' job roles, their work priorities, and key relationships, including with material objects; and how their work processes were enabled or constrained by the new building.

Initially, the researcher did not regard gender as an important analytic category. WCC espoused explicit equality goals, both in relation to the public services it provided and to the composition and treatment of its workforce. Although occupational and hierarchical gender segregation was evident, women were represented at senior levels. The organization thus appeared to be one in which gender inequality was progressively being "solved." However, it was notable that all the organization designers were men, and that women outnumbered men by 2:1 in informants

who volunteered to participate in phase 2. Then, as the fieldwork proceeded, Alison also noticed that the building seemed to make a difference to how she and others were performing gender. For example, she was surprised by the unusual amount of care she took over her own appearance, a degree of self-consciousness that she found burdensome as time progressed. To "fit in" with the modern, clean aesthetic of the building itself and a dress code that was widely adopted, she departed from her usual preference for wearing jeans and no make-up; adopting a smart trouser suit and putting on make-up. This seemed necessary, she reasoned, to establish credibility with the senior organization members present in the workspace. It would also enable her to "disappear," by complying with what she construed as a "normal" form of self-presentation; a professional, and understated but clearly heterosexual, identity. The researcher felt that she looked unremarkable and drew no attention to herself, but also that she could stand up to close inspection if necessary. Consequently, she wondered whether others were also revising their gendered performances in response to the new environment. Because of the gradual realization of the significance of gender in the new building, questions about gender did not feature in the interview schedules in phase 1 of the fieldwork (but where informants raised gender-related issues, the conversation followed). However,

in the second phase of fieldwork, interview questions about how gender mattered in the new workplace were included, where interviewees seemed at ease with this.

Analysis

Our analysis focuses on three areas: the ways in which the norms of the newly desired behaviors were identified, communicated, and understood; how these new behaviors were experienced; and how they were resisted. We began by reviewing the field notes, interview transcripts, and other documentary materials, including a comprehensive search for all references to gender. From this, we identified observations indicating the possible significance of gender in the design of the workspace and in women's efforts to claim membership there. We coded informants' accounts based on when and where gendered norms surfaced as an issue to be managed, the responses called for, and the strategies women devised to deal with them. Following West and Zimmerman (2009), we inferred what cultural conceptions of gender were salient and the extent to which they were accepted, ignored, or resisted.

As far as possible, we adopted a grounded theory approach, basing our analysis on informants' emic constructions of gender, rather than imputing our own theories to them (Charmaz and Mitchell, 2001). However, when analyzing the interviews with the organization designers, we attributed meanings to the masculine metaphors they used, of which they may have been less conscious. As such, we are drawing on the use of metaphor in organizational research as a heuristic to surface "theories-in-use" (Schwabenland, 2012) and analyze what Schön (1979) calls "problem setting," where metaphors frame the problem to be solved in a way that points to specific solutions. As Schön (1979, p. 255) argues, the metaphor casts a spell whereby the nature of the problem seems obvious, "[b]ut this sense of obviousness depends very much on the metaphor remaining tacit." Thus, our analysis aimed to surface the more latent meanings suggested by the use of specific metaphors by our informants. In general, working as an "insider/outsider pair" (Lingard *et al.*, 2007), we carried out the analysis both independently and together, taking different but overlapping roles. As the insider, the first author had participated in the field and had partial access to emic constructions of gender while the second author, the more independent outsider, was able to surface and question these constructions.

Enterprise House as Conceived Space: The Gendered Norms of the New Desired Behaviors

At the time of the interviews with the four organization designers, Enterprise House had recently been completed and staff had begun to move in. The project was widely spoken of as a bold and ambitious move that had proved extremely successful. The two senior managers, James and Marcus, exuded a confident, "bullish" air, and their accounts of the move expressed, in Cassell's (2005) words, an "image of themselves as organisational heroes" (p. 175). Marcus (Director of the Project Board), for instance, compared WCC's successful acquisition of the building with the failure of another local authority to make a similar move, observing that *"we didn't just talk about it, we get on and do it."*

The organization designers initially described the transformation they wanted Enterprise House to achieve by contrasting it with the old campus. This contrast included the image of WCC these buildings projected (Hirst and Humphreys, 2013): according to Marcus, external audiences would see the buildings and infer qualities of the staff from their images:

If you were coming into dusty old Weston Court, that immediately says to you…dusty, crusty, fallen-down, tatty, shabby. So what sort of service am I going to get from somebody here? Whereas if you go into glitzy, smart, efficient, modern, you think well these people must be pretty switched on, I'm not going to mess with these people.

James, the Chief Executive, suggested that the compartmentalized "old campus" buildings encouraged staff to behave passively:

Where we were before was absolutely dreadful buildings. I found them deeply, deeply depressing, I used to hate them with a passion. I hated them because they were disconnected. Like the Tardis,[2] people went in at half past eight in the morning, they went into a time warp and then they'd be spewed out at 5:30 at night. They would never come across anybody else other than their immediate peers…. So partly it was a kind of revulsion with our old buildings but also a sense that they didn't work, they didn't enable people to know each other in any kind of real, meaningful connecting way, they created a separation even within the departments because they were very much cellular offices. So it's fine if we thought that the vision for WCC was something that monks and hermits could achieve, but monks and hermits don't achieve the connections, actually they were valuing separateness, insularity…they were valuing the quiet deliberative approach to life, and they were not valuing what I see as fundamentally the important networks.*

It is striking that James expresses what is now regarded as "incorrect" behavior in WCC using gendered metaphors—monks and hermits are celibate men, who, whether through choice or exclusion, exist at the margins of society. The *"quiet deliberative approach"* may be diligent and pious, as are monks and hermits, but it is disconnected. We, therefore, suggest that in his use of these metaphors, James associates passivity, insularity, marginalization, and isolation with a "failed" (and highly undesirable) masculinity.

In stark contrast to these obsolete routines, the organization designers described the new spatial practices they wished to establish in terms of movement, interaction, and visibility. In various ways, they suggested that Enterprise House could initiate and sustain these practices by acting on the body. The architect, Rory, expressed his hope that the building would be:

Something that makes you just feel good to be in the space and the spirit of it. I would like to feel that people came to the building and felt they belonged to a team that was doing something, going somewhere and they were looking forward to it, put a spring in their steps as they walked into the building to start work.

The experience of being in the building could energize the body, harness its generative capacity, and evoke feelings of togetherness and optimism. The Chief Executive also spoke enthusiastically about his new freedom to conduct work by just wandering through the building and interacting with people spontaneously, and he stressed that others were equally free to approach him. However, the new walking freedoms were also described in terms that Lefebvre would code as masculine. For instance, Simon, the Project Consultant, described the ideal worker as a mobile worker who could move through the space at will:

The mobile worker is someone who can work from various, different locations including home... you know, he's out and about, he's moving around. Technically the infrastructure here is capable, anybody can log on to any of the PCs in the building, work

at any desk in the building...at any time, they just come in and plug and play.

Although the argument was that everyone can participate in these new spatial freedoms and the resultant exchanges can be reciprocal, this new behavior can also be inferred as active and sexualized, in the sense that the space is there to be penetrated.

The organization designers also argued that the building would stimulate the development of more informal, deeper relationships. Rory suggested that relationships could become:

Informal, which means that people feel able to talk to each other, and not held back in the strictures of some formal business approach, whether it's wearing a suit and tie or acting in a way where a meeting is very formal and has to be minuted. So hopefully, that informality would be productive because people would be communicating and understand other people's desires and needs and understand the way they work together.

Using a masculine dress style to exemplify "stricture," Rory argues that the building can release occupants from formality in dress, manner, and protocol and that this can enable more authentic, intimate communication. This is a place where members can be who they "really" are.

In the early phase of occupation, the visibility of the building was one of its most striking features. Marcus, the Director of the Project Board, stated that "*the intention*

was to have a more relaxed environment, a more open environment, so the designing in was all glass, so that people can see us." He recognized the potential for panoptic surveillance, but suggested that the condition of mutual visibility in which "*everyone's a warder*" would generate power in a productive sense. He stressed the equality and lack of differentiation involved in this form of regulation: there is constant surveillance; but it is subtle, not overt. It is also multi-directional, and consequently, the environment is more relaxed.

However, Rory suggested that it might take time to generate a more relaxed environment in the highly visible workspace. He used an analogy with a "nudist beach" to explain how the "settling in" process might work:

People are being told that it's better. It's not necessarily better, I feel watched now, now why is that better? But I think it's like going to a nudist beach, you know, first you're a little bit worried that everyone's looking at you but then you think, hang on, everybody else is naked, no-one's looking at each other. I think that's what'll happen, they'll get on with it.

Rory suggests that people's anxieties about being exposed will initially surface but will then subside as exposure becomes part of shared, unnoticed experience. However, Douglas and Rasmussen's (1978) ethnographic study of a nudist beach suggests that Rory's interpretation is problematic: their findings indicated that naked people do continue to look at one another, although surreptitiously, and men, in particular, often in groups, look obsessively at women.

Explicit mention of gender was made only twice in the conversations with the organization designers. In his role as leader of the Project Board, Marcus led a formal consultation that invited prospective occupants to express their concerns about the new building:

I was consulted by lots of people, women who were very worried about wearing skirts in an open plan building and going upstairs. And people were going around saying things like well I can't start an affair here, what happens if you're having an affair now? [laughter] But why not? Surely, you start any relationship by, you know, talking to people, you don't suddenly grope somebody in a corner. Which I thought was interesting, I think that's what he must have thought.

In the consultation Marcus reported, the women's concerns appeared to reinforce the similarity between the office and a nudist beach, and in turn, the "people" (a man) joked about its capacity to inhibit office romance. Each reference to gender is about sex, and both place women and men in conventional roles. But Marcus refers to women specifically in the first example, while initially using the ungendered term "people" in the second, although it becomes clear that only one man raised this issue.

The second overt reference to gender was made in the context of an event that caused widespread ripples. When staff first moved in, one disgruntled manager bypassed the official consultation and complained publicly in the local press. An article was published listing various alleged problems with the building, including the lack of urinals in the men's toilets. The unhappy manager was reprimanded by the Chief Executive and the episode formed the basis for humorous stories that circulated throughout the organization. As one employee joked, the manager had suggested that *"there were no urinals and we'd all be standing outside like a bunch of girls"*—as if humiliated by the comparison to those *"girls"* who, by necessity, are visibly proclaiming their female anatomy and bodily functions. The manager's outburst implies that hitherto taken-for-granted masculine dignity appears not to be reliable, and thus, anxieties are surfaced. And indeed, in interviews and conversations, many men said that they found the absence of urinals disconcerting.

The overt suggestion in these accounts is that differences should, and will, disappear. But this is evoked using highly sexualized metaphors. We suggest that Enterprise House's design was informed by latent heterosexual norms and definitions of identity. From the beginning, sex has to be on show (on the nudist beach, the monks forced out of their cells) and the new space must be penetrated and appropriated. We now turn to the various ways in which women responded to the new space in order to claim their membership of it.

Negotiating New Forms of Gendered Spatiality

Our data suggest that for some women, the new office appeared to have the effect that the designers spoke of, in terms of shaping a social realm composed of equals whose identities were not prejudged through their association with a particular space, and whose choices over who they could become had been extended. As Diane (Transport Planner) argued:

I like the fact that we've got open offices and you're not pigeonholed, that you can talk to everybody. You can see everybody and you just feel that you're all part of the same thing.

Elizabeth (Learning and Development Manager) observed that people were dressing more smartly, just as Marcus had suggested. For her, however, this was not an outcome forced by oppressive surveillance, but an opportunity to grow into a fulfilling new identity as both an individual and member of the collectivity:

I notice people's level of dress just went up! You know people seemed to be more—not more confident, that would be wrong—to have more respect for themselves. We've got much more acknowledgement of one another and acknowledgement of self, which we didn't have before, so that's about "I am who I am" regardless of whether I'm on a walkway, sitting at a desk or visiting the loo or whatever.

The mutual acknowledgment of self and of one another is something that appears to be new, and that the new building has done. Also as Rory, the architect, had suggested, in this workspace, it was possible to be your authentic self. The new sense of self-respect is possible, Elizabeth argues, even if your actions show your intention to "visit the loo." In contrast with the reference to "visiting the loo" as a source of shame, according to Elizabeth, this could now be done with pride, suggesting that even bodily functions such as urination could be acknowledged openly. Shahida, a temporary worker, pointed out that she had formally requested that vending machines selling tampons should be put in the women's toilets (while condoms were available in the men's toilets, in the women's, there were neither tampons nor condoms). This was not joked about publicly as had been the case for the "lack of urinals" complaint, but it suggested that female bodily fluids could be discreetly talked about—and tampon vending machines were installed.

    Estelle, a Care Procurement manager, appeared to flout conventional gendered norms by adopting exactly the assertive, penetrating spatial practices that the Chief Executive had endorsed. Estelle wore a short, spiky hairstyle and clean-cut, masculine attire, which did not seem to express accountability to conventional heteronormative ideals. Estelle

was clear in her advice about how to "get on" in this sort of work and how Enterprise House assisted her:

My advice in any team, in any job, is "ask questions." Your question is never silly. And challenge. The shrinking violet is no good. In a partnership you need to be able to speak up. You need to be able to say, "That's not what we accept. That's not the way we can do it." In Enterprise House, the people you need to talk to are there, so you go and find them. Go and stand in front of them. It's good for meeting, networking and learning.

We note the contrast between how the researcher chose to respond to the new building and Estelle's style of dress and self-presentation, which challenged those conventions. Estelle also appeared comfortable with approaching people, whether or not they expected or wanted to interact with her. Estelle did not conform to the usual heteronormative type, and as she suggested, the building worked for her.

    For gender norms to be undone, there must be both an attempt to change sex category norms and acceptance of the changed position from members of the collective (West and Zimmerman, 2009). The women's accounts above suggest that such new possibilities for claiming membership could, indeed, be negotiated and legitimated through recognition. We now, however, move on to consider more ambivalent accounts, in which the challenging of conventional norms was

attempted or accomplished through compromise.

The Reassertion of More Conventional Feminine Spatiality

West and Zimmerman (2009) point out that if acceptance of changed forms of behavior is not granted, then attempts to "undo" gender cannot be accomplished and the prevailing normative conceptions reassert themselves. In Enterprise House, we observed attempts at "undoing" in terms of adopting new practices of movement, interaction, and response to visibility that were either not granted endorsement or could only be secured by means of a conscious compromise. For instance, in contrast with Estelle, the researcher recounts in her field notes an attempt to challenge traditional gender norms by making a spontaneous approach to a staff member who happened to be a man. Alison was trying to locate an interviewee, Sue, whom she had arranged to meet at her desk, but who was absent when she approached. She wrote:

I approached Sue's desk at the appointed time, but found it unoccupied. What to do? There was a man sitting by the window next to Sue's empty desk, and a young woman opposite. I thought to myself, well I'm damned if I'm going to assume that she's the admin person! and I asked the man, very politely, if he knew where Sue was. He was visibly irritated by this interruption. He looked up long enough to inform me, brusquely, that she was at a meeting, and by the time I was thanking him he had already fixed his gaze back on his computer screen, where it remained.

The researcher had made a conscious attempt to avoid conventional assumptions about role or status based on gender. Even if the man had been a higher status employee (he was, as it turned out), in the new environment it was, in principle, possible to make a spontaneous approach even to the Chief Executive. However, this was not a successful maneuver. It is not possible to say exactly why the man expressed irritation, but the rebuff suggested to the researcher that she should, after all, have assumed that the woman was the "admin person" and that gender and hierarchy were expected to be performed conventionally in this situation.

The visibility of the workspace meant that being observed was a constant possibility. The architect had argued that as time went on, this increased visibility would become more or less ignored, and as we suggested above, some women recounted experiences of visibility and movement as useful, pleasurable, and fulfilling. For others, though, this newfound visibility was perceived as uncomfortable or oppressive. For example, Pat (Highways Officer) described how women attending job interviews had been "marked" for their attractiveness by men in her team:

One of the things that the young guys used to do, is if there was an interview being held and there was a stream of young ladies coming through, they'd actually be marking them. And sometimes I used to think, that girl hasn't actually got out of the door yet, please!

Visibility enabled these men to judge and rank women according to their sexual attractiveness, just like men on the nudist beaches described by Douglas and Rasmussen (1978). Although visibility placed curbs on this kind of behavior—"watching" had to be done surreptitiously—the building provided a space where it was much easier for men to exercise this kind of "male gaze." Conscious of this possibility, some women spoke of the anxiety they felt and the restrictions they placed on themselves to avoid being judged in this way. For example, the researcher asked interviewees whether they would walk into another office area unannounced:

You don't do it, do you. You just don't, do you? Right, this is going to sound extremely sexist but remember I do work with a lot of men. [laughs] If you were a female, that would definitely get a comment from all the men because they would notice you. (Wendy, Transport Researcher)

Many women observed that *"there isn't anywhere that you don't feel watched."* Several chose to manage their visibility by adjusting the way they dressed. Women did not simply present themselves more smartly in a uniform way, however, but did so in ways that would signal their belonging to a particular status. For example, Annabel had recently moved from a senior management position in the NHS, where she worked in what she described as a *"poky"* building. Her new management role in WCC involved networking as a way of "joining up" services, and Annabel expressed enthusiasm for all the spaces in Enterprise House that facilitated networking. However, she also said that she had changed the way she presented herself in order to signal her seniority:

In the NHS, the emphasis was on patient care and a more casual attitude to how you were dressed. And then suddenly here everybody looked quite smart and on-trend and I felt quite old-fashioned. So I spent a lot of money on clothes. And also where I used to wear a cardi at work, it's a jacket now.

Researcher: So what would a cardi say about you?

Well I think a cardi says admin. There's a whole subtle ranking and I think for women it's particularly significant. So, regular haircuts. Roots and shoots, very important. Make-up; essential, but yes, you realise that really subtle is good. Before I came here I would sometimes wear jeans, but people in jeans does so not happen here you know.

Annabel's interpretation of the "new" spatial rules was that, on the one hand, she could use the building exactly as the organization designers had intended, by appropriating it opportunistically. On the other hand, she was careful to present herself both as an attractive woman and as possessing the high status that could persuade others that it would be worthwhile cooperating with her. Alison made a similar interpretation of the new rules. Her tacit interpretation of the "deal" in Enterprise House was that, in order to be successful at roaming about and interacting with high-status colleagues, she had to adjust her appearance and look conventionally business-like and feminine.

In subsequent interviews, the researcher inquired further into the tacit rules relating status with dress and movement, and was informed that many senior women managers could be identified by their smart clothing and assertive gait. Certain women Councillors were noted for wearing eccentric, but very expensive, designer label clothing. And while women occupying lower-status roles also appeared to recognize the "subtle ranking," or rules of membership that Annabel had spoken of, they adopted a different response. Brenda (Helpdesk Officer) used her dress to downplay her status:

I like wearing suits and I like wearing jackets but where I am working now I have to tone down the way I dress. Otherwise you look like you're trying to be a bit full of yourself sometimes.

Unlike Annabel, who made full use of the building's collective spaces, Brenda was one of several women who stated that they were inclined to remain within their departmental "home" office, commenting "*I don't tend to come out into the atrium to eat because you always feel so overt if you sit there.*" And indeed, the researcher often noticed men watching women walk through the long, uninterrupted spaces of the building, sometimes appearing to struggle between their wish not to appear rude and their wish to watch the woman.

Managing Alterity

We have suggested that the ways in which women moved around the space and presented their bodies played a significant part in their attempts to negotiate and take up roles in Enterprise House. However, as Lefebvre points out, the body is generative and does not always comply with our attempts to manage "it." The visibility of the new workspace made management of some of the body's "discharges" more difficult, because they were exposed. For instance:

If you're upset about something, there's nowhere to go. Where can you go? All you can do is go to the Ladies, so there's nowhere that you can go and speak to somebody on a one-to-one basis where you can't be observed. (Samira, Adult Care Manager)

Similarly, Jean had been "on the end of a bad appraisal," was in tears in the glass meeting room, and felt that everyone was looking at her. Although she said that she "just wanted to get out," her manager appeared not to react or show much sympathy—perhaps also wary of being observed or of drawing attention to the appraisee's distress. Others spoke of the difficulties they had trying to suppress the appearance of menopausal symptoms:

Because I'm a woman of the age that I am, I do have hot flushes. We can't have fans, but just to have a small fan on my desk would be wonderful, just to be used every now and again. Even then it would be so obvious…so I just have to sort of work through it [laughs]. (Ruth, Purchasing Adviser)

Keeping these "discharges" private is rendered more difficult because the building exposes them, and attempts to mitigate them would also draw attention to the fact that they were happening. This seemed to create a situation in which everyone, including, in Jean's account, her manager, was obliged to pretend the "leakages" were not happening.

Discussion

We began our inquiry with two research questions: what are the *particular* gender norms materialized by the workspaces of the "new office"; and what types of spatial and embodied responses do women make? First, we conclude that the image of the ideal worker embodied and communicated by the "new office" is both conventionally masculine and feminine, but is still implicitly assumed to be a man: the worker strides around unflaggingly, is well presented, is ever-ready to engage and innovate, and is capable of deep relationship-building. Second, we have demonstrated that women enacted a range of responses to these new norms of movement, interaction, and exposure. Some women spoke of the new building as a liberating space that opened up a broader range of choices about who to be and how to act, and where gender appeared not to be relevant; for others, the building imposed harsh constraints, as its insistence on constant visibility clashed with norms dictating how the female body must be managed. We also observed a middle ground whereby women would consciously change their appearance or patterns of movement in line with the specific roles they aimed to take up within the new collective.

THE GENDERED OFFICE

Along with Lefebvre (1991), Tyler and Cohen (2010), and Wasserman and Frenkel (2015), we argue that conceived spaces such as offices incorporate complex constructions of gender as part of the enduring patterns of relations they are designed to realize. The "new office" in our study was designed to encourage modes of movement that were energetic and penetrative, but also to foster consensual and authentic relationships. The senior managers suggested that it also provided an antidote to another gendered space, the traditional, closed offices of the "old campus" and the emasculated spatial practices that it had helped to construct.

The organization designers expressed several related and interdependent official aims. The removal of markers of status was claimed to be necessary because fluid networking could only happen if hierarchical control and surveillance were relaxed. The building could energize the bodies of its occupants and infuse them with optimism and a sense of belonging. It would encourage mobility and allow the freedom to approach any other person. Relationships could become less formal, more intimate, and more authentic. The experience of constant visibility, regarded as a precondition for networking, might cause initial discomfort, but the staff would quickly become accustomed to it because they were all in the same boat, so to speak. Much as Duffy (1997, p. 10) suggests, the new office is designed to press occupants into "unremitting teamwork," create networked, boundary-crossing structures, and enable non-dominating relationships characterized by equality, reciprocity, freedom, and removal of hierarchical power, to unfold.

As we also observed, although the organization designers made few direct references to gender, all the metaphors (e.g., *"monks"*) and metonyms (e.g., the constraining *"suit and tie"*) used to represent the opposite to these new desired practices were masculine. These latent meanings suggest that the problem the building was designed to solve was that WCC had been held back by an unsatisfactory, obsolete kind of masculinity; Enterprise House proved instead to be an attempt to impose a new kind of super-energized hegemonic masculinity. The

building's ability to shake up old, entrenched spatial routines could also reconfigure these routines along more sexualized lines.

The fact that expressions of gender in relation to both the old campus and the new workspace were almost wholly implicit is worthy of further consideration. As Harquail and King (2010) point out, not all embodied knowledge is accessible to be articulated verbally, but resides unexpressed in our bodies. The latent expressions of the gendered-ness of the workspace and their references to other bodies, such as those of hermits, were perhaps traces of this embodied knowledge. The two senior managers involved in the design project expressed strong distaste for the old campus. Was the old campus something that they disliked so strongly because they found their association with it emasculating?

Similarly, Blum and Nast (1996) indicate that Lefebvre's understanding of the spatiality of gender bubbles just under the surface, and that he implies a dichotomy between the "active" masculine and the "passive" feminine. In our case, the initial division was made, not between masculine and feminine, but between the "wrong" sort of masculinity and a "better" ideal, which combined behaviors that are thought of as conventionally masculine (active, mobile, seeking out encounters) and feminine (openness, authenticity, and willingness to listen). However, men were implied to represent both the old and new occupants generally. In contrast, women were mentioned explicitly as women and in connection with sexual matters—having someone look up your skirt, as someone to have an affair with, as a bunch of girls queuing outside the loo. The move to Enterprise House appeared to provoke anxieties among prospective occupants about how gender might forcibly be redefined, and it introduced the fearful possibility of abjection. Referring to her large, pregnant body, one of Gatrell's (2013) informants remarks, "It was like *pointing* to my femaleness" (p. 633). Queuing outside the loo (even when done by men) could similarly point to their leakiness and enable colleagues to dwell on it, thus risking abjection. Hassard *et al.* (2000) have highlighted how the male body is the implicit norm, which makes female bodies stand out as different, although this norm too can be challenged. In our case, both of these processes appeared to be at work: female bodies remained problematic and potentially disruptive, but the detached, passive male body also had to be stirred up.

RESPONSES TO THE GENDERED OFFICE

We now turn to the ways in which women sought out membership of the strategic collective, in a situation in which they had to manage different "rules" of membership—one in which the building disrupted rote practices and encouraged its occupants to engage in unconstrained networking, roaming freely, and "being themselves," and other, implicit norms associated with sex category incumbency.

Some women appeared to embrace the norms of mobility, interaction, and self-presentation that the building designers espoused. They spoke of new freedoms to be more fully themselves; they walked across and confronted people; they looked actively at others; they requested adaptations to the loos; and they accepted and enjoyed being visible. These new practices appear to have become endorsed and established, in the way that West and Zimmerman (2009) argue is needed for laying down a changed norm (although attempts to change norms were not guaranteed to be accepted, as the researcher's experience indicates). In these responses, the informants made no reference to their status as women at all, and so, as Risman (2009) might suggest, these actions and events seem to point to the non-relevance of gender in this situation. The new office, thus, seems to offer the potential for new forms of action that women experience as positive, liberating, and authentic, and do not accord with the "passive" status that has been traditionally associated with being feminine.

In a second type of response, gender was highly relevant as women engaged in detailed self-scrutiny and self-management, in order to "do" gender and hierarchy simultaneously and successfully. For example, successful accomplishment as a high-status networker required dressing up (wearing a jacket rather than a "cardi," which might cause one to be misidentified as "admin"), whereas taking up a lower-status role was accomplished by dressing down and "staying put" in one's own office. Through these changed practices, women were expressing accountability to particular roles and statuses, and reducing the risk of being mistaken for persons of higher or lower status. West and Fenstermaker (1995) similarly cite the case of a maid caring for a rich family's children: the mother/employer insisted that the maid wore a uniform to the beach, even though it was unsuitable. But "[w]ithout a uniform, she could be mistaken for one of the guests and, hence, not be held accountable as a maid" (p. 27).

These examples also illustrate the point that gendered norms are not coherent but a sort of historically assembled hodgepodge—in order to behave in a more masculine way (roaming) women might judge that they must at the same time behave in a more feminine way (applying subtle make-up). Lewis (2014) notes the emergence of multiple femininities in organizations, but also observes that even when such feminized modes of behavior are seen as desirable, a subtle hierarchical ordering is still achieved, with white, middle-class, and heteronormative modes being privileged. In our case, there appeared to be such an implicit ranking system in these aspects, so that senior women presented themselves and acted in a way that expressed "look at me!"

and their junior counterparts sought to achieve the opposite move and blend into the background.

A third category of responses related to situations in which the body does very awkward things—its "discharges" (Lefebvre, 1991) or its "tendency to overflow" (Trethewey, 1999)—that gender rules dictate must be concealed. For example, the appearance of tears or hot flushes had to be suppressed rather than managed actively, because this would draw attention to their occurrence. However, the building dictates that occupants must be revealed, because herein lies incipient networking. The gulf between the two sets of gender rules was at its widest in this situation. Tears, hot flushes, and blood point directly to the fact that you have a woman's body, and must be hidden to avoid deep humiliation, as Trethewey (1999) says. But in the new office, it is difficult or impossible to hide. Therefore, women had to react with "stoicism" (Gatrell, 2013)—a form of body-work that involves "working through" the body's overflows without complaint, in order to protect their worth to the organization and reduce the risk of marginalization. In Enterprise House, stoicism was not a choice as it was for Gatrell's (2013) informants; it was the only realistic option, because attempts to alleviate symptoms would draw attention to them.

How might gender be seen differently as a result of this study? In answer to our research questions, we conclude that although Enterprise House was ostensibly designed to promote the realization of an idealized worker embodying both masculinized and feminized performance of gender for all staff, this was underpinned by an underlying, and gendered, hierarchy of valued and less desirable attributes and behaviors. This leads us to ask, if the "new office" offers a model of new masculinity that incorporates aspects of behavior and presentation traditionally thought of as feminine, as Lewis (2014) suggests and our findings support, where does that leave women? What is "new femininity" in relation to it? We suggest that gender is constantly in contestation, as different elements are reproduced, discarded, and recombined in many different ways. The physical spaces in which these actions occur are not neutral but shape them in myriad ways, both implicit and explicit. They also influence the extent to which attempts to "do" gender differently are accepted, resisted, or marginalized.

Like all case studies, ours has limitations, which point to the need for further research. We have identified some of the ways in which workspaces might be expressing organizational expectations about gender and the broad categories of response. These analytic generalizations will not necessarily apply to other new office settings (Yin, 2013); different processes may emerge within different empirical settings. For example, in our study, all the "organization designers"—for instance, the architects, facilities managers, and senior managers—were men. While this gender representation is typical of the architecture profession (Caven *et al.*, 2016)[3] and the UK public sector, further studies could usefully consider workspaces where women feature significantly in the design teams. Such studies might elicit very different observations and, thus, different theoretical interpretations.

DECLARATION OF CONFLICTING INTERESTS

The authors declared no potential conflicts of interest with respect to the authorship and/or publication of this article.

END NOTES

1. All names are pseudonyms.

2. The "Tardis" (Time and Relative Dimensions in Space) is the mode of transport for Dr Who, the eponymous character in a UK TV series.

3. See John Hill, "A Short Survey of Women in Architecture," *World Architects Magazine*, April 13, 2015, https://www.world-architects.com/en/architecture-news/insight/a-short-survey-of-women-in-architecture.

REFERENCES

Blum, V., & Nast, H. "Where's the Difference? The Heterosexualization of Alterity in Henri Lefebvre and Jacques Lacan." *Environment and Planning D: Society and Space* 14 (1996): 559–80.

Brewis, J., & Sinclair, J. "Exploring Embodiment: Women, Biology and Work." In *Body and Organization*, edited by J. Hassard, R. Holliday, & H. Willmott, 192–214. London, UK: Sage, 2000.

Butler, J. *Gender Trouble: Feminism and the Subversion of Identity*. New York: Routledge, 1990.

———. *Undoing Gender*. New York: Routledge, 2004.

Cassell, C. "Creating the Interviewer: Identity Work in the Management Research Process." *Qualitative Research* 5 (2005): 167–79.

Caven, V., Astor, E. N., & Diop, M. "A Cross-National Study of Gender Diversity Initiatives in Architecture." *Cross Cultural and Strategic Management* 23 (2016): 431–49.

Charmaz, K., & Mitchell, R. G. "Grounded Theory in Ethnography." In *Handbook of Ethnography*, edited by P. Atkinson, A. Coffey, S. Delamont, J. Lofland, & L. Lofland, 160–74. London, UK: Sage, 2001.

Dale, K., & Burrell, G. *The Spaces of Organisation and the Organisation of Space*. Basingstoke, UK: Palgrave Macmillan, 2008.

Douglas, J. D., & Rasmussen, P. K. *Nude Beach: Sociological Observations*. London, UK: Sage, 1978.

Duffy, F. *The New Office*. London, UK: Conran Octopus, 1997.

Gatrell, C. J. "Maternal Body Work: How Women Managers and Professionals Negotiate Pregnancy and New Motherhood at Work." *Human Relations* 66 (2013): 621–44.

Gregson, N., & Rose, G. "Taking Butler Elsewhere: Performativities, Spatialities and Subjectivities." *Environment and Planning D: Society and Space* 18 (2000): 433–52.

Halford, S., & Leonard, P. "Place, Space and Time: Contextualizing Workplace Subjectivities." *Organization Studies* 27 (2006): 657–76.

Hancock, P., & Tyler, M. "Un/doing Gender and the Aesthetics of Organizational Performance." *Gender, Work & Organization* 14 (2007): 512–33.

Harquail, C. V., & King, A. W. "Construing Organizational Identity: The Role of Embodied Cognition." *Organization Studies* 31 (2010): 1619–48.

Hassard, J., Holliday, R., & Willmott, H. "Introduction." In *Body and Organization*, edited by J. Hassard, R. Holliday, & H. Willmott, 1–14. London, UK: Sage, 2000.

Heyl, B. S. "Ethnographic Interviewing." In *Handbook of Ethnography*, edited by P. Atkinson, A. Coffey, S. Delamont, J. Lofland, & L. Lofland, 369–83. London, UK: Sage, 2001.

Hirst, A., & Humphreys, M. "Putting Power in its Place: The Centrality of Edgelands." *Organization Studies* 34 (2013): 1505–27.

Lefebvre, H. *The Production of Space*. Oxford, UK: Blackwell, 1991.

Leonard, P. "Organizing Gender? Looking at Metaphors as Frames of Meaning in Gender/Organizational Texts." *Gender, Work and Organization* 9 (2002): 60–80.

Lewis, P. "Emotion Work and Emotion Space: Using a Spatial Perspective to Explore the Challenging of Masculine Emotion Management Practices." *British Journal of Management* 19 (2008): S130–S140.

———. "Postfeminism, Femininities and Organization Studies: Exploring a New Agenda." *Organization Studies* 35 (2014): 1845–66.

Lingard, L., Schyrer, C. F., Spafford, M. M., & Campbell, S. L. "Negotiating the Politics of Identity in an Interdisciplinary Research Team." *Qualitative Research* 7 (2007): 501–19.

Nentwich, J. C., & Kelan, E. K. "Towards a Topology of 'Doing Gender': An Analysis of Empirical Research and its Challenges." *Gender, Work and Organization* 21 (2014): 121–34.

Pilgeram, R. "'Ass-Kicking' Women: Doing and Undoing Gender in a US Livestock Auction." *Gender, Work and Organization* 14 (2007): 572–95.

Risman, B. J. "From Doing to Undoing: Gender as We Know It." *Gender & Society* 23 (2009): 81–4.

Schön, D. A. "Generative Metaphor: A Perspective on Problem-Setting in Social Policy." In *Metaphor and Thought*, edited by A. Ortony, 254–83. Cambridge, UK: Cambridge University Press, 1979.

Schwabenland, C. *Metaphor and Dialectic in Managing Diversity*. Basingstoke, UK: Palgrave McMillan, 2012.

Simonsen, K. "Bodies, Sensations, Space and Time: The Contribution from Henri Lefebvre." *Geografiska Annaler. Series B. Human Geography* 87 (2005): 1–14.

Singh, V., Kumra, S., & Vinnicombe, S. "Gender and Impression Management: Playing the Promotion Game." *Journal of Business Ethics* 37 (2002): 77–89.

Taylor, S., & Spicer, A. "Time for Space: A Narrative Review of Research on Organizational Spaces." *International Journal of Management Reviews* 9 (2007): 325–46.

Trethewey, A. "Disciplined Bodies: Women's Embodied Identities at Work." *Organization Studies* 20 (1999): 423–50.

Tyler, M., & Cohen, L. "Spaces that Matter: Gender Performativity and Organizational Space." *Organization Studies* 31 (2010): 175–98.

Wasserman, V., & Frenkel, M. "Spatial Work in Between Glass Ceilings and Glass Walls: Gender-Class Intersectionality and Organizational Aesthetics." *Organization Studies* 36 (2015): 1485–505.

West, C., & Fenstermaker, S. "Doing Difference." *Gender & Society* 9 (1995): 8–37.

West, C., & Zimmerman, D. H. "Doing Gender." *Gender & Society* 1 (1987): 125–51.

———. "Accounting for Doing Gender." *Gender & Society* 23 (2009): 112–22.

Wolf, N. *The Beauty Myth*. London, UK: Chatto & Windus, 1990.

Yin, R. K. *Case Study Research: Design and Methods*. London, UK: Sage, 2013.

Alison Hirst & Christina Schwabenland

Sondra Perry (b. 1986, Perth Amboy, NJ) lives and works in Perth Amboy. She received her MFA from Columbia University in 2015 and her BFA from Alfred University, NY, in 2012. Recent solo exhibitions include: *A Terrible Thing*, Museum of Contemporary Art Cleveland, which traveled to Kunsthal Aarhus, Denmark (2019); *Typhoon coming on*, Serpentine Galleries, London, which traveled to the Institute of Contemporary Art Miami, and Luma Westbau, Zurich (all 2018); *Chromatic Saturation*, Disjecta, Portland, OR (2018); *Sondra Perry: flesh out*, Squeaky Wheel Film and Media Art Center, Buffalo, NY (2017); and *Resident Evil*, The Kitchen, New York (2016). Selected group exhibitions include: *New Order: Art and Technology in the Twenty-First Century*, Museum of Modern Art, New York, *The Body Electric*, Walker Art Center, Minneapolis (both 2019); *Family Pictures*, Columbus Museum of Art, OH, *Art in the Age of the Internet: 1989 to Today*, Institute of Contemporary Art, Boston, *Signal or Noise / The Photographic II*, S.M.A.K., Ghent, Belgium (all 2018); *We Just Fit, You and I*, Carpenter Center for the Visual Arts, Cambridge, MA, *Myths of the Marble*, Institute of Contemporary Art, Philadelphia, *Trigger: Gender as a Tool and a Weapon*, New Museum, New York (all 2017); *Disguise: Masks and Global African Art*, Brooklyn Museum (2016); *Greater New York*, MoMA PS1, New York, and *A Constellation*, Studio Museum in Harlem, New York (both 2015). Perry's videos have been screened at the Serpentine Galleries, London, the Museum of Contemporary Art, Los Angeles, Tribeca Cinemas, New York, Lu Xun Academy of Fine Arts Museum, Shenyang, China, and Les Voûtes, Paris. Perry is the recipient of moCa's inaugural Toby's Prize (2018), the Nam June Paik Award (2018), and the Seattle Art Museum's Gwendolyn Knight and Jacob Lawrence Prize (2017).

A. Will Brown is an independent curator and writer based in Chicago. Most recently, he was Assistant Curator at the Museum of Contemporary Art Cleveland from 2016–19. He has held curatorial positions at Monument Lab, Philadelphia, the Museum of Art, Rhode Island School of Design, Providence, KADIST, San Francisco, the Wattis Institute for Contemporary Arts, San Francisco, and Triple Base Gallery, San Francisco. He received his MA in Curatorial Practice from California College of the Arts, San Francisco, and a BA in Psychology and Art History from Goucher College, Baltimore, MD.

Mario Gooden is Principal at Huff + Gooden Architects and Professor of Practice at the Columbia Graduate School of Architecture Planning and Preservation, where he is the codirector of the Global Africa Lab with Mabel O. Wilson. Huff + Gooden Architects were recently commissioned to design the California African American Museum in Los Angeles and, in 2005, won the competition for the Virginia Key Beach Museum in Miami. Gooden graduated from Clemson University in 1987 with a BS in Design, he received a Masters of Architecture from Columbia University in 1990, and is a recipient of the McKim Prize. His work, writings, and lectures frequently examine architecture and the translation of cultural landscapes defined by the parameters of technology, race, class, gender, and sexuality. In 2006, he completed the installation *UnSpoken Spaces: Inside and Outside the Boundaries of Race, Class, and Space* at the Gibbes Museum of Art in Charleston, SC, and most recently, Gooden authored *Dark Space: Architecture, Representation, Black Identity* (Columbia University Press, 2016). His work has been featured in many journals and publications including *Architecture Magazine, Architectural Record Magazine, Metropolis, New York Times, Architecture & Urbanism (A+U)*, and *Artforum*.

Alison Hirst is Director of Postgraduate Research at Lord Ashcroft International Business School, Anglia Ruskin University. Her current research interests include the sociology of organizational space and artifacts, and ethnography as a way of researching and writing about organizations. She has published in the *Journal of Organizational Change Management* and *Organization Studies*, and is a member of the Editorial Board for *Organization Studies*.

Christina Schwabenland is a Reader in the School of Business at the University of Bedfordshire and the Director of the Research Centre for Leadership Innovation. She has published in human relations, organization, and culture and organization as well as authored two research monographs: *Stories, Visions and Values in Voluntary Organisations* (Routledge, 2006, 2016) and *Metaphor and Dialectic in Managing Diversity* (Palgrave, 2012). Her most recent publication is an edited anthology, *Women's Emancipation in Civil Society Organizations* (Policy Press, 2016). She is a member of the Editorial Board for the online journal *Murmurations*.

Jill Snyder was the Executive Director of the Museum of Contemporary Art Cleveland from 1996 until 2020. Snyder provided visionary leadership for the realization of an internationally heralded $35 million building project designed by renowned architect Farshid Moussavi, which catalyzed a new urban district in University Circle, a premier cultural center. A museum professional for over thirty years, Snyder has held administrative and educational positions at the Solomon R. Guggenheim Museum and Museum of Modern Art in New York, and served as Director of the Aldrich Contemporary Art Museum and Freedman Gallery at Albright College. Snyder has participated in various leadership programs at the Getty Leadership Institute, Stanford University School of Business, Leadership Cleveland, and National Arts Strategies. She is cofounder of the national association of Contemporary Art Museum Directors and serves on the Boards of the Cleveland School of the Arts and University Circle Incorporated. She received a BA from Wesleyan University and conducted graduate studies in art history at New York University's Institute of Fine Art. Snyder is a member of the Association of Art Museum Directors and the 50 Club.

Sondra Perry has emerged as one of the most significant voices in a generation of rising artists. As such, I am incredibly proud that she was the inaugural recipient of Toby's Prize, a new biennial award given to an artist who has shown exceptional promise early in his or her career. The award, selected by a distinguished group of independent curators, enables the production of new work, a solo exhibition at moCa, and an accompanying publication, all made possible through the continued generosity of philanthropist and Honorary moCa Director, Toby Devan Lewis. Toby's Prize represents moCa's continued support of artists at crucial moments in their careers, as well as our commitment to offering supportive spaces for artistic experimentation.

While not an aim or requirement for the work that is made as part of Toby's Prize, Perry approached this project by looking closely at the history of Cleveland and weaving together past moments from the city's once-bustling Euclid Avenue corridor—part of which is now called Uptown—with the planning, construction, and internal operations of moCa's architecture. The result is a poignant installation that explores the fraught construction of place, asking us to examine the very infrastructure in which we reside.

Titled *A Terrible Thing* (2019), the work traveled from moCa to Kunsthal Aarhus, and I could not have been more excited to see how it took on new form and life in this context. One of the rewarding aspects of working alongside and with an artist on the commission of new work is the ability to follow the piece's lifespan, seeing it in new locations and watching as it becomes part of a larger artistic adventure. I want to extend my sincere thanks to Kunsthal Aarhus's Director, Jacob Fabricius, and his talented team, Nadia Donnerborg, Iben Mosbæk, Trine Friis Sørensen, and Joaquin Zaragoza, for their impressive work in realizing Perry's vision anew in their space.

Perry's exhibition and catalogue are a testament to the steadfast, collaborative approach of moCa's former Assistant Curator, A. Will Brown, who worked closely with Perry and moCa's exhibitions and curatorial team to make *A Terrible Thing* an engaging reality. I would like to acknowledge moCa's Chief Curator, Courtenay Finn—whose vision and generous approach guide the team—for her skillful management of this volume. Her efforts are supported by the hard work and dedication of moCa's curatorial and exhibitions team: Kate Montlack, our Director of Exhibitions, whose attention to detail and deft handling ensure the museum runs smoothly; our Senior Exhibitions Manager, Ray Juaire, who brings his thoughtful, measured approach to all facets of moCa's program; our former Exhibition Project Manager, Eli Gfell, whose creative approach to problem solving and enthusiastic approach to working with artists exemplified our collaborative structure; and moCa's Gund Curatorial Fellow La Tanya Autry, who offered invaluable support along the way.

This catalogue includes new scholarship and writing on Perry's work alongside the thoughtful reprint of "Doing Gender in the 'New Office'" by Alison Hirst and Christina Schwabenland, which we are extremely grateful to be able to include. I would like to offer a special thank you to A. Will Brown and Mario Gooden for their rigorous texts, each of which provides new entry points into Perry's practice. The publication is published by Hatje Cantz, and it has been a joy to work with their team, Julianne Eisele, Lena Kiessler, Vinzenz Geppert, and Heidrun Zimmermann. Special thanks go to Sarah Stephenson for her thoughtful editing of this book and to Michael Aberman, the catalogue's designer, who captured the essence of Perry's practice in this inventive publication.

We are very fortunate to have the continued, resolute support of moCa's Leadership Circle, each of whom makes immersive, thoughtful exhibitions like *A Terrible Thing* possible. I would like to thank our anonymous donors, Yuval Brisker, Joanne Cohen and Morris Wheeler, Margaret Cohen and Kevin Rahilly, Becky Dunn, Harriet Goldberg, Agnes Gund, Richard and Michelle Jeschelnig, Donna and Stewart Kohl, Jan Lewis, and Scott and Kelly Mueller for their continued generosity and support. I would also like to extend a very special thank you to Toby Devan Lewis for funding this award and making this and all future Toby's Prize exhibitions and catalogues a reality. She is a visionary and a leader who has long championed and built spaces for contemporary art and artists to thrive, and we are forever grateful for her support of moCa.

This exhibition was funded in part by the Andy Warhol Foundation for the Visual Arts and supported in part by the residents of Cuyahoga County through a public grant from Cuyahoga Arts & Culture, the Cleveland Foundation, the George Gund Foundation, and the continuing support of moCa's Board of Directors, patrons, and members.

And last but not least, I offer my sincerest thanks to Sondra Perry for creating and sharing this astounding, captivating new installation with moCa's audiences. It has been a truly wonderful experience to get to know her and our own building through her work.

—Jill Snyder
Former Executive Director, moCa Cleveland
(1996–2020)